This book is dedicated
to my grandfather, Francis P. Preve,
for believing in me.

Contents

THE REMIXER'S BIBLE

Build Better Beats

FRANCIS PREVE

Backbeat
Books

San Francisco

Published by Backbeat Books
600 Harrison Street, San Francisco, CA 94107
www.backbeatbooks.com
email: books@musicplayer.com

An imprint of the Music Player Network
Publishers of *Guitar Player, Bass Player, Keyboard, EQ,* and other magazines
United Entertainment Media, Inc.
A CMP Information company

CMP
United Business Media

Distributed to the book trade in the US and Canada by
Publishers Group West, 1700 Fourth Street, Berkeley, CA 94710

Distributed to the music trade in the US and Canada by
Hal Leonard Publishing, P.O. Box 13819, Milwaukee, WI 53213

Text and cover design by Doug Gordon

ISBN: 0-87930-881-8

Printed in the United States of America

08 09 10   5 4 3 2

Introduction

When I first started producing dance music back in the early '80s, there were few resources for learning the craft. However, there were many rules for what constituted "good production techniques." It didn't help that — unlike today's world of ultra-powerful and relatively inexpensive home studios — studio time with a seasoned engineer ranged from $50 to $200 per hour and a good polyphonic synth started at $1,500. The nascent field of remixing was a wild frontier populated by trailblazers like Francois Kevorkian, Shep Pettibone, Arthur Baker, and Jellybean Benitez, and they weren't giving away their secrets anytime soon. So I learned the art and science of electronica via two time-honored methods: trial-and-error and reading every issue of Keyboard magazine from cover to cover.

Fast-forward a couple of decades. In 2000, with a few Top 10 remixes under my belt, my own studio, and the distinction of being on the team that developed Tascam's Gigastudio, I was approached by Greg Rule to become a regular contributor to Keyboard magazine's monthly Dance Mix column. It took me a few milliseconds to say yes, and thus the process came full cycle. I was now entrusted with the responsibility of training thousands of bedroom producers in the esoteric art of creating ferocious grooves, just as I'd voraciously consumed the knowledge of masters like Jim Aikin and Craig Anderton (both contributors to this book) when I was in my teens and twenties. It is unlikely that anyone will ever truly know how deeply honored I was by this opportunity, no matter how much I hug them.

Shortly thereafter, I started thinking. If I developed a significant portion of my skill set by reading Keyboard, and then I contributed countless goodies from my own bag of tricks, wouldn't it be cool to assemble all of this knowledge in neatly organized book? I proposed this to my publisher after completing two books in their Power Tools series, and they loved the idea. Slam dunk.

The next step was to determine how to structure the content. There are a few books on the market and numerous websites that tackle the process of getting started in remixing and creating dance tracks. What's more, nearly every piece of sequencing and recording software has its own array of "How To" manuals. But strangely, there wasn't a cohesive book for producers who already knew what they were doing, but wanted to go deeper into the myriad processes that separate the middling from the great. That was the book I wanted to create, and that is the book you now hold in your hands.

This is not a tutorial for beginners. It is a manual for making great dance music.

With that in mind, the next questions arise. What material should I include in this ambitious tome? How far back through the Keyboard archives should I go? At the rate that technology progresses, what's still relevant to modern remixers?

After years of working in and studying the remix scene, one thing has become crystal clear to me: Dance music is fashion for the ears. It goes through extremely well-defined stylistic cycles, where a sound begins in the underground, rises into the mainstream, then ends up in Walmart, at which point it is promptly cast aside as "dated." From there, this now unfashionable genre lies dormant for about 15-20 years, after which it is picked up by the next generation. That generation then sifts through the ashes of the discarded style, picking and choosing, then reinterpreting the various elements that defined the style. One case in point? The '90s obsession with French house, which looped classic '70s disco grooves, then ran them through constantly evolving resonant lowpass filters, resulting in a genre that brought the fun back to house music. Another example? Today's growing obsession with '80s British electro-pop, now fused with minimal house beats and the occasional retro a cappella.

As I sifted through the past decade or so of Keyboard articles, I was faced with a few challenges based on the above observations. First off, I had to determine how many hardware-oriented articles were needed. As we move toward a completely virtual, software-only universe, how relevant would it be to include topics such as working with hardware samplers? Then I reflected upon the origins of house and techno music during the '80s. During this period, everyone was pawning their old analog gear in order to raise money to buy glittering digital synths like Yamaha's DX7. As a result, thousands of cast-off TR-808s, TB-303s, and Minimoogs were snapped up by cash-strapped disco producers, who seemingly inadvertently created a sound that remains relevant to this day.

Accordingly, I decided to include a smattering of articles that covered hardware, revised slightly to keep them up-to-date with today's production techniques. For older software, I applied the same logic wherever possible. After all, not everyone can afford to update their computer workstation once a year (as much as the industry seems to presume otherwise), thus the inclusion of material that also applies in some cases to earlier versions of software, as well as to the latest and greatest updates. Fortunately, since many developers keep their software generally compatible with previous versions, a tip that applies to an earlier release will usually be equally relevant to the current version.

Tips and anecdotes from electronica artists were a slightly different matter. Since dance music is like fashion, remixers will come and go with the seasons. Like designers, some will change with the times, whereas others will fall by the wayside, fading into memory until they are resuscitated by a future generation. There were some tough decisions to make in predicting a producer's future relevance, but I think I managed to keep a decent balance between current stars, potential legends, and still-interesting footnotes.

Even so, a second dilemma remained: Some of our most interesting interviews were surprisingly devoid of real technical information on production techniques or business wisdom. This is partly due to the annoying fact that quite a few artists are simply too cagey to share the inside scoop with readers. Sadly, those are the artists who will not be immortalized in this tome. Too bad for them.

So as you sift through this book, keep in mind that it is a grab bag of information —in terms of both real-world production knowledge and historical anecdotes — for remixers and dance artists who already have a handle on the essentials of their craft but want to reach the next level.

That said, keep it funky.

—Francis Preve

On the CD-ROM

The included CD-ROM contains PC and Mac demo versions of Ableton Live. This is fully functional software that can be used to remix and re-arrange the included remix session files. The only limitation is that you cannot save your mixes or export audio; you'll need to purchase the full version for that. As this book goes to press, Ableton has just announced a new version of Live, so if you have a broadband connection, you may wish to visit the Ableton website (www.ableton.com) and download the latest demo version.

Also included on the CD are four Live Sets containing actual studio tracks from established dance and electronica artists Coldcut, Gabriel & Dresden, Jacinta, and Meat Beat Manifesto. Using the Live software you can remix, time-stretch, rearrange, process, and generally go nuts with this material, exploring the techniques described throughout the book with the aid of Live's comprehensive suite of tools.

Using the Live Sets

In addition to the music and vocal material, each Live Set includes its own brief tutorial on how to manipulate the audio content. This tutorial panel is located on the right side of the Live interface when you first open the set, so be sure to read it carefully before you begin. There is also a ReadMeFirst file for each session that contains important information on getting started.

The included remix sessions are as follows:

Coldcut: "Everything is Under Control"

Gabriel & Dresden: "Tracking Treasure Down"

Jacinta: "Solution"

Meat Beat Manifesto (MBM): "Wild"

End User License Agreement

All of the above remix content is protected by copyright, so here are the legal terms you need to abide by in order to use the material on the CD.

End User License

The "Licensor" (artist and/or record label) guarantees that the product has been created and recorded especially for this project and any similarity to any other recording is unintentional.

1. The sound samples recorded on this CD remains the property of Licensor and is licensed, not sold, to you for use on your sampling software or equipment.

2. A right to use the enclosed sounds is granted to the original end-user of the product (Licensee) and is *not* transferable.

3. The Licensee may modify the sounds but *may not use the sounds, modified or unmodified, for commercial purposes including, without limitation, within musical compositions.* Licensee must obtain a separate license from Licensor in respect of any intended commercial uses.

4. This license expressly forbids resale, relicensing, or other distribution of any of these sounds or any modification thereof. You cannot sell, loan, rent, lease, assign, or transfer all or any of the enclosed sounds to another user, or use them in any competing product.

5. Licensor will not be responsible if the contents of this disc do not fit the particular purpose of the Licensee.

6. Use of the included sound samples in isolation such as, but not limited to, video game soundtracks (where they appear in isolation or as sound effects) is not permitted without first obtaining a separate License from Licensor.

7. Use of the included sound samples in 'library music' (also known as 'production music') intended for commercial exploitation is not permitted without first obtaining a separate License from Licensor.

Chapter I
ESSENTIALS

To kick off this book, let's take a look at how a few pros approach the art of remixing. While later chapters are devoted to specific technical details on crafting grooves and unique sounds using a variety of popular software packages, this first chapter is a bit of a hodgepodge. We'll look at some concepts, techniques, and tried-and-true practices, from setting up and maintaining a soft studio to essential business practices. Also cued up: some very insightful advice on how to approach building a great remix that defines your sound. Once we've set the stage, we'll dig in deeper.

Let's begin with your workplace, the studio. While some remixers still prefer hardware, software is definitely the more cost-effective approach these days. In fact, I daresay that software-only production will become the norm before the end of the decade.

In this column on software studios, which first appeared in the April 2005 issue of *Keyboard,* Craig Anderton detailed how to prepare your studio for maximum efficiency.

April 2005
Who's the Boss?
Does your technology control your creativity, or do you?

Training your software-based studio is like training a dog. You reward it when it's good, punish it when it's bad, always let it know who's the boss, and give it a lot of love.

Last night I recorded a song in my computer-based studio. So what? Here's what: *Everything worked the way it was supposed to.* And believe me, it took a lot of effort to make sure I wouldn't have to spend a lot of effort. For example....

THE COMPUTER
My studio is bi-platform, although most work gets done on Windows XP because I use several Windows-specific programs. But no matter what platform you're using, the first step in a clean recording experience is to maintain your computer. This means:

Defragment your hard drive. Some say defragmentation is overrated. And in a way, that's true. Fast hard drives and a lot of RAM can cover a multitude of sins. But a fragmented drive can start messing with you when you're in the thick of a project, which is precisely when you *don't* want to be distracted. A word to the wise: Defragment often. That way it also takes less time than if you do it infrequently.

Some people recommend having a separate hard drive to use exclusively for audio. If you do this, it will make backup easier, and will also mean you won't need to defrag so often. The audio drive will contain fewer and larger files compared to your system drive, which contains lots of small files that often change.

Clean up your system. Get rid of programs you don't use. With Windows XP, go to Start > Run and type msconfig. Under the Startup tab, uncheck all those little useless thingies that load at start-up. (Is it really a priority to check for updates to RealPlayer every time you boot up, or load some accessory that lets you use your computer as a TV?) If you're not sure what a specific item is, don't uncheck it. A good clue is to look at the Command column. It's not advisable to uncheck items that start "C:\WINDOWS\system32," because your system probably needs those.

While you're at it, uncheck any unneeded services under the Services tab. For example, if you don't have a printer connected to your music computer, you can uncheck the Print Spooler service. *Caution: Some of these services are essential to running your computer.* Your local bookstore will have books about Windows XP that explain what each service does. With a little research, you can decide whether you need a service or not.

Turn off System Restore on your audio drive. Go to Start > Programs > Accessories > System Tools > System Restore. Click on System Restore Settings. Leave System Restore enabled on your main drive, but turn it off for the others. You can always turn it back on again if you need to, but the correct procedure to restore your audio projects is to save frequently!

THE OPTIMUM TEMPLATE FILE

When you load your host program, what happens? First, it probably scans for plug-ins, and that takes a while ... and if it doesn't like a plug-in, the program might even hang. So move any plugs you don't use out of your main plug-ins folder into an "old plug-ins" folder. You can always bring them back if you miss them.

Second, it should load all the tools you need at your disposal to start recording immediately. For example, when I open Sonar, there's an Acidized loop providing an audio metronome track in track 1 and the IK Multimedia SampleTank 2 multitimbral module installed in track 2, with four MIDI tracks set up to drive it. All I have to do is select a sound, put the focus on a MIDI track, hit record, and I'm busy recording a bass line, drum part, or whatever. There's an audio track with EQ already set up for my vocals, and a few other blank audio tracks.

Sure, "workstation" plug-ins might not have the ultimate Minimoog bass sound, or a 35GB grand piano. But that's the beauty of MIDI data. Play a part worthy of the ultimate Minimoog bass or a 35GB piano, and you can always assign that part to a different plug-in that you load up while mixing.

THE SHORTEST DISTANCE...

...is usually a keyboard shortcut. I'm shocked when I look over some people's shoulders and see them mouse around for everything — including cut, paste, open files, save, etc. It's really worth making a commitment to learning at least some of the most important keyboard shortcuts, because the amount of time you'll save is enormous. You'll also be less distracted during the recording process, which leads to more inspired performances.

Check out your program's Help file and do a search on "shortcuts." If there isn't a print option in the Help file copy it to a text editor and print it out. Learn a new shortcut every week. You'll thank me six months from now.

HAVE A MIC READY TO GO

This is especially true if you're a singer or songwriter, of course. But what happens if you're playing some great chord progression and get an idea for a lead line? If you're cookin' on the chords, don't try to incorporate the lead line into your part and get distracted: Sing it into the mic. Inspiration is fleeting, so be prepared to capture whatever comes into your mind. At least if it's recorded, you won't lose it. If the process of arming an audio track in your recording software is so complex that you don't want to deal with it, keep a cassette recorder beside the computer for one-button recording of whatever is going on in the room. (This has the advantage that it will work even when the computer isn't turned on.)

Once you've got the essentials of good studio hygiene in place, the next area to concentrate on is how you organize your work. Here are some of my thoughts on improving your workflow, so you can easily keep track of the numerous tracks you've already created or are about to produce.

July 2001
Workflow Enhancement
Tips for putting the "pro" in productivity

Workflow. It's a corporate buzzword these days, to be sure, but it's also the backbone of every project, creative or otherwise. How you work can definitely impact the quality of your musical endeavors. We all know how fickle the Muses can be — if you're not ready when they come knocking at 3:30 a.m., they'll just move on and leave you whining about the great song idea you thought you had.

Over the years I've discovered a few tricks that not only make composing and remixing faster, but, more important, actually improve the creative process itself. Organization is the key.

For computer users, a key ingredient in successfully organizing your creative system is having the fastest, biggest hard drive you can afford. Nothing slows a project down like hunting for a lost DVD backup, sound library, or sample CD. Having all your sounds and sequences ready for action with the click of a mouse can make the difference between a terrific session and an exercise in frustration.

Hard drive prices are plummeting. A 250GB or even 300GB drive can be had for $200 or less. With deals like this, it's a no-brainer to upgrade. The boost to productivity will be immeasurable.

Here are some of my favorite workflow enhancers:

DIRECTORY ASSISTANCE

When you begin a project, always make an effort to keep every file associated with the song (patch libraries, sequences, samples, audio tracks, even MIDI system-exclusive dumps — remember those?) in the same folder or directory. If it means duplicating a file that resides elsewhere on your hard drive, that's okay. It only takes a few extra seconds while you work, but it makes it easy to keep track of all of the song's components. Better still, once you've completed the composition, you can simply burn a CD with the folder contents — and the final mixes — in one quick step. This makes archiving your work for safekeeping a breeze.

LIKE A VERSION

Who hasn't worked on a track over a sustained period of time, only to find that earlier versions had a better groove, mix, or arrangement? Saving a copy of every version of a file during development is common practice in the software industry. Fixing one problem sometimes creates a new, more irritating obstacle. Being able to revert to an earlier version, or at least cue it up so you can listen to it, can be the only solution when confronted with this type of situation.

Even in these days of multi-level undo, which is found in many software sequencers and audio editors, it still makes sense to periodically save a copy of your most current file to a backup folder. The trick here is numbering the files in sequential order so you can keep track of each change to the project as it develops.

Here's my system: I include a three-digit number at the end of every filename, separated by hyphens (for example "MySong2-3-7.lso"). For small changes, like tweaking levels or adding effects, I increment the last digit. For medium-sized changes, like the addition of new parts or samples, I increment the middle digit. For major changes, like revising the arrangement or recording new audio tracks, I change the first digit. This way, if I find that a track has meandered off course, I can revert to the last decent-sounding version and pick it up from there. If all those numbers seem like more hassle than you're prepared to deal with, try the simpler approach of appending v1, v2, v3, and so on to your sequence files. Whichever technique you use, this is an extraordinary timesaver in the event that you need to go back to an earlier, better version.

MAKE A LIST AND CHECK IT TWICE

When you begin a project, make a plain text file that contains a list of every synth, software app, plug-in, and patch used in the piece. Update this list as the project progresses, and be sure to keep it in the same folder as the rest of the digital components. If even a few weeks pass between work sessions, it's easy to lose track of where you were — especially if you're using pre-MIDI, pre-programmable vintage gear. When the project is completed, print a copy of the component list and file it in a safe place. Having a record of everything in one place could save a few headaches in the event of a mix recall or hard drive trauma.

RIP DRAG MIX

Every time I buy a killer new sample or loop library, I rip the CD contents to AIFF or WAV format and stick them in their own folder on my hard drive. As I work on a track, I can immediately audition each sample without having to find the CD, wait for it to spin up in the drive, sift through the samples, rip the sample that strikes my fancy, then add it to the song. When you're communing with the Muses (or working with an impatient client) every second counts, especially when you're in a state of "flow." Having hundreds of gigabytes of inspirational audio at your fingertips can really put your creative process into hyperdrive.

JUST A BIT OFF THE TOP

If you work on multiple projects simultaneously — or are incredibly experimental/prolific — you may find yourself with dozens or even hundreds of sequences with cryptic names like "doodlesong" or "phunkybeat." Determining which track is which often consists of opening the file in your sequencer, turning on all your synths, setting up the mixer, etc. One of my all-time favorite workflow tricks is to record the audio for 32–64 bars of each composition in rough format at the end of each session, keeping an mp3 file of each mix in the appropriate sequence's folder. This way, when you sift through your catalog of ideas looking for nuggets of inspiration, it's a simple matter to listen to each audio snippet as opposed to powering up your entire rig only to find that the track in question wasn't the one you were looking for.

Hopefully these tips will help smooth the creative process. The secret is staying organized. Computers have changed the way we work and compose, so don't be afraid to dive in and take advantage of everything silicon has to offer.

One of the interesting aspects of remix culture is that there is no set of rules as to what skills a remixer must have. Countless DJs hire and/or collaborate with synthesist/producers. The latter are often referred to as "programmers" in the industry, though their contributions are far more extensive than simply entering data into a sequencer, as the word would seem to imply.

On the other hand, there are some brilliant remixers who got their start as musicians and performers, like BT, Moby, and Scissor Sisters. These artists often work alone, since they already have the skills to produce everything themselves. Even so, quite a few musicians choose to collaborate with DJs, since their unique vision and knowledge of dance music enables them to contribute the type of ideas that traditional musicians wouldn't think of

> initially or might even consider "wrong."
>
>   Over the years, I've worked both alone and in collaboration with DJs like Roland Belmares and Licious The Diva. Here are some thoughts on why the combination of skills can lead to results that are far more than the sum of their parts.

August 2004
Grab a Partner
Working with DJs

Occasionally I'm asked why I collaborate with DJs when I do a dance remix project. In fact, the question usually comes out like this: "Why do you work with DJs? You're already a keyboardist and producer. What the heck does the DJ do when you're remixing a track?"

The answer is as varied as the collaborations themselves. Some DJs have experience with grooveboxes and audio editors. Others have an encyclopedic knowledge of music and beats. Consider how much time you spend learning about filters, sequencers, and the latest effects plug-ins. Well, professional DJs spend the same amount of time honing their craft, perfecting segues, checking out new tracks, and spinning live sets.

While I love doing remixes on my own, there's a lot of knowledge that these cats bring to the table, and we all know that more knowledge is a good thing, right? So let's assume for a minute that you're on the musician side of the fence, looking to hook up with a DJ. Let's look at the various ways you can collaborate with a DJ to break new ground.

THE COLLEGE OF MUSICAL KNOWLEDGE

One of the indicators that a DJ is worth his or her salt is the depth of their musical knowledge. If they're obsessed with having the latest tracks before everyone else and they can rattle off a litany of every significant hit and underground white-label record, including the genre, label, and year, then you know you've struck gold.

Why is this important? For one thing, someone with this degree of meticulous attention can turn you on to tons of new tracks that are likely inspire and move you. For another, they can listen to your mixes and make recommendations based on what the current trends are. Like it or not, remixes are to music what fashion is to clothing. If you're doing something that's sooooo last month, a good DJ will steer you in the right direction.

What's more, because of their practical experience in clubs, they know what the crowds like. Accordingly, they can tell you what kind of response your track will get and which labels will be most receptive to your sound. In a way, knowing a successful and knowledgeable DJ is almost like having a virtual A&R veep on your team.

ARRANGEMENTS

Arranging a dance mix is very different from writing a three-minute pop song. Often, newbie remixers miscalculate how long the various segments of a remix should be, with introductions that are too short and breakdowns that aren't long enough. One of the keys to dance floor success is to build momentum with your arrangement.

Because their livelihoods depend on it, good DJs instinctively understand the elements of a remix arrangement. They know how to hype up a crowd with the right type of breakdown and how to bring the choruses back at the right time for maximum impact. For example, Licious The Diva helped me develop some techniques for constructing killer intros that are easy for novice DJs to mix into, yet are also interesting enough to keep the crowd's attention as they evolve. One very simple formula is to start with drums or percussion only, introducing new elements every eight measures. Then wait at least 24 bars before bringing in the bass or rhythmic synth parts.

MASTERING

Club sound systems often sound radically different from your home studio monitors. It can be hard to get a handle on how to deal with the low end, much less the overall EQ and dynamics of your mix. If you've partnered with a DJ who has a residency at a local club, they'll often let you try out your mixes on the club system before the crowd arrives. Better still, your DJ can mix your tune into another song, so you can hear your track in relationship to an established hit. This ear-opening courtesy has saved my butt on more than one occasion. Until I heard them on the club system, I would've sworn those mixes were club-ready. While the track plays at the club, grab some paper and take notes. Sometimes there are many subtle adjustments that you'll want to make, and your notes will ensure that you remember them all.

August 2004
THE MIX MAN COMETH

Gabriel and Dresden are quickly becoming one of the hottest progressive remixing teams around, reworking tracks from top artists like Annie Lennox and Britney Spears. In a recent discussion with Josh, the keyboard-playing and programming half of the duo, he explained how working with Dave Dresden raises his mixes to new heights.

"With over 30 remixes under our collective belt," says Josh, "I can tell you without a doubt that working with Dave has changed the way I make — and think about — music, for the better. Dave's 17 years of buying music and DJing gives him a perspective that is unique. His ear is tuned to what will work on the dance floor as well as what will still be remembered when the lights turn on.

"I'll admit that it took me a while to get used to the idea of working with someone who wasn't a Logic wizard or a synth-programming god, but now that we've done so much together, the lines between the technical and creative roles have blurred. We communicate on a musical level, and whatever needs to be done on the computer to make that happen, I just do it. I view him as an equal even though I'm working the gear. It's sometimes hard for us super-technical geeks to let a bull/DJ into our china shop/studio, but I couldn't recommend it more. It will seriously change the way you do things in ways you couldn't predict."

Sometimes collaborating with a DJ can require working long-distance. This would have been nearly impossible a mere decade ago, but now that the Internet has threaded the world's computers together, this type of collaboration is starting to become commonplace. The next section outlines a set of techniques that can make the process not only easy, but enjoyable and productive.

May 2005
Internet Collaboration
Getting hooked up

Recently, I was lucky enough to score a top-ten *Billboard* dance single, Debby Holliday's "Half a Mile Away." This remix was a long-distance collaboration between myself and circuit DJ Roland Belmares. After doing the initial preproduction, keyboards, and drum programming at my studio, we completed the mix by bouncing a Logic Pro song file back and forth between L.A. and Austin through the magic of broadband. In preparing for this endeavor, I discovered quite a few tricks for smoothing the process of connecting two studios via the Internet.

GETTING STARTED

It's critical to make sure both parties have identical software suites for the project. Apps like Ableton Live, Apple Logic, Propellerhead Reason, or even Apple GarageBand are all excellent candidates for long-distance collaboration, since they include a huge assortment of softsynths and effects, minimizing the need for additional third-party plug-ins. It can be problematic if both parties don't have identical collections.

It's possible to collaborate even if your systems are vastly different, but you'll have to do it by transferring audio files and submixes back and forth. The housekeeping (versioning and file management) required to do this is not trivial.

Another decision factor is cross-platform compatibility. While Logic and GarageBand are Mac-only products, Live and Reason come in both PC and Mac flavors and are packed with the tools needed to create finished product, though Reason isn't capable of recording audio tracks, a definite consideration if one of the collaborators plays an instrument like fiddle, turntable, or anything else for which there's no software equivalent.

Be aware of the CPU and RAM specs of both systems. If one computer is considerably more powerful than the other, you could easily run into compatibility issues if either collaborator piles on effects or softsynths, especially those with complex algorithms like reverb, physical modeling, and high-quality virtual analog synth plug-ins. In this situation, consider rendering or freezing resource-heavy tracks and working with audio and loops as much as possible, as this will minimize CPU overhead.

Once you've got the software and PC configurations finalized, you should designate a reference system for the final mix. This decision is based on multiple factors: who's got the best monitors, who's got the best acoustics, and who's got the best ears. Don't let egos get in the way! The collaborator who consistently creates the most balanced mixes should be the final link in the production chain. If both parties are tweaking EQs and one studio is better equipped than the other, the mixing process can become an unproductive tug-of-war. As you begin putting the finishing touches on a project, set aside some time to talk in-depth with your collaborator about direction and vibe. Communication is the key in any partnership. You can always agree to do separate versions of a track if your creative visions diverge too sharply.

Figure I-I

For well-heeled remote collaborators who are concerned about digital security as well as convenience, Digidesign's high-end DigiDelivery system is a cross-platform solution for secure high-speed file transfer. Two hardware component choices are available: the 500GB Serv GT at $9,995 and the 80GB at $3,295. Both boxes do the whole job, from providing a file server where files can be uploaded to notifying the recipient that a file is ready for download.

BRIDGING THE GAP

For any Internet-based project, a broadband connection is crucial. If you're going to be transferring audio, loops, and multi-megabyte sequence files, it's simply not practical to use a dial-up account (unless finances are an issue and you have the patience of a saint).

To complicate matters, all broadband services are not created equal. A connection with high-speed download and upload times is essential, so beware of ADSL (Asymmetric Digital Subscriber Line) services that receive data at speeds of approximately 1.544 megabits per second, but send (upload) data at speeds of only 128 kilobits per second. With ADSL, you may think something is terribly wrong with your connection when you send your files to your partner and they take much longer to transmit than the songfile you just received.

When shopping for a broadband provider, double-check to ensure that the upload and download speeds are roughly the same. For what it's worth, my Internet service provider (ISP) is cable-modem-based; the service works well and has sufficient bandwidth for the majority of my data transfer needs. The downside is that some cable-modem services degrade noticeably when shared by many users in a single neighborhood. If in doubt, ask around to see what services your neighbors use and if they're satisfied.

Another thing to watch out for is the fact that some ISPs have a limit to the size of files you can attach to email. This can be problematic if both parties are adding audio files to the project. Since it may not be practical to change your ISP — and your email address in the process — try using My Yahoo (my.yahoo.com) or Google's new Gmail service (gmail.google.com). Gmail offers a full gigabyte of advertiser-sponsored email storage. The downside of these services is that both currently have a cap of 10–15MB for attachments.

If you need to transfer larger files, you may want to consider a paid service like www.sendthisfile.com or Apple's .Mac suite of online tools. While sendthisfile offers a free basic service, there are bandwidth limitations that may make it necessary to upgrade to one of their paid plans. Apple users who are doing a lot of Internet collaboration should give some serious thought to the .Mac service, which includes 125MB of dedicated storage, email, and backup utilities for a $99 annual fee. Your collaborator will be able to log onto your .Mac account and transfer files even if he or she is using Windows.

LIKE A VERSION, REDUX

Finally, one of the keys to bouncing files back and forth between studios is the versioning trick discussed earlier in this chapter. Be sure to create a new version as soon as you receive the project file from your collaborator. That way, if your online experiments take a wrong turn, you can always revert to an earlier mix and save yourself a lot of headaches in the process.

Doug Beck has written countless articles for *Keyboard* on his experiences as half of the remixing duo Boris & Beck. In this column, he gives a wonderfully candid account of what happens when a label and the remixer(s) fail to communicate.

October 2000
Communication Is Key
The story of a remix gone bad . . . then good

Let's face it: There are very few producer/remixers who can get away with a "here's my mix — take it or leave it" attitude. It doesn't matter if you're a seasoned pro or a new producer doing your first spec mix. Maybe it's your first opportunity with a new label, or a new client. Whatever the situation, one thing's for sure: If everyone isn't totally clear about what's expected from the remix, it just might be your last. There aren't too many second chances in this business.

As remixers we sometimes forget that what we ultimately do is a work for hire, a job. Yes, there is artistry, craft, and technological skill involved, and it's important — even necessary — to bring all of your creative and technical skills to each project and make the best record you can make. But at the end of the day, the people who are paying your fee have their own specific reasons for hiring particular producers/remixers. A record label has a vision and marketing plan to which they have given considerable time and thought. The reality of the business means that a remix is actually a collaboration with your client, and as in any collaboration, good communication is absolutely necessary.

I've heard nightmare stories from some of the biggest names in the industry about remixes that were rejected by a record label simply because there was no clear understanding of what the label people wanted from the outset. Many hours and dollars have been spent on big-budget projects that never saw the light of day because producer and label just weren't on the same page. Solid business relationships can become strained because of a simple miscommunication or misunderstanding. Most of us genuinely want the label to be happy with the work we've done, and we want to accomplish this with a minimum of drama. Clear communication with the person you're working for is imperative.

This is the story of a communication breakdown, the tools we used to prevail, and how the whole thing might have been avoided in the first place.

COMMUNICATION BREAKDOWN

My partner and I (Boris & Beck) were hired by a fairly large label to remix a single of an established artist (no names will be mentioned to protect — well, me). We were told that we were hired on the strength of our previous work and our demo reel. The label provided no real direction; we were simply told to "do your thing." (Those words still echo in my head....) After a few days in the studio, we delivered a trancey vocal mix at 140 bpm. We were very happy with it. It had lots of energy, big buzzy keys, and floating arpeggios, in a style similar to records we had done recently that were working well in the clubs. We really thought we had a winner. Wrong!

When the phone rang, we were already onto the next project. "We like the mix but the tempo is too fast. You're going to need to slow it down. We don't like the bass sound. We want you to put in more vocal and add some percussion from the original version. By the way, where's the second mix?" Second mix? What second mix? We didn't know anything about a second mix. My first thought was that this project was a total wash. I was ready to say the hell with it, but decided the best thing to do was fix it, whatever it took. We recalled the mix.

TEMPO FIX

My first challenge was the tempo issue. The mix consisted of about half MIDI tracks and half audio samples. The MIDI tracks would be a no-brainer: slow down the tempo on my sequencer program, and the MIDI tracks follow. The audio would be another matter. I had imported audio samples from various sources into Cubase, and had spent hours chopping, tweaking, and editing them. It wasn't going to be practical to simply go back to the source audio and time-stretch it to the new tempo. It would never be tight, and I would essentially have to do it over.

Determined to lose as little of our work as possible, I tried taking a percussion track and, with the software's built-in time-compression/expansion facilities, changing the tempo of the entire track. While the result was close, it wasn't close enough. Then I tried it on a vocal track, and to my surprise it turned out well, needing only small nudges here and there to tighten it up. I went back to the percussion tracks and the other bits of audio and used the audio export function to write new WAV files to my drive in one- to four-bar phrases. For instance, the kick track was basically a four-on-the-floor pattern, with rhythmic breaks and transitions every 16 to 32 bars. I exported a one-bar section of the four-on-the-floor part, and then exported each of the breaks and fills so they became single audio files instead of a bunch of little files. Next, I imported my new files into [Sony] Acid, slowed the session tempo down to 135 bpm, and listened carefully to make sure everything was tight. Once I was satisfied, I used Acid's export function to write WAV files at the new project tempo of 135, then imported these into my original Cubase session.

Using the old kick track as a reference, I reconstructed the kick pattern, making sure I had all of the breaks and fills in the right places. I followed these same steps with the rest of the audio tracks, which ended up taking about two more hours.

WE'RE REMIXERS, NOT MAGICIANS

The second major issue we were facing was the request that we use a specific percussion loop from the original mix. After fruitlessly searching the DAT for the sample, I phoned up the A&R guy and asked him if he forgot to put it on the DAT. His response was, "Can't you just take it off the original record?"

This is another instance where good communication at the very beginning would certainly have come in handy. You cannot assume that the person hiring you has a clear understanding of music technology and how these tools work, and, regardless, it's your job to make sure you have all of the parts you'll need to do the remix. I can't count the number of times a record label has delivered a vocal that had all of the parts on one stereo pass, with effects. You need to specify that you want the lead vocal separate from backgrounds, and no effects. Any other signature parts that you and/or the label want to include in the remix can also be provided on the DAT. Until there's a magic extraction software program that lets you pull individual parts off a record, this is the way it is. Fortunately, most clients are happy to oblige your requests, but the time for you to speak up is at the beginning of the project.

We went back to the original single, and as it turned out, we got lucky: The percussion part we needed was isolated in a breakdown section for a couple of bars. To capture it, I imported the entire mix into my audio editor via the CD, chopped out the percussion part, and looped it. I dropped the loop into Acid, exported the file at 135 bpm, and imported it into the Cubase session. Painless. We made a few additional minor changes here and there, and then constructed a dub version at 140 bpm from our original mix. When we delivered our new vocal mix and dub, everyone at the label was happy, and we were only about a day behind.

This story could have had a very different ending. Fortunately, the awesome technological tools we have available make these kinds of recalls much less painful than they would have been even just a couple of years ago. However, the whole mess could have been avoided if there had been clear communication between our camp and the label up front. We were very lucky that we were given an opportunity to make it right, and in the end we saved

March 1998

THE ANGEL'S GUIDE TO COMPENSATION

1. Appraise what you're worth. Obviously the more and higher-profile work you've done, the more you can ask for.

2. Get it in writing. If it's not in a contract, I don't care who agrees with you on it.

3. Work "points" into the contract. Points have got to be in the mix. I've been working those provisions into agreements so that if the track is used outside of the context for which I've been hired, then I would be compensated for it.

4. Don't do it alone. Have good management and a good cross-section of friends who are very knowledgeable in the industry. Having a lawyer is essential. It's tedious and time-consuming, and often it takes longer to get through the stupid agreement than it does to do the project, because lawyers will take their time and they're busy. It may not be the biggest deal in the world to them, because it's a one-off thing for one song, but protecting yourself is very important.

our relationship with a new client. As a result of this experience, we now have a check-list of issues we deal with before we start the project:

- Talk about tempo issues or concerns. Know what the client has in mind regarding a specific tempo or tempo range for each mix.
- Discuss what parts should be on the DAT. [*Editor's note: These days, a CD would be used instead of a DAT cassette.*] Some labels will invite you to be at the session, so you can listen to the master and print exactly what you want to a DAT. This is a good time to get the client's thoughts on what "signature" parts they feel are important on the remix.
- Discuss the client's expectations clearly, so you're sure you understand exactly what they need from you. It might seem obvious, but being extra specific about what's expected can save everybody a lot of time and trouble.

"Do your thing...." Those words still echo in my head, mocking me. Based on those words, we made some assumptions that turned out not to be the same ones the label was making, and neither of us knew it. Communication is key!

June 1998
ARMAND VAN HELDEN TALKS COMPENSATION

Back in the late '90s — before downloading helped to implode the dance music market — a good remixer could command tens of thousands of dollars per remix. Back then, Armand Van Helden was one of the premier pro-ducers. Here's a little interview tidbit from June '98 to make you very, very jealous.

Are you still getting flat fees, or are you getting into points now?

Flat fees. The amount of time and phone calls you have to put in to collect points is a nightmare. Even for an artist signed to a label, it's a nightmare. They [the record labels] will hold out 'til the very last minute, until you're about to sue them. And it's just a fucking game that all the labels play. It's a part of major label business. Their whole thing is, "Don't sweat nothing until the dire last minute — until we're about to go to court." That's how they work. So me and my manager finally said, "Fuck all this drama trying to get paid! Let's just set the rate high to compensate, and just get it flat."

Some people might argue that a flat fee could be a rip-off to an artist whose remix hits big.

My Tori Amos remix blew up, and you know what, I didn't see nothing from that. Zero. But at the same time I got about 40,000 other mixes because of it. You see what I'm saying? So, in a way I did get paid back from it. And prob-ably easier and faster than trying to collect it from the label.

Word on the street is that you pull in anywhere from 25 to 50 grand per mix. Is that true?

Yeah, but again, a lot of it's my manager, cause I really don't do any of the talking. The whole thing started out last year. I was doing mixes at that time for about $25,000. And that's high, but that's pretty much what the best peo-ple were getting. But what happened was, I wanted to do a hip-hop album, and I said, "I don't want to do any remix-es. Set the price crazy high so nobody will bite." And people bit. So, we were like, "If they're going to bite at $30,000, lets go to 35. And then if they're gonna bite at 35, let's go to 40." And that's how it ended up. It's just business. You know? I mean, you create a demand, and if you're turning in quality stuff, you jack the price.

Even the best grooves sometimes fail to stir a crowd. A great remix often requires more than vocals, percolating synths, and slammin' beats — you need a killer hook to bring your mix to the next level. Doug Beck breaks it down and explains his approach.

April 1999
Signature Synth Lines
Drop one of these hooks into your next dance track
and watch the club go nuts

I recently spent some time hanging out in dance clubs in NYC, Miami, and Chicago, and noticed a trend at every venue I visited: At peak time, when the club is totally amped and the grooves are banging, playing over the groove is a relentless, infectious synth line that drives the track — and the crowd — right over the edge. How is it that a quirky synth sound playing a simple melody can inspire nearly every person in the room to throw his or her hands in the air and scream? And how do the people making these records come up with such hooky, biting synth sounds and parts? This month I'd like to share with you some tips on creating a synth line frenzy of your own, the kind that will have people hanging from the rafters and screaming for more.

THE STARTING SOUND
Creating an infectious synth line is easier than you might think. You don't need an arsenal of synths to do it — in fact, you can work wonders with just a sampler. But let's start with the synth. The first thing I do is look for a biting synth sound that will really cut through a mix, usually something with a lot of high-midrange frequencies and not too much bottom. I've found that synth brass or analog string-type sounds are a good starting point, but you'll most likely want to edit the sound to give it a character that's more unusual. At the very least, you'll need to make sure it has a fast attack and almost no release time.

Once the attack and release are tight, it's time to engage the filter. If your synth has different filter types, you can try all of them until you find something that strikes you, but a lowpass filter will almost always do the trick. It's also helpful if you can assign the filter cutoff to your synth's joystick or mod wheel, as this will give you greater control over the filter. I'll often assign another track on my sequencer the same MIDI channel as my synth line, so I can record the filter modulation movements separately.

KEEP THE PART SIMPLE
Once you've got the right synth patch at your fingertips, you're ready to play your part. While there's no magic formula, there are a few guidelines I try to adhere to. First and foremost, it's important that the part be simple. A signature synth line in a dance record is not unlike the vocal hook of a pop record: The melody should be catchy and memorable, not overly complicated.

It's also important to take into account the mood that the melody conveys, since the synth line is often the main melodic part in the track. Melodies based on minor scales tend to convey more of a sense of urgency than those based on major scales. Exotic, Eastern-sounding melodies can provide a darker, more trance-like flavor, yet still sound manic.

When you come up with a line you like, loop it and listen to it replaying. Is it infectious and haunting? Can you listen to it for a while without getting tired of it? Does it groove? If so, you've got your signature line.

SHAPING THE SOUND

Once the part is captured, it's time to make sure it works with the track. Since the line will be prominent in the mix, it often requires some serious fine-tuning and tweaking for maximum impact. If you've assigned filter cutoff to a joystick or mod wheel, try opening and closing the filter at key times during the track, or concentrate on riding the filter to color the part in a dramatic and unusual way. I also like to overdo the reverb and chorus, using much more than I might on any other part; it gives the sound a siren-like quality.

Layering two or more sounds can work wonders too. A sound that's great by itself doesn't always work when you put it in your track. On a recent project, I had a pretty good synth sound, but it wasn't quite right. I started randomly going through sounds and came across an odd, synthesized percussion sound — kind of like a low-pitched electronic timbale. The sound itself did nothing for me, but when I layered it with what I already had, the percussive attack gave the sound just what it needed. I never would have guessed it would work so well! You never know, so it's worthwhile to loop an eight-bar section of the track with the synth line playing, and layer various sounds over it.

Another good trick is to sample your part, or sample just the sound that you've created. Once it's inside your sampler, you can modulate and effect it even more. Try playing with the sample start and end times. You might find that the unnatural, harsh attack created by shaving the sample's start time really works. Adjusting the loop time can alter the feel of the synth line in an interesting way.

The signature synth line has been a staple of dance music for many years, but what's new is the emergence of tracks with fresh sounds and powerful hooks so prominent in the mix that they are often the singular defining feature of the track. It's this marriage of sound and melody that can push a track right over the top.

In the essay below, Doug Beck and DJ Boris give you the skinny on how they use transitions as a tool for adding tension and release to a remix.

November 1999
Ebb and Flow
Build it up, take it down

The pacing of a remix or dance track intended for club play has everything to do with the impact it will have on the dance floor. A good club track never starts with a washy synth sound and then blasts right into the bass line or groove all at once; it builds up tension gradually and releases it in an exploding rush, then cools off again, taking the crowd on a wild ride. Playing with that energy is the domain of the DJ, and it is definitely an art form.

Though I do spend a fair amount of time in dance clubs, I am not a DJ. My partner DJ Boris, however, is a fixture in the clubs of NYC, the Hamptons, Miami, and Boston. What better resource to explore the ebb and flow of energy that makes for an effective track or remix? Below, DJ Boris and I discuss how the elements of an arrangement impact that intangible current of energy. While we follow no strict formula when we work on a remix, we wanted to offer some guidelines and ideas to consider that will help you give your track a dynamic flow for club play.

I've added my own comments at the end of a couple of Boris's sections.

Doug: What do you like to hear at the beginning of a club record? What's important to you?

Boris: The most important element is the way the intro is put together, which in essence builds the track into what it is. If the intro doesn't grab me, the rest of the track usually doesn't satisfy me either. An intro gives a taste of the track, like a tease. The most important thing is, without question, the drums. Is the kick solid and banging? Are there some interesting percussion parts? This is what I look for immediately. Also, it can't get too creative with rhythms and effects; it has to have a really solid beat, since this is where the track gets mixed in. [Thunderpuss 2000's mix of "It's Not Right" by Whitney Houston is a good example of a track with an excellent intro.]

Doug: Once you're past the intro, what elements are you looking for to build energy?

Boris: Synths. I want to hear an interesting synth sound playing a cool part that lifts the track. Occasionally, I hear records where a synth part comes in and actually brings the energy down. You must have that high level of energy piercing through the track. Drum and percussion parts that mark a new phase of the track have to be dynamic and interesting, too. [For cool percussive elements, listen to a Hex Hector or Victor Calderone remix.]

Doug: Also, it's not enough to just slam in a new part at measure 64. New parts that are added have to make sense musically and rhythmically. Transitions can help this process tremendously. A transition can be as simple as a cymbal crash on the eighth-notes before the new section begins, but a lot of the time something more elaborate is called for. For instance, we often use sweeping synth transitions to bridge different sections together. So Boris, what is it specifically about a synth line that grabs you?

Boris: What I like seems to be the perfect combination of the sound and the part that it plays. It has to be an instant hook, but part of what makes a hook work is the synth sound. They have to complement each other. [Check out Razor-n-Guido's "Do It Again" for an example of a track with a great sound/melodic hook.]

Doug: Let's talk about what's next, after a synth hook has been established and the energy is rising.

Boris: For a remix, a vocal record, you have to set up the point where the vocal comes in so it has maximum impact. If there's a high-energy chorus with a wailing vocal, that almost always cranks the energy way up. We might let the chorus loop for a while, then drop out most of the heavy synths and drums when the first verse comes in to take it back down a little bit.

Doug: In a vocal remix, the structure of the song dictates a certain energy flow. The chorus usually has the most energy, verses less, and short bridges and pre-choruses can work like transitions. It's like having a map to work from, and you have to follow it, especially for a shorter radio edit. But the same principle works for dubs [minimal vocal versions] and tracks [instrumentals], too. You can drop a high-energy sample over the most banging groove for a while, then pull the sample and a few other parts out, and get the same effect as the chorus and verse of a song.

Boris: After the track has built to a frenzy, a big breakdown can be dramatic. People really dig it. Everyone's been building up to a peak, and then the record basically takes a breather so everyone else can, too. If it's done right, people just go nuts. It really takes them over the top. And at this point, the track should just ride for a while with the energy peaking. After another 32 bars or so, the track can start to break down. It's important that the final breakdown is gradual and that the beat remains solid so the DJ can mix out of the track into the next record. Then the whole ride starts over again.

Doug: If you think about it, it's like a rollercoaster. The good ones build up tension and expectations and then release all that energy in a big rush. Then there are smaller waves, and another buildup, another drop, until it finally coasts out. There are many great rollercoasters, just like there are many great dance tracks, and no two are ever the same. What they all have in common is, when you get it right, the crowd is in for one wild ride.

Most remixers are also dance artists and producers themselves, So before we move on to the more technical and musical details of producing the various elements of a good remix, let's take a look into the development of the dance artist in general. In this column, Rob Hoffman details his role in creating the early demos for a pop artist you may have heard of — Christina Aguilera — as well as his work developing Michelle Crispin.

November 2000
The Demo
Artist development and presentation

If you've found it difficult to get noticed in the music industry, you aren't alone. As remixer/producers, we're constantly battling for recognition and the big break that can set our careers on fire. While we'd all like to get that call from Madonna to remix her next single, it's not very realistic. One of the more interesting and practical ways of getting noticed in the industry is the development or "spec" deal. Basically that means finding an artist who you think has potential in the current market and producing their demo, then shopping it to record labels. The goal is to either get paid for the work you've done for the artist or the ultimate reward: producing some portion of the artist's debut CD. Unfortunately, there are no guarantees in this world, so get things in writing. It can be a simple deal memo stating what your intentions are and how both you and the artist expect to get paid. As with all things involving money, it doesn't hurt to have a lawyer draw up the paperwork.

It was this strategy that brought my partner Heather Holley and I together with pop diva Christina Aguilera. Two and a half years ago her management team contacted me and asked if I would write and produce her demo on spec (*i.e.*, no guarantee of payment). They sent a video from her Mickey Mouse Club days and a demo of a song she had written with another producer. Upon hearing her voice, we quickly agreed to do the deal, and scheduled time for her to fly out from the East Coast. We wrote five songs the week before her arrival. She sang all five songs, backgrounds and leads, in five days and I mixed them three days later. It added up to about two weeks of work, generally about 15 hours a day. Both her management team and mine sent the demo to every major-label contact we had, and within a few months she signed a deal with RCA. My partner and I were fortunate enough to be able to write and produce a song for her debut CD — an opportunity we probably wouldn't have gotten had we not developed a working relationship with Christina and RCA from the beginning. We are truly blessed to be in such great company on such a successful record.

So how does this apply to the dance world, especially remixes? Fast-forward to today.... My team has been applying this development strategy to dance music artists, and we are enjoying great success with it. It's always difficult to find raw tracks to practice your remixing skills on, but here you have the opportunity to create the raw material and devise a series of mixes and remixes that shows off your skills not only as a remixer, but also as a writer and producer.

Over the last year we've been developing an artist named Michelle Crispin. We originally set out to record a three-song demo, but that plan was modified. We ended up creating a fully marketable CD and vinyl single complete with a pop radio mix and five club-ready remixes, plus a short-form video. With this single we've created quite a buzz around town. The record industry loves to see sales figures. It shows them that groundwork has already been laid and means that they can concentrate on a larger marketing plan.

The dance world is particularly well suited to independent promotion. Record pools (services that provide music to club DJs) regularly accept vinyl and CDs from unsigned artists and indie labels, or you can go direct to the DJs themselves. It's quite gratifying to walk into a club and hear one of your mixes playing; try that in the pop or rock world and Top 40 radio! Most DJ pools also provide a weekly chart allowing you to keep track of your progress. They also provide you with marketing material as your single rises up their individual charts. It's even possible to chart on the *Billboard* Club Play chart by servicing the *Billboard*-reporting DJs. This is a group of DJs that supplies *Billboard* with their playlist each week. These playlists make up the Club Play chart. No politics, no payola, just spins in a club. The *Billboard* DJs are very influential in the dance community, and success there means that labels will want to find out who you are and what you're about. This may lead to remix and production calls from both major and indie dance labels.

With an artist who's willing to tour, you may gain even more club exposure. When Michelle goes out to play a gig, we usually send out vinyl, CDs, and a promo video to the club two weeks prior so the DJs can start to add her track to their rotation. If the club has a video wall they might play the video as well.

In addition to increased visibility for you or your production team, there's also the opportunity to make money via online distribution. We began distributing Michelle's single about ten months ago on the Internet. Amazon.com offers its Advantage program; there's also the Orchard, CDbaby, and others who require you to do nothing more than fill out an online form and send them product. Our online presence has also led to many dance specialty stores calling us to request product. Not bad. We've turned the art of demo production into a money-making marketing machine.

Chapter 2
DRUMS, BEATS, AND GROOVES

It's hardly a secret that drums and drum loops are the bedrock of every remix. People just don't dance to tracks that don't have a killer beat. End of story. With that in mind, let's take a good look at how producers nail that combination of sounds and syncopation in their mixes, starting with a few salient points from Doug Beck.

June 1998
Building a Better Groove
How to make a sampled beat mesh with the track

When we're talking about dance music, nothing is as important as the groove. Without a slamming, high-energy beat, you simply don't have a dance track. The good news is that there are lots of tools available to help today's dance music producer or programmer put together a great groove — sampling CDs are plentiful. Instant groove, right? Well . . . you might feel kind of strange using someone else's canned loop from a CD, no matter how good it is. You want something that sounds original, not the same loop that anyone can download or pop into their sampler.

I'd like to take you through some of the ways you can "dress up" a loop to make it sound significantly different from the original source. In this way, you can incorporate sampled drum loops into your music without it being obvious that you've used an identifiable loop.

There are many benefits to using a sample CD. One big one is that once you find a decent loop, a lot of work has already been done for you: The drums are mixed, EQ'd, panned, compressed, and even mastered. Also, there are many good choices available, no matter what type of dance music you're into. Sample CDs are generally royalty-free for music production, which means you don't have to pay royalties if you use the material on a commercial release. (Note that this is not *always* the case, so be sure to read the fine print on the packaging.)

Almost every track I do consists of both drums that I program, with sounds originating from either a synth or a sampler, and some sampled loops. Layering a loop with programmed drums is an important first step, just to make sure the sampled loop locks up with the MIDI programming. If the loop locks with a programmed four-on-the-floor kick, for instance, and the groove feels okay, you can be assured that all of your subsequent MIDI programming will lock too. In addition, by layering the loop with programmed drums, you have already taken a step toward disguising the loop.

A common problem I experience when working this way is that the kick drum in the sampled loop "fights" with the kick I've programmed. Regardless of how you tweak the tuning of the loop, sometimes you will hear a slight flamming between the kicks, or a phasing or flanging effect. In fact, whenever you use a sampled drum loop with a programmed kick, you will most likely run into this. There are a couple of tricks you can try to remedy this situation. The quickest fix might be to simply roll all the low end off the loop. If your loop is playing from a sampler and the audio is coming up on a dedicated channel on your mixer, the channel EQ may be enough to do the trick. Alternatively, if the loop has been imported as an audio file into your sequencer, sound editing software can help out. Most software-based sound editing programs have filter effects and EQ that you can use to process your audio file. When you filter out the low end, the loop retains its feel and the programmed kick drum sounds clean.

Which brings us to effects. Different filter settings can dramatically change the sound of a loop while still retaining the feel and the groove. A simple delay clocked to the loop can sometimes create a great feel. Flanging can create very interesting effects. Another phenomenal software tool is Propellerhead's ReCycle program. In a nutshell, this program takes a sound file (*e.g.,* a drum loop) and chops up the audio into discrete slices so it can be edited in some very practical and precise ways. Depending on the loop, you can sometimes remove a kick drum manually without affecting the rest of the loop. You can also use ReCycle to change the tempo of the loop, or to scramble or rearrange the contents of the loop, which can create some extreme variations on the original. ReCycle can also create a MIDI file from an audio sample, so you can retain the feel of the loop while utilizing drum sounds from a sampler, synth, or drum machine.

Another way to spice up a groove is to layer several loops together with your programmed drums. This may take some experimenting, but the results can be quite good. Adding a single percussion loop to a drum loop can really make a track slam, and you can play with the feel by offsetting the percussion loop slightly in either direction. Experimenting with dif-

November 2001
BT ON BEATS

Brian Transeau delivers the details on how he creates his trademark stutter edits and sample-accurate layered grooves.

Let's talk about the mechanics of how you make your breaks.
There are two ways I do things. Every time I program a break in [Propellerhead] Reason and time-correct it in [Apple] Logic, I make it a WAV file and throw it into [Sony] Acid. So I already have thousands of beats that are my Reason breaks, but if I want to do something at a different tempo, everything's already cut up ready to go in Acid. I might take a dope kick drum and hi-hat from one loop and snares and ride cymbal from something else, but it'll all work together because I've time-corrected everything to the same grid.

And I have hundreds of DATs of amazing stuff, like Omar Hakim playing hubcaps with brushes or whatever. I've cut up all this stuff and put it into my Acid library.

I have a bunch of gear, so the beats start in a bunch of different places. But mostly my beats start with Reason and Acid and the MPC, although a little less frequently now with the MPC3000. Before Reason, I was using the MPC and Acid, and taking sounds that I now use in Reason and cutting them up and arranging them in Logic.
Why the switch to Reason?
Reason helps minimize the tedium of fine-tuning a loop, finding good loop points and so on. It's so easy to use, and the rendered files I get from it are really close to being perfectly time-corrected, so it makes that process easier.

I use the compressor in Reason too, because it's so ghetto it's good. It kind of reminds me of a dbx 160.

ferent pan settings is also worthwhile; by panning various elements of your drum tracks, you can create a wider sound. Adding a sampled loop played an octave lower than its intended pitch can evoke a darker, half-time feel.

And don't forget the breaks. Even a great groove can get boring if it just repeats over and over. Insert breaks at key points in the track to add impact or build tension. For instance, drop the kick out for a measure before you add a clap, and when the clap comes in bring the kick back in. Bringing percussive elements in and out of your track will let it breathe and build, and will help keep it dynamic and interesting.

> **As Doug mentioned, sampled loops are a great shortcut when it's time to lay the groundwork for your groove. Another path to beat bliss is to create everything from scratch, including drum sounds and effects processing. In the next essay, Craig Anderton describes the process of working with samples of single drum hits.**

August 2001
Better Drum Parts Through Programming
Using a sampler's voicing parameters to customize the sound

With so much rhythmic emphasis in today's music, it's no surprise that drum generators — whether in the guise of soft synths, samplers, or hardware grooveboxes — are enjoying a surge in popularity. I've been particularly enjoying two VST instruments that complement

Sometimes I'll do separate bounces of just kick, just snares, and just hi-hats, then do the shelving EQ to each of the files in Logic, then bounce it all together. It's so easy to get a good vibe happening with Reason. My general approach with that is to take a Redrum, compressor, and two REX players. I'll highpass-filter the REX files, pan the ReCycle breaks out in stereo, then use Redrum for the backbeat. I have the mod wheel maybe assigned to filter cutoff so I can make different parts of the ReCycle loops filter differently.

How do you work with drum loops of live playing, which inherently have slight timing variations?
I love using live drums in my stuff to pick up the intensity of a track. But I'll shelf the live drums at around 200Hz, so all of the ass-end comes from a 909 or that kind of kick drum. You hear the overheads, the snare cracking, and all the hi-

hats and ride, but all the bass comes from an electronic kick. I did that on "Never Gonna Come Back Down" [from *Movement in Still Life*].

I like that super-compressed overhead sound. I've taken a 909 kick, a programmed snare, and a live loop shelved at 200Hz. Or you could take a live drum loop, shelf it at 80Hz, then put an 808 kick with it — that sounds banging too.

When I'm recording live drums I like to go into the studio and use a bunch of vintage mics and compressors, record [with analog tape] at 15 ips and everything. Then I'll take everything back to my place, and when I look at the waveforms of all the drum tracks it's like, "It doesn't sound like the kick and hi-hat are flamming but you can see that they are." So I'll time-stretch past the beat and then hard-cut the hi-hat and the kick drum together and bring everything up to the downbeat, and it just punches.

each other perfectly: Steinberg/Waldorf Attack (which synthesizes drum sounds) and Native Instruments Battery (which plays sampled drums). *Editor's note: Attack is unfortunately no longer available, but numerous other programs have taken its place, including Apple Logic's Ultrabeat.*

To get the most out of these programs — or, for that matter, samplers playing drum sounds, software suites with percussion instruments (such as Propellerhead Reason), and even dedicated hardware units — you'll want to take advantage of the many editing possibilities. By tweaking a few parameters, you can create more expressive and powerful sounds, while personalizing what you do. Here are some of my favorite drum tweaks.

PITCH SHIFTING

The pitch control parameters are surprisingly useful. You can:

- Tune drums to the song's key. This is particularly applicable to toms and resonant kick drums (such as the famously overused TR-808 "hum drum"). If the kick is out of tune, it can fight with the bass to make mud, or just confuse the song's sense of key. If fine tuning is not available as a control (sometimes you can change tuning only in semitones), you may be able to feed in a constant amount of pitchbend as a workaround.
- Create multiple drum sounds from one. Want to play a two-hand shaker part, but you have only one shaker sample? Copy it, then detune the copy by a semitone or so to provide a slight sonic variation. Detuning can also create a family of cymbals or toms out of one cymbal or tom sample.
- Accommodate different musical genres. Some house music styles pitch drum sounds lower, whereas drum and bass often pitches sounds up. You may not need a new set of samples; try retuning the ones you have.
- Use radical transpositions to create new sounds. Most drum boxes don't have a gong sound, but don't let that stop you. Take your longest cymbal sound and detune it by –12 to –20 semitones. Create another version of the cymbal and detune it by about –3 semitones. Layer the two together. The slightly detuned cymbal gives a convincing attack, while the lower-pitched one provides the necessary sustain.
- (A note for trivia fans: You may wonder why detuning can't create the wonderful cymbal effects that happen when you shift the pitch of a sample on an E-mu SP-12 or 1200. This is because those boxes used a different type of sample transposition — technology based on sample skipping rather than stretching/compressing. Sample skipping, which is an older technology, introduces new overtones when a sound is pitched up or down.)
- If your drum sound source lets you assign velocity to pitch modulation, you can increase dynamics by programming high velocity levels to add a very slight upward pitch shift. This works best if you apply velocity to the amount of pitch envelope, and then modulate the drum's pitch from the envelope, so that after attacking at a higher pitch, the drum will fall back to the normal pitch. Of course, the increase doesn't have to be slight if you want to create a disco-type falling tom sound. A small increase emulates a drum's skin being stretched, hence pitched higher, when it's first hit.

CHANGING THE SAMPLE START POINT

Altering a sample's start point under velocity control can add convincing dynamics (see Figure 2-1). Most drum machines won't do this, but many synths and samplers will. Generally, you set the initial sample start point several tens, or even hundreds, of milliseconds "late" into the sample so it's past where the attack occurs. Now assign negative velocity to modulate the sample start point. At low velocities, you don't hear the signal's initial attack; higher velocities will kick the start point further toward the beginning, until at maximum velocity you hear the entire attack.

If you already have a good MIDI drum part but it lacks dynamics, you can add sample start modulation after recording. Simply overdub a controller track using a mod wheel or MIDI fader, and assign the controller to sample start time.

FILTER MODULATION

For dynamic control beyond tying velocity to level and/or sample start point, assign velocity to filter so that hitting the drum harder produces a slightly brighter sound. This gives extra emphasis to the hardest hits, making the drums feel more "alive." Soft taps will sound a bit muted.

HI-HAT AMPLITUDE ENVELOPE DECAY MODULATION

One of the most annoying "features" of electronic drums is the hi-hat. A real drummer is constantly working the hi-hat, opening and closing it with the pedal, but the electronic version is an unchanging snapshot. Sure, you can program a combination of open, half-closed, and closed hi-hat notes, and assign them to a mute group (described below) so each will cut off the others, but programming a rhythm with three hat sounds is tedious, and doesn't always sound realistic.

A more expressive option is to use a MIDI controller, such as mod wheel, to vary an open hi-hat sound's envelope decay time. Shorten the decay for a closed hi-hat. As you extend the decay, the hi-hat opens gradually. I usually play the hi-hat note with my right hand and

Figure 2-1

The highlighted section of Battery's virtual front panel shows the controls for modulating, setting, and monitoring the sample start point. (Note: I've modified the front-panel graphic to focus attention on the sample start point elements.) On the waveform display, the red line indicates the initial sample start point, as set by the Start control. In the Modulation section, velocity is modulating Sample Start by –92, so higher velocities cause more of the attack transient to be heard.

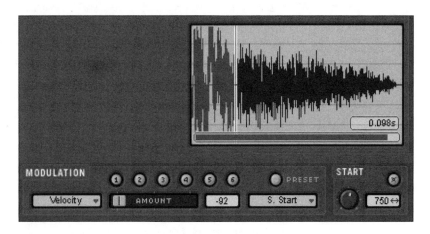

move the mod wheel with my left, but this is also an operation that lends itself well to "post-processing" — record the part, then overdub the MIDI controller changes necessary to create a more expressive track.

OVERDRIVE

Most drums have a quick initial attack, followed by an abrupt decay. Adding a bit of overdrive distortion will "crunch" the first few milliseconds of the attack, while leaving the decay untouched. This affects the sound in three important ways:

- You can raise the overall average level of the drum for a louder perceived sound, because the overdrive effect will limit the percussive attack.
- It creates a short period of time where the sound is at its maximum level, thus contributing a feeling of punch.
- It increases the attack's harmonic content, producing a brighter attack.

MUTE GROUPS

When drums are assigned to a mute group, hitting a drum that's part of the group will cut off any other drum from the group that's still sounding. This is mostly intended for hi-hats, so that playing a closed hi-hat sound will shut off an open hi-hat. But there are other uses for mute groups:

Assign toms with long decays to the same mute group. Too many simultaneous tom decays can muddy up a track. When you assign them to the same mute group, not only do tom rolls sound cleaner, but you conserve polyphony, which can be a problem with older samplers.

If you have some rhythmic loops loaded into your sampler along with individual drum sounds, make the loops part of a mute group (assuming, of course, you don't plan to layer them). This is particularly useful if you're playing live. Suppose you have a bunch of four-measure loops, but you're hitting a build and you want to switch quickly between the first measure, or first two measures, of various loops. Assigning loops to the same mute group means you can start them with impunity, knowing that the other ones will shut up when you do. [*Editor's note: Today, Ableton Live is more often used for this application. When multiple loops are assigned to the same Live track, triggering one of them will automatically mute another.*]

SINGLE-CYCLE LOOPING

This sampling-oriented trick can turn a quick hit into one with a looooooooong decay, particularly with toms and kicks.

The object is to loop a single cycle in the drum's decay tail, and have it repeat indefinitely. You then apply an amplitude envelope to give the decay the desired length. Try different individual cycles for looping. They may appear almost identical in the waveform display, but some will usually loop better than others, and the harmonic content may be significantly different as well.

February 2005
PRODIGY

Liam Howlett didn't want *Always Outnumbered, Never Outgunned* to be too similar to *Fat of the Land*, but he didn't want to lose the signature funky-punk sound of the band. He succeeded in keeping the energy and aggression of the previous albums, but also infused a little sex into the mix. "Hot Ride" seems to distill it best for him. "I did the instrumental before I hooked Juliette [Lewis] up for the vocals," he says. "I recorded a live drummer in the studio. I wasn't bothered about getting the mix perfect with the drums. I got it roughly right and balanced it out, but I wanted to be sure to keep that raw sound. I knew what I could do with it once I got it into Reason, so I didn't bother with compression. I chopped it up and had the separate hits, but it kept the room tone as well. That gave it the raw live sound I was looking for."

CLICK LAYERING

Sometimes modulation of an existing sample just isn't enough to create serious dynamics. This is where a click sample or sound can come in handy.

For samplers, create a click sample. I made mine by simply drawing some spikes in a digital audio editor for about 35ms, and saved that as a file. With synthesized drums, you can make a good click by applying maximum, extremely short pitch modulation to a white-noise source or buzzy oscillator, then impose a very quick amplitude decay.

The goal is to layer the click with another sound, such as kick. But the key is to choose a velocity curve where the click is very quiet at lower velocity levels. The click's entire dynamic range should be given to the upper dynamic range of the sound with which it is layered. As you play harder, the click will become more audible, adding punch to the drum sound. A little lowpass filtering on the click will help you blend the two sounds to taste.

In closing, remember that machines don't kill music — people do. If your drum parts aren't all they could be, use some of these tricks to help them come alive.

When is a drum machine not a drum machine? Doug Beck offers some unique groove advice on getting a bit more mileage out of those old MIDI beatboxes before you post them on eBay.

August 1998
Everything Old Is New Again
Finding inspiration in obsolete gear

Every few months I go through a crisis of sorts. I convince myself that the way I've been making records has become stale.

The truth is, one can only do so many projects using the same methods before things get a little dull and predictable. To combat this, I try to challenge myself to find interesting new ways to make music with the technology I already have at my disposal. This forces me to dig deeper into the potential of my instruments and tools to put them to use as creatively and effectively as I can. Sometimes I'm amazed at what happens. In this column, we'll explore ways to get great results by using an instrument in a fashion altogether different from the way it was intended to be used.

It's easy to get caught up in a new piece of gear and forget that some of the best recordings ever made employed technology from the '70s and '80s. I'm very fortunate to have some of the newest technology in my studio, but I often get so caught up in learning new operating systems and interfaces that I long for the early '80s, when all I had was a drum machine, a synth, and a silly haircut. (Okay, I still have a silly haircut.)

A recent trip to a friend's studio reminded me that it doesn't take the latest technology to make great records. As I looked around his studio, among very few new pieces of gear I saw several old drum machines, a couple of older synthesizers, and a very inexpensive sampler (a Boss SP-202 Dr. Sample). When we chatted about the unusual way he employs some of his older instruments in recordings, I got inspired. As I made my way back to my studio on a crowded subway train, the ideas started flowing. I couldn't wait to start connecting cables.

THE DUSTY OLD DRUM MACHINE

I have an older-model drum machine that has been in my closet for a few years. It has no special vintage appeal, like a Roland TR-909 or TR-808, so it really wouldn't be worth much if I decided to sell it. The sounds are kind of ordinary, but I always thought it had a good feel: The quantize functions offer various grooves and swing settings. I pulled it out of the closet, dusted it off, and connected its MIDI output to one of the MIDI inputs on my computer's MIDI interface. This configuration would allow me to trigger any synth or sampler in my rig from the pads on the drum machine without having to reroute any MIDI cables. Now it just so happens that the drum machine was still full of internal patterns. Since the pads are assigned various MIDI note numbers, you can imagine the random nature of what came pouring out of the connected synth when I played a pattern on the drum machine. I can tell you that the results were, well, sometimes just crap. But then again, depending on what was called up on the connected synthesizer and the pattern playing on the drum machine, things began to get interesting.

My first order of business was to try to create synth lines that were rhythmically and harmonically unlike anything I would ever think to play. By making small adjustments and changing programs, I began creating pattern after pattern of rhythmic synth lines. Using the groove and swing quantize functions on the drum machine, I could change the feel instantly. I could also randomly change the MIDI note numbers assigned to the drum machine pads to trigger different notes on my synth.

Bass lines were next on the agenda. By the same method I was able to create dozens of interesting bass lines, all ready and waiting to be plugged in on my next project. The obvious next step, of course, was to create drum and percussion sequences using my newly

August 1997
FRANKIE KNUCKLES

"The single most important instrument that signified the house sound was and is the Roland TR-909. It set the standard, and is still being used. It's pretty much a staple of what we do today at Def Mix."

October 1997
DJ SHADOW

"I did the *Endtroducing* album on the Akai MPC60II with nothing else, really. By the time I got the MPC, I was so ready for something new. I'd fantasized about it for so long that when I got it home I was shaking and sweating."

rediscovered old friend and my shiny brand-new sampler. I spent hours calling up samples and triggering them in different combinations. Let me tell you, I was like a mad scientist, and I might still be there had I not gotten hungry. The results of all this experimenting were so interesting that I recorded all of the note data directly into the sequencing program on my computer. This will allow me to edit and tweak all of the sequences I had just recorded at a later time. I was also able to easily organize the dozens of sequences by category, so when I'm looking for something next time I'm working on a track, it will be easy to find.

I realize that I've just scratched the surface here. I've spent the last few days looking around my studio and digging through storage to see what old, forgotten treasures I can use to spice things up. I've even been poking around at shops that sell used gear to see what they can't wait to get rid of. Hey, anyone who remembers when Roland introduced the TB-303 can tell you it was just a sad excuse for a bass arranger. Retail music stores couldn't give them away until years later, when somebody put one to work to make acid tracks. Now there's a host of new hardware and software products trying their best to reproduce the 303 sound. Food for thought.

August 1999
DAVID MORALES

When it comes to drum machines, Morales finds that "different machines have different feels. Some have a cheesier, rougher edge. I can sample the same sound into the Akai MPC60, S950, or S3000, or into the [E-mu] SP-1200, and they'll have different feels." That's why he keeps a stable of beatboxes and percussion modules on hand — which also includes an E-mu Procussion and a classic Roland TR-909. "What I use depends on what I'm looking for sound- and feel-wise. If I'm making a commercial remix, for example, the 909 may be too dark for the track."

If you don't have access to all of the latest technology, my hope is that my experience will give you some new and interesting ideas. If you have older gear you've been thinking about unloading, you may want to reconsider. For what it's worth on the used equipment market or as a trade-in, that old piece of gear just might be worthwhile to hang on to. You might find some creative ways to put it to use.

Figure 2-2
Though the Roland TR-909, E-mu SP-1200, and Akai MPC-60 are among the most coveted drum machines for remixers, the Roland TR-808 is arguably the granddaddy of the bunch. Here's what the original looks like.

It's amazing how many uses there are for classic drum machines. In the late '80s, the TR-808 ruled house. In the '90s, everyone craved the TR-909 for everything from house to techno and even trance. In the new millennium, all bets are off as the new wave revival brings the entire pantheon of early '80s beatboxes to the ears of the next generation of clubbers. No matter what you label this nouveau nostalgic sound, here's how those beats are created.

April 2003
Electroclash of the Titans, Part 1
Back to the future . . . again

Generation X'ers rejoice — or beware. The '80s are back. Only this time the beats are harder, the timing is tighter, and everything is punchier. As with most revivals, the Emperor's New Clone has a name: electroclash. While I prefer my own moniker, "retronica," "electroclash" is what the mainstream press is calling this movement.

Electroclash artists such as Fischerspooner, Felix Da Housecat, Scissor Sisters, Soviet, and Ladytron are reprocessing the essence of '80s pop into nouveau nostalgic dance music. The faces and po-mo approach may have changed, but the hallmark sounds remain: spiky analog synths, classic beatboxes, and distressed signal processing (for evoking that stone-age digital grunge).

BOXES OF BEATS

Arguably, one of the most important aspects of "that '80s sound" is the sputter of analog drum machines. Fortunately, there's no shortage of retro samples ready to be imported into your favorite beat-box or sampler. Visit a few of the major soundware developers' websites. In building your retronica kit collection, be sure to snag the following essential drum machines:

Roland TR-808. While technically not the first analog beat-box, the 808 has been a part of nearly every dance music movement since 1980. Unless you've been living in a cave, you'll immediately recognize the cheesy bombast this drum machine delivers. When working with 808 kits, be sure to keep an ear peeled for the trademark synth cowbell, wet-n-slappy claps, and the humming kick drum that launched a thousand sleazy Miami jams.

Roland CR-78. Only slightly less ubiquitous than the TR-808 are Roland's earlier forays into rhythm tools for the home organ set: the CR-78 and its little sister, the CR-68. Sounding like a cross between a flea circus and a swarm of locusts, the cheerful electronic sounds of the CR-78/68 served as the basis for numerous early OMD and New Musik tracks, as well as finding their way into a fair number of contemporary downtempo and lounge mixes.

Simmons SDS5. Strictly speaking, the SDS5 was not a drum machine, though it was often triggered by one. Instead, the SDS5 was the first commercially successful analog drum kit. Remember those freaky hexagonal drums in old Spandau Ballet and Duran Duran videos? Yep. They're Simmons. The kicks were thwocky and the snares were splashy noise bursts, but the toms were the defining factor for these kits. The SDS toms' lush pitch sweeps with a bit of fizzy sizzle found their way into hundreds of '80s tracks.

ROLLING YOUR OWN

If the above drum machines are already old hat to you, then roll up your sleeves and start programming your own electro sounds. There are quite a few hardware and software options for creating original electronic kits. Korg's Electribe series have a huge following thanks to their super-friendly array of knobs and switches, perfect for real-time twiddling.

On the software side, Logic's Ultrabeat includes many of the same features as the late, lamented analog-style Waldorf Attack, along with the ability to process and mangle sampled material. Ableton Live's Impulse beat box also allows some serious modification of drum samples.

In the area of add-on plug-ins, it's worth noting that FXpansion DR-008 has also gained a following among programmers thanks to its hybrid approach to kit design. Want a kit that's mostly sampled with a few analog-modeled surprises thrown in for flavor? No sweat. Want to dig in deep and design all your drums from scratch using a variety of synthesis approaches? DR-008 has you covered.

DISTRESSED TO KILL

While it's still a bit early to guess which processing techniques will define the electroclash sound over the next few years, two classic effects are already becoming quite prominent: distortion and degrading/bit-crushing.

Distortion is available in several flavors, and is pretty easy to use: add a distortion effect and crank it up until you like what you hear. Sample-rate degrading and bit-crushing are trickier. Essentially, these plug-in tools allow users to resample sounds at lower sampling rates and bit-depths in real time, thus adding aliasing and other digital artifacts to percussion tracks (or anything else for that matter).

The important thing to consider *vis-à-vis* sample-rate reduction and bit-crushing is that first-generation samplers and sampling drum machines were decidedly lo-fi by today's standards. Remember, back in 1981, a $40,000 Fairlight Series II sampler with all the trimmings recorded and played back 8-bit sound. So, in order to really capture that ghetto '80s sound, you need to beat up your bytes a bit.

Quick tip: Macintosh users should check out MDA's freeware Degrade plug-in (and a slew of others) at www.mda-vst.com.

Lastly, for ultra-punchy retro rhythms, try keeping all of these drums as dry as possible, that is, after you've applied any degradation, EQ, and/or distortion. Apply some compression, set your levels and panning, then be done with it. Wet, cavernous reverbs didn't really come into vogue until the mid-'80s, so getting that tight Kraftwerk/Mirwais electro sound requires keeping the beats up-front and in your face. My favorite tool for getting this result is Waves' L1-Ultramaximizer.

Now go dig out your old checkered Vans and start making cheesy beetz.

Once you've got your groove on, it's time to spice it up with fills and other incidental percussion effects. Read on as Doug Beck describes his tried-and-true processes.

January 2000
Breaks and Rolls
Tips for setting up sections and building drama

As I reflected back on a few recent projects, something occurred to me: In order to make an effective dance record, you need more than just a slamming groove and a catchy synth hook. I mean, that goes without saying, right? But in clubland it's all about drama, and the most dramatic club records have dynamic rhythmic breaks and unconventional snare and tom rolls that momentarily interrupt the groove. Done right, the effect creates a buildup of tension followed by a rush of release when the beat slams back in, and the club crowd responds with heightened energy and enthusiasm.

Here we'll discuss some concepts and ideas for programming and creating dramatic breaks and rolls.

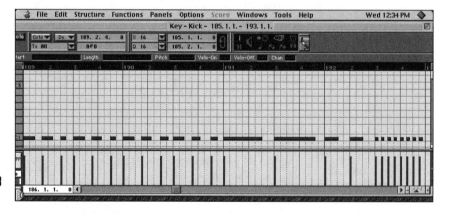

Figure 2-3

SYNCOPATED BREAKS

Let's start with rhythmic breaks. A stuttering or syncopated break can be used as a transition into a new section of the record or to set up a new element of the arrangement. Breaks are most commonly used to introduce high-energy parts of the track, such as choruses. Typically, every instrument and part is playing the same rhythm in unison, which creates a huge sound. This type of break usually works best in four- or eight-bar doses, but it can be shorter or longer if it feels right — whatever works.

While there are many approaches to programming a good break, I usually start with the kick drum. I'll program about four bars of a kick pattern (see Figure 2-3), then copy the pattern to every percussion part in the track (claps, hat, toms, cymbals, etc.). I'll edit each copied track by shifting its notes up or down so they trigger the desired percussion instrument. Now I have all of the percussion instruments playing precisely the same, tight rhythm. I like to set the velocity of the notes to around 100. If I open up the note velocity all the way to 127, it can be a bit of a letdown when the break is over and the groove comes back in. There should be a contrast in intensity between the rhythmic break and the high-energy segment that follows.

Next, I program bass and synth parts to play the same rhythm. What I end up with is a huge passage made up of all the instruments playing in unison, and this inevitably focuses attention on the rhythmic break.

The downside of this technique is that it can lead to polyphony choke, timing slop, or CPU overload depending on your rig. One workaround is to record a single hit from the break into your sampler, then edit the sequence so it triggers only the sampler. Instead of triggering ten or more notes, the sequencer now only has to trigger one.

For a vocal production or a remix, I often find a way to work a vocal snippet into the break as well. I look for something high energy to add to the hype of the break: a scream or high note that I can loop as the break plays. Check out an audio example of this on the new Boris & Beck remix of Jennifer Holiday's "Think it Over."

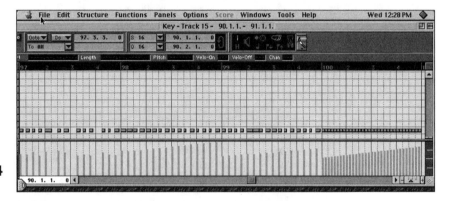

Figure 2-4

ROLLS

It's becoming more and more of a challenge to create a unique snare roll — something a little more interesting than the usual sixteenth-note variety. Here are a few ideas.

First, I like to use step-time programming for my snare rolls. In step-record mode, you can program very precise rolls, and in doing so you can sometimes stumble into happy programming accidents. One example: Let's say I want a four-bar snare roll. I go into step-record mode in my sequencer, and set the note value to sixteenth-notes. I'll program three bars of sixteenth-notes, then switch the note value to 32nd-notes for the last bar. Now I have a relatively simple four-bar snare roll. Then I like to "draw" the velocities of the notes. I tend to bring the note velocity up and down a couple of times during the roll to add tension, and then I go for a higher velocity level in the last bar. (See Figure 2-4.) You can experiment with any values for any number of measures. Change it up, and try different combinations — you just might stumble on something great.

Also, don't limit yourself to eighths, sixteenths, and 32nd-notes. Try including some triplets. And if your sequencer has swing quantizing, experiment with various settings for all or parts of the roll.

November 2001
BT DESCRIBES "FREQUENCY-SPECIFIC SWING"

Another technique that BT developed and refined in his productions is something he calls frequency-specific swing. "Your brain interprets things at higher frequencies as swinging harder, and lower frequencies as swinging less," he explains. "So you can get away with swinging more at lower frequencies. 'Somnambulist' is a good example of this. The beats like the kick and snare that fall in the middle, they're swinging really hard; I pushed them by 1,025 samples. Then the acid line on the Roland JP-8000, and the little percussion bits, those are swinging by 202 samples.

"So you don't hear it. When you look at it on the screen, you can see that the sounds are actually flamming. But your brain doesn't perceive it that way. It's like the top percussion is propelling the thing forward, but underneath it is this really funky swing."

Effects can dramatically color your snare roll and give it a unique character. Delays and flangers are great effects to try, but be careful with reverb. A little goes a long way, and the roll can end up sounding muddy or drowned out. I'm a big fan of filtering snare rolls. To add an interesting dynamic to the part, record the opening and closing of a low-pass filter as the roll plays into your sequencer. Start with the filter closed, and, as the roll comes to a crescendo, open the filter. This is a simple but very effective trick.

Breaks and rolls should be more than afterthoughts. They're essential elements of a track. The energy of a good groove can be dramatically heightened when set off by a rhythmic break. Likewise, a great hook can be highlighted by a dramatic roll. It's worth investing the time to experiment with different approaches, using all the resources at your disposal.

Sure, breaks and fills are a tried-and-true way to emphasize transitions between sections of your song, but that's just the tip of the proverbial iceberg. Greg Rule is not only the former editor of *Keyboard*, but a seasoned remixer whose credits include Faith No More, the Fixx, and KMFDM. He's got a few more transition tricks up his sleeve that should get your juices flowing as you produce your next track.

Fall 1999
Transitions
There and back again . . .

Dramatic sweeps and fills can do wonders for kicking a chorus or bridge into high gear.

Blame it on my background in percussion. When it comes to building tension in a dance mix, few things pound my pulse like big fills or transition effects leading from a verse to a chorus, from a chorus to a bridge, and so on. Sweeps, zippers — whatever you call them, almost all dance tracks and remixes have some sort of whiz-bang fill or effect that leads you from section to section. Sometimes they're just a beat or two long. Sometimes they last for several bars. Here's how I go about creating my transitions.

Probably the most non-fill famous transition effect is the backward cymbal. This soft-to-loud swoosh of noise works well in many tracks because it doesn't contain much, if any, melodic information, and therefore won't collide with pitched material. The only problem with the reverse cymbal trick is that it's been used to death ... and I'm among the offenders.

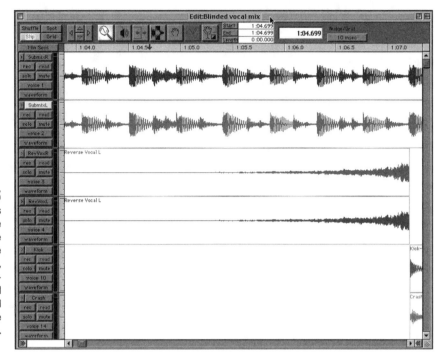

Figure 2-5
A reverse vocal swell. In this example I isolated a syllable from the first word of the verse vocal, then ran the slice through a huge reverb, sampled it, flipped the sample around backward, and aligned it so it faded in and reached peak energy on the downbeat of the verse.

This doesn't mean the idea should be abandoned, though. The reverse/swell principle can be applied to many other sound sources, such as vocals. Try this trick: Isolate the first word or syllable of a chorus or verse vocal, and run it through a cavernous reverb. Sample that performance. Flip the sample around backward and align it so the peak of the swell occurs on the downbeat of the chorus or verse. Drive it home by putting a kick and crash on the downbeat (see Figure 2-5). Some words or syllables work better than others, so experimentation is the key. When it works, it's a dramatic effect.

If you've listened to much drum and bass music, you're well aware of the "ReCycled" breakbeat sound. But you don't have to own Propellerhead ReCycle software or make drum and bass music to incorporate this stuttering effect into your songs. On a recent remix I did for Christina Aguilera, I recorded a one-bar breakbeat into Digidesign Pro Tools (although any sampler or hard disk recorder will do). Then I selected the snare drum region of the breakbeat, copied it,

November 1999
DAVID FRANK

A key part of Christina Aguilera's "Genie in a Bottle" is the drum pattern. Frank created it note by note in Logic. "I had two kick drums going," he explains. "I had one triggering the [Akai] MPC60 — it was playing the basic kick pattern — and the second one from the [Korg] TR-Rack doing the 32nd-note pattern. At first, it wasn't grooving at all, but I played around with the 32nd-notes in Logic until I came up with the pattern you hear in the song." To round out the percussive elements, he added a reverse hi-hat track, a triangle hit on beat 4 of each bar, a high-frequency noise burst from a Clavia Nord Rack, and a "zap" sound, reverse swell effect, and fuzz guitar sample from the Yamaha EX5.

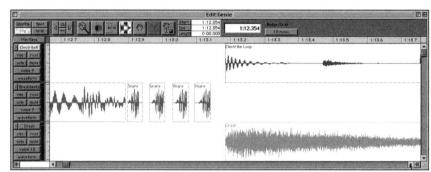

Figure 2-6
Machine-gun snare. Here's a jungly stuttering snare effect I created by crudely chopping a snare from a breakbeat and positioning the slices as 32nd-notes at the end of the bar.

and pasted it four times in a row at 32nd-note intervals at the end of the bar, with gaps between the samples (see Figure 2-6). This jungly chopped snare effect, short as it is, really helped set up the next section.

Another thing I like to do is incorporate pitch and filter modulation into snare rolls. The zipper, I call it. I've built a library of MIDI files that contains rolls of different lengths and resolutions. Sometimes I'll layer two or more of these together to create a more interesting effect. Leading out of the breakdown section of my Faith No More remix, for example, I used a layer of three rolls: I started with a four-bar sixteenth-note snare roll, then added a one-bar sixteenth-note roll at bar 4, and finished off with a one-beat 32nd-note roll on beat 4 of the last bar. For extra expression, I'll often twist the filter and/or pitch knobs and experiment with delay effects during playback while a DAT recorder captures the performance.

July 2001
DALLAS AUSTIN

Describe your current method of making beats.
Rick Sheppard [engineer/programmer] usually sits next to me. He has two screens: one for virtual keyboards and one for the sequencers. I might say something like, "Let's try something at 95 bpm. Bring up a bank of rim shots, some 808 hi-hats," and so on. He'll load up a bunch of different samples — fill up the whole controller with whatever kinds of sounds I've requested — and I'll make a beat. That's how it starts.

So you tend to build your beats note by note, as opposed to using loops.
I used to do it with loops. Back when we were doing Boys II Men and ABC, I would have 25 to 30 tracks of loops going. I think that became "my sound" at that time. Sometimes the loops would even be out of sync with each other — out of tune — and I'd go write a song on top of it. But once sample clearance became tighter, I stopped using so many loops. I mean, you put 25 samples in a song now . . . it's just impossible. I was talking to Chuck D of Public Enemy, and he said they used to have, like, 75 samples in a song.

Now I tend to build the beats. I'll say, "Give me some sounds from the [E-mu] SP-1200." I love that thing; I have four or five of them. It has a dirty ring that you can't get from anything else. The filters they used. . . . I also use the [E-mu] Turbo Phatt or Proteus 2000.

Do you prefer to build songs from the bottom up — drums, then bass, and so on?
After the beats are done, I'll usually add chords, a lead line, or something melodic to match what I'm singing in my head. The bass usually comes last.

DECIPHERING DELAY

If your effects processor doesn't display delay times in beats per minute, you can use the following formula to convert bpm (quarter-notes) to milliseconds:

60,000 divided by bpm = ms per quarter-note

Alternatively, I sometimes record the controller data into a sequencer along with the notes. Either way, this rollercoaster fill is a winner. Check out two versions of the zipper in my "One Thing Leads to Another" and "Stand or Fall" remixes for the Fixx.

When it comes to creating percussive transitions like the ones mentioned above, don't limit yourself to drum-related source material. In my "Stand or Fall" remix, I sliced a syllable from a word in the vocal track and used it the same way I would use a snare in a drum fill. Similarly, I chopped a small slice from a crunch guitar riff in a remix for German rockers Subway To Sally and used it as I would a drum sample in a fill.

Last but not least, if you're looking for a pre-fab source of these types of sounds, check out *TranceFusion* from Ilio — a top-notch sample CD packed front-to-back with transitional sweeps, swoops, fills, and effects.

Chapter 3
BASS

One of the most creative and flexible areas of dance music production is in creating a unique bass sound that's big enough to rock the floor without overwhelming the mix. There really isn't a right or wrong type of texture or bass line as long as it's in tune and emphasizes the groove — these sounds run the gamut from Timo Maas's legendary "wow" one-note bass to Soulfuric-style live bass. So this chapter will focus on the technical nuances of fitting your synth or electric bass into the mix.

Michael Cooper is the owner of Michael Cooper Recording, located outside the small resort town of Sisters at the base of the Oregon Cascades. In this tutorial, he discusses the thorny issue of stereoizing synth bass parts.

July 2000
Mixing Monster Synth Bass Tracks
A wide stereo bass can still be tight

It's a common dilemma: The killer synth bass track you recorded in fat stereo sounded awesome when you first laid it down. But now that it's time to mix, that nice wide bass has the song's foundation swimming all over the map. Sure, the bottom end sounds huge. But it also lacks focus. The bass is panned so wide that it's detached from the kick drum, and the groove is suffering because of it. What can you do? You could use only the mono output on the synth and pan it dead center; that would anchor the mix, all right, but now the bass sounds about half as big as it did before. If only you could anchor the mix and keep the bass fat.

Good news — you can.

I'll show you how to create a huge stereo bass track that's both focussed and wide. This stereo mixdown technique works best with clicky synth bass sounds that have a snappy attack. Real and sampled electric bass guitar tracks usually don't work as well for this application. For one, you want plenty of high-frequency content on the attack of every note, something electric bass generally lacks (the exception being slap bass). Also, real bass guitar has been consistently panned dead-center on recordings for so many decades that stereoizing it to fill up more of the field makes our indoctrinated minds rebel. But rules are meant to be broken, so feel free to try this technique whenever you're seeking a larger-than-life sound.

GIRTH IS GOOD
Stereo instruments that are hard-panned across the entire stereo field sound inherently bigger than those panned dead center. Adding a stereo chorus effect to a lackluster mono synth bass track can turn it into a barreling behemoth.

But sounds with a lot of low frequencies are generally best panned dead center in a mix, for two reasons: First, this tends to anchor the mix and make the groove more solid. Second, it also gets bass-heavy instruments out of the way of high-frequency instruments, which are often panned off to the sides of a mix. Panning high-frequency sounds (such as cymbals, tambourine, and acoustic guitar) to the sides creates a subjectively wider stereo field — a big-sounding mix.

By applying all of the above principles to our bass track, we can have our cake and eat it too. The key to mixing monster synth bass tracks is to pan the bass patch's low frequencies dead center to anchor the mix, while spreading the high-frequency content across the stereo field to make it sound physically larger. To do this, we must split and equalize the original, dry signal.

Whether you're mixing a sequenced MIDI bass track or an audio track recorded on your DAW, the technique is the same. In both cases, you'll be taking a mono signal either from your synth's mono output or from one side of a stereo audio track.

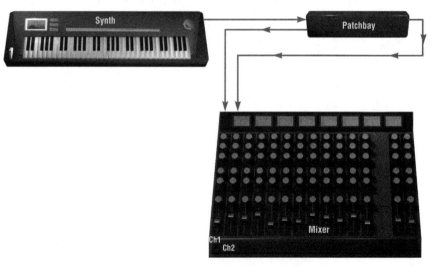

Figure 3-1

Depending on your studio setup, there are several ways to mult (or split) a mono synth bass sound into two signals. The method shown here requires a patchbay. If you use a patchbay that can be half-normalled (inserting a plug into the top socket allows the source signal to continue to be heard because the signal path to the mixer channel hasn't been broken), patch the bass track out of the top socket into an additional mixer channel at the patchbay.

BASIC SETUP

You'll need a mixer that's equipped with shelving EQ or highpass and lowpass filters. First, "mult" the synth bass's mono output to bring it into two separate mixer channels. Multing (or splitting a signal to create two or more identical signals) can be accomplished using a patchbay (see Figure 3-1). If you don't have a patchbay, use your mixer's bus or direct outputs (see Figure 3-2). A simple Y-cord will do in a pinch.

Once you have the same signal duplicated on two mixer channels, it's time to equalize them. Using the mixer's lowpass filter or high-frequency shelving EQ, roll off all highs above roughly 1kHz on the first channel and pan the signal dead center. (If you're using shelving EQ, cut the highs by the maximum amount possible, typically anywhere from 12 to 18dB.) This is our "anchor" channel, so we only want bass and lower midrange frequencies to remain here.

Figure 3-2
If you don't want to use a
patchbay, connect the direct
output of the mono synth
bass mixer channel to the
input of another channel.

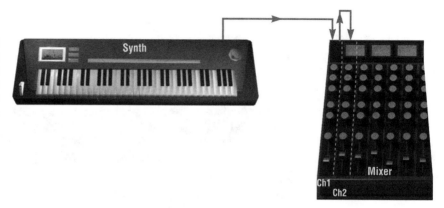

Figure 3-2
If you don't want to use a patchbay, connect the direct output of the mono synth bass mixer channel to the input of another channel.

On the second mixer channel, roll off all the frequencies below 1kHz, using either a high-pass filter or low shelving EQ. Use the same corner frequency (in this case, 1kHz) on both mixer channels to cut out highs and bass frequencies, respectively, so the combination of both EQ'd channels contains virtually all of the original frequencies from the mono output of the synth.

Once you've rolled off the bass frequencies on the second channel, send its EQ'd signal out to an effects processor via your mixer's bus outputs or dedicated effects send. Set the effects unit to produce a fat stereo chorus. Return the left and right outputs of the effects processor to two channels of your mixer (or to a stereo effects return channel, if your console is so equipped), and pan the channels hard left and hard right. Next, remove the high-frequency bass channel from the main stereo bus so you hear only the center-panned mono low-frequency bass track and the effects unit's right and left returns. Experiment with setting the effects processor's wet/dry mix somewhere between 50 and 100% wet.

You should now have stereo chorus applied only to the high-frequency content of the synth bass track, creating a really wide stereo image. The bass track's low frequencies are center-panned, where they'll meld with the kick drum track to anchor the mix.

FINE-TUNING

In the previous example, we used a center (or cutoff) frequency of 1kHz as a starting point for splitting the synth bass track into two bands. But every mix is different, and 1kHz may not always be the perfect choice. If the center-panned bass needs more presence, try raising the crossover frequency to 2 or 3kHz. If, on the other hand, it competes with the lead vocal too much, try lowering the frequency to 500Hz. The synth's chorused high frequencies may also compete with other hard-panned tracks such as guitars and other keyboards, in which case raising the crossover frequency should help clarify things. It's a juggling act to find the right center frequency to complement all elements of the mix, but that's what mixing is all about.

If you find that the composite bass track is still not focused enough, slowly fold in the left and right chorus effects returns toward center pan until the desired balance between a compact and wide sound is achieved. Reducing the delay time on the chorus effect to between 10 and 15ms should also tighten things up. Make sure the effect's modulation rate and depth parameters are set to low values to prevent the bass from sounding wobbly.

Once you've found the right balance, the synth bass track should sound downright colossal, yet firmly rooted in center field where it belongs.

With its roots in classic funk and disco, electric bass guitar has been the foundation for hundreds (thousands?) of house and retro R&B tracks over the years. Guitarist/songwriter/producer/engineer Jay Graydon has been nominated for 12 Grammies and won two, whereas Craig Anderton is the author of *Home Recording for Musicians* and a world-renowned expert on electronic music production, not to mention a brilliant guitarist and keyboardist. In this segment, they deliver the goods on how to compress electric bass for maximum punch and presence.

Their advice is tailored to using hardware mixers and compressing the bass on input, which was standard operating procedure in 1999. Today, you may prefer to record the bass player to an uncompressed 24-bit track and then add compression after the fact, as that will give you more options.

May 1999
Compressing Electric Bass
Tame the low end of the mix

Want a solid foundation for your music? Rein in your bass player's dynamics with compression.

Most musicians (and recording engineers) want the bass to provide an even, uniform bottom end. Compression, which reduces dynamic range variations, can help achieve that goal by boosting low-level signals and reducing high-level signals. This results in a smooth sound that provides a consistent foundation for the other instruments.

First we'll describe how to patch the compressor into the system, then how to adjust its parameters.

COMPRESSOR ROUTING
- Before patching in the compressor, plug the bass direct box output or bass mic into a mixer input.
- Assign the mixer channel to a recorder track (using a bus or the channel's direct output).
- As the bassist plays, EQ the sound to taste, then adjust levels (don't exceed −4dB peak with a digital recorder. For an analog recorder, aim for an average level of 0dB).
- Patch in the compressor using the mixer channel strip's insert patch points. If these aren't available, patch the channel's direct output (or the output of the bus to which the module is assigned) into the compressor, then patch the compressor output into the recorder track input.

COMPRESSOR PARAMETER ADJUSTMENTS

Following are suggested points of departure for the most common compressor parameters. As you tweak parameters, note that one of the most important tools for achieving the right amount of compression is the compressor's gain reduction meter, which shows how much the compressor is restricting the dynamic range at any given moment. For example, if the gain reduction meter shows –3dB, that means the gain has been reduced by 3dB to bring down a peak.

Unless you're going for a heavily compressed sound (there are no rules in sonic land), compress by an average of 2 to 4dB, with occasional peaks being compressed by no more than –6dB.

Recognize that the various parameters interact. It's often necessary to go back and forth among several parameters until you dial in the exact sound you want.

Begin by setting the ratio control to a 3:1 ratio. This means that for every 3dB increase in input level above a specified threshold, the output increases by only 1dB. Try a higher ratio if the bass signal is extremely uneven, but bear in mind, the higher the ratio, the more it will "squash" signals above the threshold. This often results in a smaller, thinner sound.

Now set the attack and release controls. (Release is sometimes called decay.) The attack knob determines how long it takes for compression to kick in once the signal exceeds the threshold, while release sets the time required to return to a non-compressed state once the signal drops below the threshold. Many compressors include an "auto" setting for these parameters, which is usually the easiest way to go and often nails the right values. Otherwise, start with a fast attack (0–5ms) and medium decay (100–150ms).

Next comes the threshold control, which determines the level at which compression begins. Initially set it to the highest available value (usually 0dB), which means only notes exceeding 0dB will be subject to compression.

While the bassist plays his instrument, look at the gain reduction indicator (VU-style meter or LEDs) and lower the threshold so that there's an average of 2 or 3dB of compression. The peaks (loudest notes) should indicate 4 to 6dB of compression. This is a common, "industry standard" type of setting that avoids extremes.

If you need more compression to keep notes even-sounding, lower the threshold (in other words, the compression will kick in at lower level signals) or increase the ratio. But remember, overcompressing can thin the sound. Ideally, the bass player will have a sufficiently good "touch" so that lots of compression won't be needed.

The process of compressing the dynamic range lowers the overall level, so use the compressor's output (makeup gain) control to bring it back up. While observing the input level feeding your mixer or multitrack, adjust the output so that the maximum peak (not average) levels of the compressed and uncompressed signals are identical. However, note that you can also tweak the output control a bit if you need more or less overall level feeding the multitrack to hit the optimum levels mentioned earlier.

As a general rule of thumb, the amount of output gain should equal the amount of gain reduction. For example, if the gain reduction meter shows 4dB of gain reduction on peaks, set the output control to give +4dB of gain.

HARD OR SOFT KNEE?

Now it's time to adjust the hard/soft knee switch, if present. A hard knee clamps down with full compression as soon as the signal exceeds the threshold, so select it to add more punch to the sound. For a ballad, soft knee may be more appropriate. (Note that dbx uses the term "Over Easy" compression for soft knee operation.) Since it adds compression based on how far past the threshold the signal has gone, soft knee doesn't clamp down on the player's dynamics quite as hard.

ATTACK TIME

Once the general settings are squared away, you might want to re-tweak the attack and decay settings. A fast attack compresses the beginning of the note's transient, which keeps the attack level even but reduces "punch." This may be helpful with a digital recorder, where you have to be very careful not to exceed 0dB for more than a few milliseconds on individual tracks (in fact, we strongly recommend not going over –4dB to allow for some headroom).

However, if you're hitting analog tape really hard (+6dB or more past 0), experiment with increasing the attack time to 20–30ms to let through some of the attack. Unlike with digital recording, tape saturation will absorb the transient, and you may prefer the extra "smooth punch" compared to clamping it down with a really fast attack time.

RELEASE TIME

The release time is a bit of a compromise. It needs to be fast enough that it doesn't affect the attack of the next bass note, but not too fast. Because of the bass's very low frequencies, a short decay setting may actually follow individual cycles of the string vibration, which will cause a subtle distortion.

Try selecting a very slow release (*e.g.*, 250ms) and listen to what happens. As other bass notes are attacked, they will be low in volume because the release time has not yet passed, so the gain is still reduced. The best way to find a good release time is to increase the duration slowly, starting from the fast setting. When you damp (hand-mute) a bass string, the gain reduction meter should move back to 0 at a rate slow enough for you to detect, but not so slow as to take a significant amount of time.

USING EQ WITH COMPRESSION

If the sound gets too "small" with lots of compression, add more low-end EQ (boost around 100Hz). Remember that placing EQ before the compressor increases the amount of compression in the frequency range being boosted, as the EQ is increasing the level at those frequencies, causing them to go over the threshold more often (or compressing them more if they're already above the threshold). If you do add low-end EQ, consider raising the threshold (which gives less compression) so that the lows don't get overcompressed compared to the rest of the signal.

Nothing kills a remix faster than bass and kick parts that just don't fit together sonically. Emphasizing either incorrectly will quickly result in either mush or the absence of one or the other. Rob McGaughey is a mastering engineer, pro audio consultant, recording engineer, and musician, and has also done mastering work for several major labels, which makes him well qualified to help you get the most from your bass/kick blend.

November 1998
Team Players
How to make the bass and kick drum fit together

The challenge: The low end of a mix is very important, and getting it right is a difficult art to master. Bass instruments and kick drum need to fit together to form the guts of the rhythm section in many styles of music. Whether you use a bass guitar, synth bass, upright bass, tuba, or whatever, you need to blend this bass instrument with your kick drum while still maintaining the individuality of each instrument. There is no magic formula that will work with every mix or every style of music. The goal of this article is to give you the tools and knowledge to experiment and find your own perfect mix.

A little knowledge and some experimentation are the keys to success.

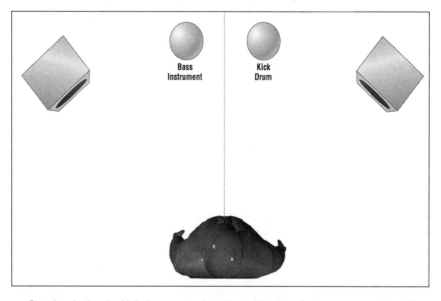

Figure 3-3
Carefully placing bass instruments in the stereo field will help them remain distinct in the mix.

Start by placing the kick drum panned center and the bass instrument panned to either one o'clock or 11 o'clock — just a little bit of offset can make a big difference (see Figure 3-3). If bass frequencies are panned too far to the right or left, they carry a lot of weight to that side of the mix when they are played, making the mix sound lopsided.

Solo the kick drum and listen to it. EQ to taste. You can make it rounder by adding 1–3dB around 60–90Hz, bring out or hide the "click" of the kick drum beater hitting the head by finding and EQing the "click" frequency (often in the 5–8kHz range), add some rumble by adding low-frequency EQ, or make the drum tighter by using a highpass filter set around 30–65Hz.

Solo the bass track and listen to it. EQ the bass instrument to taste. Round out the bass tone by EQing around 80–200Hz, add punch and presence in the 500Hz–2.5kHz range, and bring out harmonics, attack, and articulation around 4kHz and up.

Figure 3-4
Using complementary EQ will allow bass guitar/synth and kick drum to peacefully coexist in a mix. Here the bass guitar has been EQed to emphasize lower mid frequencies, while the kick drum is emphasizing the low frequencies and the attack of the beater.

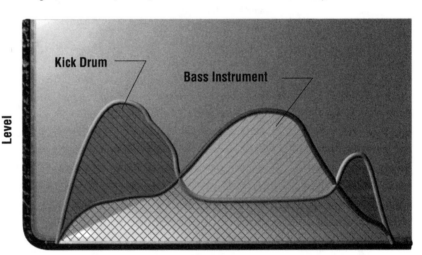

Solo both the kick drum and bass together. Listen to how well they blend with one another dynamically as well as timbrally. Can you easily differentiate the two instruments from one another, or do they tend to blend together? EQing the bass and kick drum to accentuate different frequency ranges (see Figure 3-4) will help each instrument stand out in the mix and not sound muddy. Play with the EQ and levels to get the best sound you can.

Listen to the entire mix. How does the bass fit in with the other tracks? You may want to move any bass effects slightly to the left or right to give the kick and the bass their own space. If you're panning a vocal directly in the center, it may sound better to have the kick drum panned very slightly left and the bass slightly right (or vice versa).

You may want to add a little light compression to the entire mix and listen to how that affects the bass levels. If necessary, solo the kick and bass tracks and add compression to one or both tracks to balance the levels or to add more punch. The key is to get the best mix and tone with as little EQ and compression as you can. If you overprocess the bass tracks, it may result in a hollow sound. Always reference back to the entire mix when adding processing.

When you have a mix that you like, make a copy and listen to it in a variety of environments. Bass will sound very different in your car, home stereo, boombox, and other environments.

Every engineer's nightmare is the mix that sounds great in the studio and terrible everywhere else.

It's hard to take a poorly recorded track or a crappy synth voice and fix it in the mix. You'll be more successful if you start with good-sounding raw tracks. Make the individual tracks sound good by themselves and blend them in with the rest of the mix. You can then add compression or tweak the EQ to make them fit. Knowing what to listen for and how to get the sound you want will increase your odds for success, but you'll still have to listen and experiment. I recommend listening to CDs that have a low end you like, and analyzing the sound of the individual bass instruments, where the instruments sit in the stereo field, and how they interact with one another.

TRICKS OF THE TRADE

Stereo Placement. Low-frequency instruments carry a lot of weight in a mix, provide the foundation for the music, and draw the listener's attention. The trick is to place these bass instruments in the stereo field where they'll have the desired impact without detracting from the rest of the mix, and where each instrument can be heard and differentiated from the others. Bass instruments are traditionally placed in the center of the mix between 11 o'clock and one o'clock.

Equalization. EQ can be a valuable tool for emphasizing frequencies that are desirable, removing or reducing unwanted rumbling or buzzing, or fine-tuning for the ultimate tone. The trick is to equalize each of your low-frequency instruments differently so they're most prominent in different frequency ranges. We want each instrument to have the best possible tone, but we also need to make sure they all cut through the mix, don't fight each other, and don't turn into mush or mud.

Compression. Bass instruments will often have very wide dynamic ranges that require compression to make them stable in a mix, so they don't seem to fade in and out. Compression is a great tool to give bass instruments more impact and make them punchier and fatter. But be careful with compression; some compressors can roll off the lowest frequencies and make the bottom drop out when they're pushed too hard.

Subharmonic Enhancement. A number of bass-enhancing processors and tricks are available to artificially add subharmonic frequencies to a bass signal. Many of these add a synthesized bass tone one octave (or more) below the fundamental bass frequency. These can be very effective tools to make the bass sound bigger, make that subwoofer rumble, and make the walls shake. These tools generally work best when you're adding bass in frequency ranges where nothing else exists in the mix. You need to be careful when using these processors, as they can turn your mix into an unintelligible muddy mess or eat up valuable headroom with inaudible low frequencies.

Gates. For super-tight bass and kick tracks, use a gate to trigger the bass track when the kick drum hits; this trick will tighten things up nicely. For a huge kick drum sound, set up a gate to bring in a low-frequency synth tone with each hit of the kick.

Of course, I also have my own complementary low end theories, so here's a little grab bag of tips and tricks that have worked wonders in my own mixes. Some of them reinforce Rob's wisdom above, whereas others expand upon the information.

September 2000
Low-End Theory
How low can you go?

There are quite a few methods of ensuring that your track's low-frequency range is emphasized without overwhelming the entire mix. From compression to sub-harmonic synthesis to layering sounds, a wide range of tools and techniques is available for keeping the bottom tight.

GET THE BALANCE RIGHT

The first place to focus your attention when tweaking the low end of your mix is the balance between the kick drum and bass itself. Every kick has a specific pitch, and electronic kick drums often emphasize this pitch depending on the manner in which they are programmed.

Carefully examine the relationship between your bass line and your kick drum, not just in terms of the way they groove together, but whether they are in tune with each other. I've seen troublesome mixes clear right up when the pitch of the kick drum was adjusted slightly to make it relate harmonically to the bass.

Alternatively, consider assigning the majority of the deep low-end information to one instrument or the other. A perfect example of this technique can be found in the drum and bass genre. Often, huge bass drones drive entire tracks while the kick drum components are relegated to support roles due to the ultra-fast breakbeats that define the style.

COMPRESSION/LIMITING

Nearly every track I've worked on has included some form of compression on the bass line and/or kick drum. Used judiciously, this type of dynamic processing can yield incredibly punchy results, often defining the difference between a good mix and a brilliant one.

Earlier in this chapter, other producers and engineers discussed their methods to finessing low end, so here's my personal approach to compressing kick and bass for dance music:

Begin with a fairly strong ratio. The trick here is to improve the impact as much as possible so the instrument doesn't get lost in the mix. A 4:1 ratio is my usual starting point, but I sometimes push into the 10:1 range if the instrument really needs it.

Use a fast attack time. Start with settings in the 5–20 millisecond range, as these allow the initial attack transients to remain intact (depending on your recording medium), thus enhancing each hit of the instrument. Tweak the release time while listening for unwanted compression artifacts like pumping and breathing.

Adjust the threshold to taste. This is where the real fine-tuning lies. Due to the variables in gain structure for many home studios, it's probably best to simply use your ears when making adjustments to the threshold parameter. Again, the objective is to enhance punchiness while improving the overall presence of the signal, so be sure to adjust the final gain to make up for any major dynamic shifts.

One last trick: Consider combining the kick drum and bass signals and running them through the same compressor channel while adjusting the relative volumes of each instrument. This approach won't work for every mix, but it can be a useful shortcut to keeping the bass and kick dynamics tightly aligned by emphasizing the dominant hits in each instrument's phrasing.

SUBS FOR THE DUBS

There are several hardware products and a whole slew of plug-ins that feature a process called "sub-harmonic synthesis." While each product sports its own feature set, the principle behind the process is essentially the same.

Here's how it works: The input signal is analyzed and a pitch (or series of pitches) is generated one or two octaves below the original signal. These sub-harmonics are then dynamically blended back into the original signal, creating the illusion of deeper bass content. A similar effect can also be achieved by routing the signal into a pitch-shifter tuned down an octave, then applying a lowpass filter to the shifted signal to eliminate all but the lowest bass frequencies.

A word of caution: Due to the fact that some of these processors create fixed pitches, they should be used carefully if applied to bass synth. Unless tuned accurately, sub-harmonic synthesizers can easily create dissonant artifacts in the low end, which will be perceived as muddiness.

That said, sub-harmonic synthesizers are a terrific way to punch up a lackluster rhythmic loop or even add some depth to a completed mix. In fact, I know of at least one DJ who keeps the dbx 120XP in his arsenal for live gigging. It's his secret weapon for getting repeat gigs on the rave circuit.

SINE OF THE TIMES

Another nifty way to add subsonic oomph to a bass line is to mix in a sine wave one octave lower than the original part. Nearly every synth can generate pure sine waves (or, in a pinch, filtered triangle waves) out of the box, so it's a relatively simple matter to trigger two patches or synths on the same MIDI port/channel.

The beauty of this approach is that you can treat the sine wave patch as a surgically precise equalization tool that adds subsonic spice without muddying the bass. Adjusting the amount of bass boost is accomplished by simply raising or lowering the volume of the sine wave.

If you try this, it's essential to tune the sine wave an octave lower than the bass, not to the same pitch. Tuning it to the same pitch can cause phase cancellation, which will drastically reduce the bass instead of enhancing it.

It's also worth noting that pure sine waves are the basis for many classic drum and bass and hip-hop patches. So if you've ever wondered how that boomin' jeep bass was created, wonder no more.

There you have it. From hip-hop to house, the foundation of every good dance track lies in a rock-solid bass response. Just be sure to tame those volumes and proceed with caution, as some of the above tips could blow your woofers along with your mind.

Bottoms up!

Subwoofers: Some Parting Thoughts
Down the rabbit hole . . .

Before we close, I'd like to touch upon the issue of working with subwoofers in a home studio, as this is becoming increasingly popular with dance music producers on a budget. Subwoofers can help round out the sound of small nearfield monitors that have 5" woofers. Here are some pros and cons to consider.

The upside to adding a subwoofer to your rig is, obviously, more and bigger bass. Configured correctly, a well-designed subwoofer can give your studio a more accurate sound when it comes to mixing for a club. The key phrase here is "configured correctly." The crossover point (the frequency at which the bass response switches from the nearfield to the subwoofer) should be set to complement the frequency response of the 5" woofers, and the overall volume of the sub should be balanced in context with the output of the speakers.

Incorrectly configured subwoofers often cause more problems than they resolve. For starters, if you set your room up with exaggerated bass your mixes could well suffer from *decreased* bass. Why? Well, if your sub is pumping out big, bombastic bass, you're likely to underemphasize those frequencies in your final mix (since your subwoofer is ultimately deceiving your ears).

I recommend buying the best nearfield monitors you can afford, with full 8" woofers. If you simply *must* own a subwoofer to feel complete, then be sure to constantly compare your mix with commercially released tracks that you know sound great in a club. After comparing, adjust levels and EQ accordingly.

Chapter 4
LOOPS AND SAMPLING

Make no mistake, the art of sampling and working with rhythmic loops is one of the most crucial elements of modern dance music. Even in overtly electronic genres like trance and electro, sampling techniques play an indispensable role in the creation of memorable riffs and grooves.

Truly inspired sampling is equal parts artistic and technical skill, so this chapter will tackle both engineering and creative applications of these technologies, with emphasis on current software as well as classic hardware approaches. No matter what your preferred tools are, you can find tips you'll be able to use.

In his aptly titled "Power Tools for Sampling" feature in the October 2003 issue of *Keyboard*, Jim Aikin details the essentials of how sampling works and how you can make the most of it in your tracks.

October 2003
Power Tools for Sampling
Basic concepts and advanced tips

Programmers have developed a number of ways of coaxing a computer into making sound. These synthesis methods include not only sample playback — which is the subject of this chapter — but also such methods as analog modeling, physical modeling, additive synthesis, frequency modulation (FM), and granular synthesis. Sample playback is a relatively simple and incredibly versatile technology, which is why it's so widely used. In sample playback, the computer grabs a previously recorded digital recording of a sound and sends it to the computer's audio output so you can hear it. The recording itself is called a sample.

The big advantage of sample playback is that absolutely any sound can be recorded and then played from a MIDI keyboard. A modern sampler typically doesn't have a characteristic sound of its own. Instead, it sounds like whatever sample is being used. A number of companies are in the business of creating and selling collections of samples, called *sound libraries*, that you can load into your sampler and play. Just about any sound you can imagine is available somewhere as part of a sound library.

The disadvantage of sample playback is that making expressive changes in the sound while it plays is rather difficult. This is because the sample itself (the digital audio recording) is pretty much set in stone. There are ways to customize sampled sounds so as to make a sound library uniquely your own, but doing so is more difficult than with some other types of synthesis, because you're starting with a pre-existing sound rather than building it yourself from the ground up.

Instrument designers have developed a number of features to allow musicians to make better-sounding music with sample playback. In this tutorial we'll touch on some of the most important features.

In order to cover a number of concepts quickly, we haven't included a lot of detailed explanations. If you're not clear on how to apply the tips, you'll need to spend some time with your instrument's manual.

Pitch-shifting, multisampling, and looping are basic to how samplers work. Once you understand these concepts, you'll be well on your way.

PITCH-SHIFTING & TIME-STRETCHING

Until the hip-hop revolution picked up steam in the early '90s, samplers were used first and foremost for playing other types of instrument sounds (such as electric piano, trumpet, and bass guitar) from the keyboard. Today, they're used just as often for playing beats and special effects, but emulating the sound of other instruments is still an important aspect of sampling.

The first step in using a sampler to generate the sound associated with a conventional instrument is to record the sound of a single note — let's say a Middle *C* played by a trumpeter. The second step is to instruct the sampler that when you play a higher or lower note on the keyboard, you want the sampled trumpet note to be played at a higher or lower pitch. (Actually, there are a lot of other intervening steps. I'm simplifying here.) This is done by assigning the sample to a *key zone*, a range of keys on the MIDI keyboard.

The standard way of changing the pitch of a sample, which is called *transposition*, is by having the sampler play it at a slower or faster rate of speed depending on which key you play. Your sampler should perform transposition automatically when the sample is assigned to a key zone, so you never actually need to think about the playback speed. If the sample is played at half-speed, the pitch will drop by an octave. Also, the sample will last twice as long, so any rhythm recorded into it — if it's a drum loop rather than a trumpet note, for instance — will run at half the original tempo. Conversely, if the sample is played at double-speed, the pitch will be an octave higher than the original, the sample will only last half as long, and the tempo of a recorded rhythm will be doubled. This type of pitch-shifting, which changes both pitch and the length of the recording at the same time, is even older than sampling. You can do it with a turntable or an analog tape deck.

By assigning the sample to a range of keys and having the sampler change the speed only a little between one key and the next rather than doubling the speed or cutting it in half, we can create a keyboard layout in which the sample can be used to play chords and melodies in a familiar way.

For small changes in the pitch or length of a sample, transposition works very well. When you need a larger change, however, transposition can produce undesirable sonic changes. For instance, if you need to slow a drum loop down drastically, a low-pitched kick drum can easily become so low that it will drop out of the mix entirely, while cymbals will sound muffled and grainy.

Newer, digital-only technologies have made it possible to change the pitch without changing the sample length, or vice versa. There are three ways of performing this magic: with granular or formant-based resynthesis, or by slicing the sample apart. None of the methods is perfect, but used with care they can all produce excellent results. Some samplers let you do these types of pitch/time changes in real time, simply by adjusting a parameter. Others require that the changes in the sound be stored in memory ahead of time. Some samplers, especially the hardware variety, don't offer any of the newer pitch/time-changing methods. If you have the right audio editing program, however, you can stretch the sample, store the results as a new file, and then load the new file into the sampler.

Granular techniques tend not to work well with percussive material, because granular time-stretching involves slicing the original sample apart into numerous tiny "sound grains." To slow the sample down, some of the grains will be repeated. The sharp attack transients of a drum hit tend to be smeared and blurred by being sliced apart, and you may hear multiple attacks (called *flams*).

For drum loops, a better technique is to slice the sample into larger segments, each of which contains one isolated drum-hit — often an eighth-note or sixteenth-note in length. The individual slices can then be triggered separately at any tempo, and each slice will still sound exactly the way it did in the original sample.

This is how Propellerhead's ReCycle software works. ReCycle isn't a sampler; it's a utility program that slices up the samples for you and puts them in a format called a REX file, which can be read by a sampler or a digital multitrack recorder. Some software samplers now include their own beat-slicing utilities that operate in a similar manner to ReCycle.

In addition to separating a long beat into a number of short slices, a beat slicer does two other things: It creates a MIDI file in which individual notes trigger individual slices, and it creates a keyboard layout for the slices in which each slice is assigned to a separate MIDI key so that the slices can be played in order by the MIDI file. Some sampling instru-

Figure 4-1
In a multisample, individual samples are assigned to various ranges of MIDI keys. Each sample has a root key parameter. When the root key is played, the sample will be heard at the pitch at which it was originally recorded.

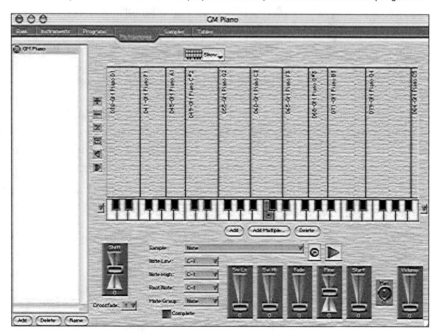

ments will play the MIDI files themselves, while others will time-stretch sliced-up loops only when a sequencer plays the MIDI file.

MULTISAMPLED LAYOUTS

When one sample is assigned to the entire range of a five-octave MIDI keyboard, it will play very slowly at the bottom of the keyboard, very quickly at the top, or both. The sonic changes produced by this amount of pitch-shift are usually undesirable. A better solution, which has been available since the early days of sampling, is to record a number of related samples — for instance, a piano playing single notes at various pitches — and spread them out across the keyboard with each sample assigned to a different zone (see Figure 4-1). Each sample only needs to be transposed up or down by a few half-steps, so the sonic changes caused by extreme transposition are avoided.

This technique is called multisampling. A keyboard layout in which a number of samples are assigned to keyboard zones is called a multisample.

Multisampling solves the immediate problem of the sonic changes caused by large amounts of pitch-shift, but it introduces a new problem. If you play a scale using a multisampled instrument, you'll hear abrupt changes in the sound as you switch from one sample to another. Getting a group of samples that are well matched, so as to minimize this problem, is not easy.

A few samplers will allow you to set up a multisample in which the key zones cross-fade from one to another. You may hear one sample when you play a *C* and another sample when you play an *E*, but when you play the *D* between them you may hear a mix of the two samples. This technique, which is called key crossfading or positional crossfading, generally doesn't work well. You'll most likely hear phase cancellation between the overtones in the two samples.

In addition to key zones, your sampler may be able to create velocity zones (also called velocity windows or velocity splits). With this feature, the sampler can do a much better job of matching the performance response of acoustic instruments. Most instruments sound different when played at low volume than when played at high volume. It's not only that the sound gets louder — in most cases it will also get brighter. That is, the upper partials (the overtones that are higher in frequency) will acquire more energy. A sampler's filter and envelopes can only go so far in mimicking the complex acoustic phenomena involved. By sampling each note of the instrument at two or more dynamic levels and then creating a multisample that uses velocity to choose which sample to play (this is called velocity-cross-switching), the sound designer can create a much more realistic multisample.

As with the samples in adjacent key zones, velocity-cross-switched samples need to match one another reasonably well in timbre, and each needs to be set at a suitable volume level. If the samples don't match, the multisample will be difficult to play in a controllable and realistic way. In practice, I find that a multisample of an acoustic or electric piano that uses more than one but fewer than eight separate velocity-cross-switched samples in each zone is just not very satisfying to play, because the sound transitions are too abrupt.

With percussive sounds, however, phase cancellation is less of an issue, so velocity crossfading can be used to smooth out the transition between a softer drum sample and a louder one.

LOOPING

In the early days of sampling, memory was much more expensive than it is today. A method had to be found for recording a short sample, yet allowing it to sustain for as long as the player held down a key on the keyboard. The method is called looping. When looping is switched on for a sample, part or all of the sample repeats over and over. Two points within the sample, called the loop start and loop end points, define the segment that will repeat.

In most samplers, you can edit the loop start and end points of any sample. Finding usable loop points is not easy, however. If the sounds at the beginning and end of the loop don't match one another, the loop will be bumpy, and you may hear a click each time the loop repeats. Several methods of dealing with this problem are found on various samplers. Some have automatic loop point finders. Some will do back-and-forth looping. Some let you crossfade the audio data at the beginning of the loop into the end of the loop, so that the transition is smooth.

Crossfading isn't useful with rhythm loops, because it will interfere with the crisp sound of drums. Back-and-forth looping is a poor choice unless you want to hear the beat play backward on every other repetition. Many people who use rhythm loops don't actually use the sampler's looping ability at all. Instead, they trigger the sample from their sequencer at each bar line (or every two bars, if it's a two-bar loop). This method has an advantage: You don't have to worry if the sample is slightly too short or slightly too long for the current tempo.

If the sample is actually being looped by the sampler and played by the MIDI sequencer as one extremely long note, you face two problems. First, the sample is quite likely to drift out of sync with the tune unless it's trimmed to exactly the right length. Second, if you want to hear the loop, you have to start playback from the top of the song each time. No MIDI sequencer/tone generator combination that I'm aware of allows you to start playing a sampled note in the middle and hear the sample start playing in the middle.

For best results when looping, prep the samples in an audio editor. A good audio editing program is a must for anyone who is serious about computer-based sampling. With an editor, you'll be able to accomplish several essential tasks:

Trim the start and end of the sample correctly. Get rid of any silence at the start of the sample so it will trigger immediately when the sampler receives a MIDI note-on message. If it's a rhythmic sample, trim the end so that it will loop without hiccuping.

Normalize the sample. Normalizing brings the whole sample up to the maximum possible level short of clipping. It's much easier to match the levels of the individual samples in a multisample if all of them are normalized. Note, however, that samples with a healthy amount of mid-to-high-frequency content will sound subjectively much louder than a low-frequency sample that has the same absolute level. You may find it easier to work with the brighter-sounding samples if their level is a couple of dB lower.

Resample with effects. If you know you're going to want a given sample to have cho-rusing, distortion, compression, or even just a touch of equalization, create a new file (don't overwrite the old one!) in which the effects are printed. This will reduce the load on your CPU. Most audio editors have a suite of plug-in effects, which are included for precisely this purpose.

Isolate and remove pops and clicks. When sampling from vinyl, you may want the funny little clicks to be part of the sample. If a click is driving you crazy, though, load the sam-ple into an audio editor and zoom in on the click. You may be able to draw it out of the wave-form using a pencil tool. If your editor won't do that, or if you don't like the results, you can copy a short segment of similar audio from nearby and paste it so that it replaces the click. When doing this, it's a good idea to copy and paste at zero-crossings (points where the wave-form crosses the zero line in the display).

BURGER OR PATÉ?

My impression is that most people use samplers for getting the job done — adding essen-tial electric piano, bass, string, brass, or drum tracks to a mix — rather than for creative sound design. But some samplers have a surprising number of sound design features. If you want to push the boundaries, read the manual and try clicking on those little buttons to see what happens.

If you're mainly using a sampler in more conventional ways, the same suggestions apply. Convincing a sampler to do a realistic simulation of a conventional instrument is not easy. Fine attention to velocity response, key-zone mapping, and other parameters is essential. But the results will be worth the effort. No matter how deeply you've explored your sampler, there's a good chance it will do things you've never considered. So have fun, get a little crazy, and make some great music!

Due to the stability of dedicated hardware, not to mention the fact that prices for used gear on eBay are extremely attractive, there's still a huge following for vintage samplers. In researching this book, I came across another of Jim Aikin's gems on the topic of integrating loops into your tracks, with equal emphasis on both soft and hard approaches.

Fall 1999
Make Music with Loops
For pointers on using sampled beats, start here

It used to be, if you wanted a hot drum beat, you hired a drummer. Likewise for bass tracks. But technology has changed all that. Thanks to sampled loops, you can produce full, professional-sounding arrangements quickly using simple off-the-shelf tools. Rather than chortling that I never have to deal with a drummer again (which would be unforgivably rude — and besides, I know some great drummers!), I like to think of using sampled loops as an easy way to collaborate with musicians from around the world — cats who have years of experience in styles where I'm strictly a newcomer. By picking up a sampling CD or two, I can add their taste and energy (not to mention their arsenal of world-class recording hardware) to my songs.

While traditional musical skills aren't vital in loop-based music, you'll need to know how to use some specialized hi-tech tools. If you're new to the idea of using loops, a few production ideas and short cuts wouldn't hurt, right? There's a lot of cool hardware and software out there, though — way too much for us to give specific tips on each piece of gear you might own. Rather than try to provide hot tips covering specific features, we've gathered some ideas that you can use no matter what gear you're using.

USING A SAMPLER

Making loop music with a sampler offers at least one important advantage over a computer-based multitrack recorder: You can use the sampler's filters and envelopes to process the audio, or even do a pitchbend for a special effect. On the other hand, once you've filled a hardware sampler's RAM with sounds for a given song, you won't be able to add any more. And unless the sampler has a keyboard or performance pads, you'll need a way to send it as MIDI, so you may end up using a computer sequencer in any case. (An old computer with MIDI sequencer software will work fine, though — even one that's too slow for digital audio.)

If you're using a sampler, here are some techniques to get you started:

■ Assign related loops at the same tempo to adjacent MIDI keys. Then start your sequencer and improvise an arrangement. And don't limit yourself to hitting keys on the downbeats. Sometimes a pickup on beat 4 (or the "and" of 4) followed by the same sample on beat 1 is just what the doctor ordered.

   You may find that it takes some practice to play the loops with tight enough timing that it doesn't sound like a train wreck. Sure, you can quantize the timing later in the sequencer, but it's worthwhile to spend some time learning to play with precision. You might want to do it at a gig sometime — and even if you never need to, you'll discover more cool layered beats once you're able to hear an idea and then play it.

■ When cutting (truncating) the start of the sample so that it will trigger right on the beat, I generally leave 10 or 20 samples of "dead air." My theory is that the sampler's envelope generator may need a little time to ramp up, even if the envelope is set to an attack time of zero. Twenty samples is only half a millisecond (assuming you're sampling at 44.1kHz), so you'll never hear it. But if the envelope generator is a little sluggish, you'll hear all of the attack transients in the sample, so it will snap.

■ If a sampled loop is a little too short, so that there's dead air at the end of every bar, try making a copy of a short segment of the background sound just before the end of the loop (or from some usable spot earlier in the sample) and paste it onto the end. If your sampler supports back-and-forth looping, and assuming you're triggering the beat on every bar line from your sequencer, you may be able to program a short back-and-forth loop at the end of the sound. This will cover up the gap.

■ Drum loops, even stereo loops, can be tempo-shifted in a sampler without developing any nasty digital artifacts, as long as the tempo change isn't too great. The math is a little awkward, so you may prefer to do the shift by ear: Just grab the sample's coarse- and fine-tune parameters and edit them until you get it in the pocket.

■ In case you're curious, the formula works like this: Each half-step a sample is tuned upward increases its tempo by a factor of 1.05935. So if the original tempo of a loop is 135 bpm, you can figure out its tempo when it's played a half-step lower by dividing 135 by 1.05935 (answer: 127.4). This formula will get you in the ballpark.

■ If you have Propellerhead's ReCycle 2.0 or earlier, you can chop up a loop and export it to a hardware sampler. (For better or worse, Recycle 2.1 and higher is only compatible with softsynths and sequencers.) With a computer and a sampler ReCycle can send files to, you can easily slice and dice your drum loops. For example, you might want to drop out the snare during a breakdown section. ReCycle creates a matching MIDI file for each loop, so you can just as easily adjust the feel of the loop's rhythm without changing the sounds. If you don't have ReCycle, you can do much the same thing by hand. It's a little more work, but the results can be worth the trouble. Start by making as many copies of the loop as you need. Delete everything from the first copy except the kick on the downbeat. Chop the second copy to leave only a single snare hit or whatever. To leave room for a fill in the middle, use the sampler's "paste silence" command to erase some audio from one of the copies without shortening the loop.

If you don't have a paste silence command, you can probably create a "silent sample" (by recording nothing, if all else fails). Then make two shortened copies of your loop, one containing only the material before the hole you're trying to create and the other containing only the material after the hole. Truncate the silent sample to the desired length, and then paste the three samples end to end. Some calculation will be required to get everything the right length, so keep a pencil and paper handy.

■ Resampling with effects is a great way to customize your loops. You can add flanging or reverb to taste, resample, and then free up the effects processor to do something else. If your sampler won't do resampling (most will), consider recording the sampler's output through the effects. With a hardware sampler, you can capture the results to your DAW, or use a tape deck and then run the tape deck's output back into the sampler. For that lo-fi sound, record the sample to a cassette deck while sending it a signal that's a little too hot, so that you get some analog overload distortion.

Speaking of distortion, some hardware effects boxes have algorithms that do guitar amp simulation. These effects might not fool a real guitarist, but they're great for drums. [*Editor's note: Guitar amp simulators have improved a lot since this was written, and today many of them are available in software.*] Run a loop through one to overdrive it: The sound can be monstrous!

■ Small amounts of time-shift can be done by retuning a loop up or down. This won't work with pitched material, of course. If you need to time-stretch a loop using DSP rather than retuning, convert it to mono first. Many time-stretch algorithms do a poor job of stretching stereo loops, especially drums. At the very least, the phase coherence will likely be lost, causing drum hits to bounce all over the stereo field. You may hear flams in one channel but not the other. Don't even try to fiddle with the parameters until it sounds good; convert to mono.

■ Trying to truncate the start of a loop, but you don't have graphic waveform editing? Assign the sample to the whole keyboard with the original pitch at Middle *C*. Then play the sample three octaves lower. The silent gap that you're trying to get rid of will be eight times as long. Move the start point up to where the sample starts promptly when you play the lowest key, but don't cut off any of the sound you can hear. Check this new start point at the original pitch to make sure none of the snap of the attack has disappeared. When you're satisfied with the new start point, perform the cut.

USING A MULTITRACK RECORDER

A standard multitrack recorder/MIDI sequencer program has many tools to make loop-based music easier. You'll be able to see your arrangement easily as graphic blocks and edit it by dragging whole groups of audio segments around the screen with the mouse. Adding automation (changes in level and panning) is easy as well. A single song can contain hundreds of megabytes of loops, because they're streaming from the disk, not being played from RAM. On the downside, your track count — the number of samples you can play at any given time — may be more limited than with a sampler, retuning samples is not so easy, and most DAWs won't let you improvise fills or breaks on a MIDI keyboard. [*Editor's note: Ableton Live and Cakewalk Project5 are noteworthy exceptions.*]

What about making loop music with a stand-alone hard disk recorder? Yes, you can do it — but such a recorder is not a good tool for the job. The fact that there's no hi-res computer-style graphic editing environment will cost you extra hours of work. And some stand-alones have a limited timing resolution when cutting and pasting audio, so you may find it hard to get the groove to feel right. Mix automation is available on some stand-alones, but some are missing this vital feature. For all these reasons, we'll restrict our focus to computer-based recorders.

Here are some ideas that may prove useful if you're doing loop-based music in a computer:

■ If you're transferring audio via the analog inputs, grab a bunch of stuff all at once and store it in one big audio file. It's easier to chop this apart later than to start and stop the recording process over and over.

■ Start each new project by creating a folder on your hard disk and making it the default directory for recording into. When it's time to back up your files, you'll be able to drag-copy the whole mess quickly rather than having to sort through a bunch of stuff.

■ If your recorder handles stereo audio as dual mono tracks, be careful not to let the left and right halves get separated when you're dragging chunks around in the track window. Getting them to line up again can be difficult.

■ To prevent clicks and pops, switch on the software's "cut at zero-crossings" option.

■ Rather than use the audio editing commands in your multitrack recorder, you may find that in the long run you'll get better results if you invest in a dedicated stereo audio editor. Among the features such an editor may offer: Compatibility with numerous file formats (or even with a hardware sampler), more types of DSP, and better input metering.

■ Get friendly with your multitrack's "snap-to-grid" options. Creating loop-based arrangements is all about lining up the rhythms, so these features can make or break a mix. For example, you may be able to insert markers and then snap the samples to markers when moving them around. With this feature, you should be able to insert a marker at a snare hit in one loop and then snap a separate snare sample to the marker so that it lines up perfectly.

■ If you're running short of audio tracks, bounce everything down to a stereo submix. Then mute the source tracks — but don't erase them. Later on, you're almost sure to want to make some changes and redo the submix.

■ After lining up several loops with the bar line and block-copying them for eight bars or so, use the track delay or nudge feature to shift certain tracks forward or back until they line up in a rhythm that feels tight to you. You may find that two loops line up flawlessly except for one drum hit that's way out of line. Make a backup copy of the offending loop, and then use cut-and-paste audio editing to remove the offending drum hit from its original position and paste it earlier or later.

■ If your recorder allows you to mute individual chunks within a track, you can start an arrangement by setting up a layer of five or six loops and then block-copy the whole mess for 64 bars or so. Then mute various chunks to create entrances and breaks.

■ Rather than snipping apart the audio, open up a hole for a fill at the end of a bar using your recorder's graphic mix envelopes. If you change your mind later, changing the mix automation is likely to be easier than re-editing the audio clip.

■ Make alternate versions of a loop by bouncing it internally to a new track (or stereo pair) while running it through various effects or combinations of effects. This will eat up extra disk space, but you'll find it much easier to juggle an arrangement than if you're trying to use one track and automate the changes in the effects parameters. This can be worth doing even if the effect is a simple EQ change: If you're not using as many real-time effects, you may have enough CPU overhead to plug in an extra softsynth.

TEMPO MATCHING

The liner notes for many soundware CDs give the tempos for their loops. The bad news is, these tempo indications may be slightly, or even wildly, inaccurate. Assuming you're using a sampler and a sequencer, it's easy enough to find the real tempo of a suspect loop. Here's how:

We'll assume you're dealing with a one-bar loop; the process for multi-bar loops is similar. Trim the loop in the sampler so that it starts promptly when triggered, and so that there's no excess audio (such as the kick on the following downbeat) at the end. In your sequencer, record a whole-note at the right pitch to trigger the loop. Quantize the whole-note so that it starts smack on the downbeat, and adjust its length so that it's just one or two clock-ticks shy of being a whole bar long. (In a sequencer with 384 ppq clock resolution, for instance, one bar is 384 x 4 = 1,536 ticks, so the note should be about 1,534 ticks long.)

Copy this note so that it plays eight or 16 times in a row, making sure to keep all of the copies quantized to the downbeat. Set the sequencer to loop over those 16 bars, and start playback. You should hear the loop playing. Adjust the sequencer's tempo until the groove sounds smooth. Take note of the sequencer's tempo — that's the actual tempo of the loop.

If you're using audio tracks rather than a sampler, the procedure is much the same. Make a one-bar segment of the loop, copy and paste it a number of times while snapping it to bar lines, and set the recorder to loop playback across a four-bar or eight-bar segment. Then adjust the playback tempo until the beat sounds right. (By default, some DAWs will adjust the tempo of the loop when you change the tempo of the sequence. Switch this feature off.)

As you speed up the tempo, the copies may overlap one another, which can cause odd things to happen. If the tempo is too slow, you'll hear a gap of "dead air" between the copies. Ignore these artifacts; just listen to the feel of the beat. Once you've got it right, you can adjust the length of the audio segment so that its end lines up with the next downbeat.

If you're using an audio recorder or editor that will display the precise length of a loop in samples, and if the loop repeats a couple of times on the source sampling CD so that you have two downbeats to work with, you can find out the exact tempo. Here's how:

1. Write down the number of samples between the start of one pass through the loop and the start of the next pass. You may be able to do this by finding the precise peak of the kick drum sound at the start of each bar.

2. Divide the number of samples by the sampling rate; this gives you the length of the loop in seconds. For example, if the loop is 170,667 samples long, and the sampling rate is 48kHz (48,000 samples per second), the sample is 3.555 seconds, or 3,555 milliseconds (abbreviated "ms"), long.

3. Divide this number by the number of quarter-note beats in the loop. Our example loop happens to be eight beats long (two bars of 4/4), so each beat is 444.44ms long.

4. To get the tempo in beats per minute (bpm), divide the magic number 60,000 by the number of milliseconds in a beat. In our example, 60,000 / 444.44 = 135, so the tempo of the loop is 135 bpm.

5. Now that you know this, you can set the tempo of your sequencer to a matching figure.

Okay, that's one sample. What do you do when you need to match the tempos of several samples that are at different tempos? You've got several options:

- If you're using a sampler, grab the coarse- and fine-tune parameters. They'll affect the pitch of the sample as well as the tempo. With drum loops, you may be able to shift a loop by a whole-step (which amounts to ten or 15 bpm, depending on the starting tempo) or even a little more without compromising its sonic quality.
- Try the time-stretch/compress DSP algorithm in your sampler or recorder. If you're slowing the tempo, listen carefully for flams (double-struck notes). If you're speeding it up, listen for swallowed notes. In either case, listen for changes in the groove, as these algorithms sometimes add or remove audio in the quiet spots between drum hits —

but without adding or removing similar amounts between each pair of adjacent hits. This can cause beats 1 and 2 to be closer together than beats 2 and 3, for example. As a last resort, you might want to slice the loop apart into one-beat segments, time-stretch each segment, and then paste them back together.

■ If you're using a sampler, use Propellerhead's ReCycle to slice the beat apart. [*Editor's note: Most DAWs now provide virtually seamless time-stretching of beats, so ReCycle is no longer a necessity.*]

■ Use a different loop.

OTHER IDEAS

Here are some creative tips that may come in handy no matter what type of instrument or platform you're using:

■ Mix and match. There's no law that says you have to use *only* R&B-style samples in a hip-hop project. Some of the most interesting music comes from unexpected collisions between sounds that nobody else has ever tried throwing together. Slow down some scratching and use it in an ambient piece, or add grunge guitar to a light jazz tune. With the right filtering and processing, it may put the mix into an exciting place.

■ If you want to use two drumbeats together, but the kicks are fighting with one another, use heavy EQ or highpass filtering to eliminate the kick from one of the loops. Or eliminate the kick from both of them and add your own kick from a MIDI module or a different sample.

■ By running a simple rhythm loop through a delay processor that's set to an odd rhythmic delay time of 3/8, 3/16, or even 5/16, you can create some bold new grooves.

■ Long sweeps are a great way to keep a one-bar or two-bar loop from becoming too static. In a sampler, try mapping a real-time controller to filter cutoff and then record a long controller contour into your sequencer. If you're using multitrack software, try a resonant flanger plug-in with a slow LFO sweep.

■ Don't make all your loops the same length. If your basic beat is one bar long, add a few other little elements (a horn stab, a scratch, an obscure thumping sound) that repeat after two or four bars.

Fall 1999
All about Loops

What's a loop? In the broadest sense, a loop is any chunk of audio that repeats. While you can make loop-based music even with an old-fashioned reel-to-reel tape deck [*Editor's note: In interviews, producer Brian Eno still mentions the influence of Steve Reich's "It's Gonna Rain," which was created on tape in 1965*], basically we're talking about recording and playing back sounds in digital form from a computer or a sampler. Once a sound has been transformed into digital data, it can be stored, played, and processed very easily.

The most common types of loops are drum beats and bass lines. Chord parts, solo lines, vocals, and sound effects are also used a lot as loops, but vocals and effects are more likely to be dropped in on top of a looped groove, and they may or may not repeat. Loops are almost always in 4/4 time, and they're usually one bar, two bars, or four bars long. Since your song is likely to be a lot longer than this, you make music with a loop by repeating it a number of times.

To make loop-based music, you need two things: some sounds, and a piece of gear that can record and play the sounds. The gear will be either a sampler or a computer and software. The sounds will most likely come from a soundware CD, CD-ROM, or DVD, but you can also make your own sounds.

In a song that's recorded using loops, quite often two, three, or more loops will be playing at the same time. This is called layering. By starting and stopping various loops at various times, you can create a song structure with an intro, verses, choruses, breaks, and so on. You can build excitement by adding more layers, and then make a dramatic break by muting (silencing) some of the layers for a few bars.

To build up a song using loops, you need to find loops that work well together. A typical sampling CD gives you hundreds to choose from. The most important consideration is tempo. If you have three or four loops that you think might sound good together, but they're at different tempos — and more often than not, they will be — you'll have to fiddle with some of them so that they're all at the same tempo. (See "Tempo Matching in the Real World," later in this chapter, to learn how to do this.)

With bass lines, lead lines, and chord parts, you may also need to get the loops in the same key. This is a trickier challenge, but many samplers and software-based audio recorders include pitch-shift processing. If you're using a sampler, you can change the pitch and tempo of a loop simply by tuning it up or down — playing it from a higher or lower key on the MIDI keyboard, for example.

This type of shifting always affects both the pitch and the tempo: As the pitch moves up, the tempo speeds up, and vice versa. In order to change one without affecting the other, you have to mess with the sample using DSP (digital signal processing). Pitch-shifting and time-stretching with DSP will sometimes add strange little glitches to the sound. The further you shift the material away from its starting pitch or length, the more obvious these sonic artifacts will become: With small amounts of shift, a good time-stretch algorithm can do a very reasonable job. Always listen carefully to make sure the results are acceptable to you. Even if you hear some minor problems, by the time you build up a full mix the glitches may be masked by other sounds.

Some CDs provide tempo-matched and key-matched loops that are designed to work together. These are often called "construction kits." A construction kit will typically give you a full-band arrangement between four and 16 bars long, followed by the drum track by itself, the bass track by itself, then the guitar licks and so on. Individual drum hits may be included as well. You can sample these separately and use them to program snare rolls or whatever you like. If several of the kits on the CD are at the same tempo, as they often are, it's quite easy to be creative by mixing and matching the samples — using the drums from one groove along with the bass from another and the scratches from a third, for example.

You can also grab loops off of the radio, or sample the cool bits of commercially released music CDs — or old LPs, for that matter. But if you do so, you won't be able to release your music commercially unless you get clearances for the loops. Clearances can be expensive or even impossible to obtain; for more on how to deal with this problem, see "Sample Clearance" at the end of this chapter. When you buy a sampling (as opposed to music) CD, you're normally buying a license to use the samples in your own music without further cost or paperwork. But be sure to read the fine print; not all licenses are alike.

Many sampling CDs are available in audio format, playable from any CD player, but these days CD-ROMs and DVDs suitable for computer use are more common. Packages containing both an audio CD and the same sounds on a CD-ROM organized in several different file formats are very common. If you're using a hardware sampler, you can sample from an audio CD by plugging your CD player's output into the sampler and recording the material. With a CD-ROM, much of the work has been done for you.

Want to make your own loops? Many sampling CDs have not only prefabricated loops but individual drum hits. You can easily put a few of these in a sampler and then create a beat that triggers them using any MIDI sequencer. If you have a microphone handy, you can record your own percussion from scratch, using anything from an old pair of maracas to a metal garbage can lid.

Fall 1999
Up & Running
From here to loop madness in nine easy steps

Let's cut to the chase. If you want to make loop-based music, here's what you need to do:

1. Get some hardware. If you prefer to use a sampler and you're on a tight budget, you'll find some very viable options in used gear. Whether you buy new or used, look for these features:

■ Lots of RAM (that's the memory where the samples are stored) and/or expandable RAM. In a new sampler, 64MB would not be out of line. If it's used, insist on 16MB, and ask to see the memory installed and running, to avoid possible compatibility problems.

■ The sampler should be ready to hook up to an external storage device for archiving your samples. This usually means a SCSI port on the back panel.

■ Resonant filters are good. So are built-in effects.

■ If you go the computer route, don't even think about picking up used equipment that's more than a year old: Get the newest, fastest computer you can find. For audio I/O, a standard soundcard will work in a pinch, but it's not ideal. In a Windows machine, most soundcards are not low-latency (that is, there will be a short gap between when you trigger a sound using external MIDI and when you hear it), but most exter-

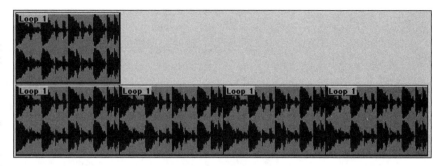

Figure 4-2
After you've found a beat that you want to use, brought it into the computer, and trimmed it, the first step in making a track is to drag-copy the chunk of audio so that it repeats a number of times, starting at bar lines. Here, a one-bar drum beat is shown before copying (top) and after being copied end-to-end (bottom).

nal audio interfaces are capable of low-latency operation. On the Mac, OS X has built-in low-latency audio, but an external audio interface will give you better quality and more features.

2. Get some sounds. Some audio software comes with starter loop libraries, and you may be able to find things on the Internet. The more source material you have to work with, the better.

3. Get some sounds into the hardware. There are two ways to do this — direct digital transfer (which could mean either loading the file straight from a CD or, in rare cases, using the digital output on a CD player to play the audio into the digital input of a sampler or computer), or by recording the audio through the sampler or computer's analog audio inputs. Consult your manual for specifics. Direct digital transfer is cleaner, but don't worry about it: Unless you've got poor cables or are producing tracks for a major-label release, analog recording works fine. Check your signal level prior to recording. If you record a sample at a low level, you can normalize it (boost the gain to maximum) afterward, but this process also boosts the noise floor. Conversely, if you record at too high a level, the input will clip, causing a very nasty type of distortion.

4. Trim the edges. After being recorded, the loops will normally have dead air or unwanted sounds at the start and end. Getting rid of this is a chore, but you'll save memory and disk space, and if you don't trim at least the start of each loop you'll find it almost impossible to get them to line up rhythmically.

5. Match the tempos. If you've grabbed a bunch of loops that are at different tempos (or in different keys), your music will be complete hash until you take care of this vital step. See "Tempo Matching in the Real World" later in this chapter for some ideas on how to proceed.

6. Line 'em up and start playback. Park the first loop on the downbeat of the first bar. If you're working in a computer recorder, copy it four or eight or 16 times, as shown in Figures 4-2 and 4-3. If you're working in a sampler, don't copy it: Trigger it from a sequencer, as shown

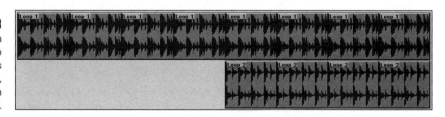

Figure 4-3
Here, the beat from Figure 4-2 is being looped so that it plays eight times (upper track). A second beat, also one bar long, enters in bar 5 (lower track).

Figure 4-4

If you're using a sampler and a MIDI sequencer, your loops will look more like this. Here (as seen in the Cubase piano-roll edit window), one loop repeats on every bar starting at bar 5. A second loop, two bars in length, begins on bar 9. The changes in color are used by Cubase to show MIDI velocity: Here, the first loop starts loud, but gets quieter before the second one enters. The MIDI notes are shown as ending just slightly before the bar line because this makes them easier to see graphically; in a real musical situation, each note should be programmed to last as long as possible, and end just before the start of the next note. The gaps shown here between notes would most likely be audible. The MIDI notes are sent to the sampler, which actually plays the loops.

in Figure 4-4. Pick another loop and start it playing at bar 5. Pick another one and start it at bar 9. When you've stopped dancing around the room in sheer excitement, you're ready to...

7. Figure out which loops work well together. You probably had some thoughts about this even before you started Step 3, but you may be in for some surprises — both pleasant and unpleasant. In fact, the surprises never end. You'll be on Step 7 for the rest of your looping career.

8. Add spice. Anything from MIDI synth pads to live vocal and guitar tracks. Instead of or in addition to your live tracks, grab some more samples and lay down a few breaks, fills, and transitions.

9. Finish the tune, mix it down, and play it for your adoring fans. Need we say more?

Jeff Taylor (a.k.a. Madjef) is certainly one of the top guns in the industry. His contributions to Jam & Lewis's production speaks for itself. In this interview with Ernie Rideout, Jeff explains in detail his production process. For Akai MPC-based remixers, it's a treasure trove of useful information.

Fall 1999
MadLoopz with Madjef
Jam & Lewis's groove guru drops some science

Working with loops making you feel like you're back in school? Take heart. Even masters like Madjef stick to the basics. Ninety percent of all the tracks that came out of Jam & Lewis's Flyte Tyme R&B production juggernaut in the mid-'90s had Madjef's signature on them — as either producer, engineer, programmer, or performer. His discography takes up more room than his Rhodes. Driven? Ambitious? "They call me Madjef," explains the artist also known as Jeff Taylor, "because I'm mad about this technology, and all this cool stuff that we get to do and call it work. How could you not be mad about this, man?"

Jimmy Jam and Terry Lewis bear some responsibility for unleashing the mad loops of Madjef on the world. "They've grown a lot of talent, and given a lot of guys a lot of opportunities," he says. "I have the utmost respect for them as musicians, as songwriters, and as mentors — they're just amazing guys." At the core of Madjef's approach to looping are several things he learned from watching Jam and Lewis work.

"I learned you have to listen carefully to your loops," he says, "and remove things that don't work to make room for the things that, though they may not be prominent, will work better. Once you take that one thing out, all of a sudden the loop jells. It's a matter of spending lots of time focusing on what is going to make your loop better. I learned from those guys that quality is what it's all about. Also, they brought out the musician in me. You see a guy like Jimmy Jam work in his studio with his rows of keyboards, and he's playing everything. How can you observe this and not want to be creative and play something yourself?"

Inspiration, hard work — okay, but there must be more to it. There is, and here follows the Cliff's Notes version of the Madjef Method.

BEAT 1: CHOOSE YOUR SOUNDS

"I've got a huge sound library. When I watch TV and I hear something that I could use as a sonic foundation for something, I'll pray for it to come on again and I'll sample it. That one sound may spark the idea for an arrangement, though it may never even end up in the final composition. The essence of my style is to come up with stuff that's not the typical, everyday style of loops. But I try to keep it funky — you gotta be funky.

"If I'm going for a mellow feel at 80 bpm, certain sounds are required. If I'm going for 94, 97, or 100 bpm to get you dancing a little bit more, then different sounds are required. I determine what the vibe of the piece is going to be, and then I'll go through my sample libraries and try to come up with sounds that fit the vibe. For example, I'll take a scratch sample that I like, drop it into [Digidesign] Pro Tools, and combine it with another sound that I find interesting. Then I'll spit that out into my Akai MPC2000, and I'll find kicks and snares and other sounds to use with it. I may take two or three snares to create another sound. I'll sample that and use it as my snare sound to create a new vibe."

June 2003
PREFUSE 73

Are you using a lot of samples on the Prefuse tracks?
Not the way you'd think. I like to take the part of the sample that you normally wouldn't want to take. Like the tail end, the echo of what you were "supposed" to take. You can create a texture out of this one random sound. You can take a piano loop. But why not take the shit in between? Those slices of sound take on their own rhythm and force you to place your drums in a different way.

When I first started, before I had the MPC, I made tape-to-tape beats. That was so hard. You could never line them up. I had a friend that could do it well, and I always looked up to him. Then the MPC came into play and made everything like cake. Everything came together and I had no restraint whatsoever. I went crazy on that.

BEAT 2: PROGRAM YOUR DRUMS

"I'm really hyped on the Akai MPC2000/3000 series drum machines. They're the greatest things for getting a good R&B feel and groove. In this case, I'm working on a little hip-hop loop. It's just a matter of saying, 'Okay, what's the first instrument going to be here?' I'll pick a sound and get a kick pattern going, a real basic thing. I'll add a snare to that, keeping it very simple. I'll look for something that will give me my vibe right here. This is my basic pattern; it won't change. I'll do things on top of it to create a busier feel, to distinguish the choruses, verses, and breakdowns.

"Everything I do is in real time. It's just so much easier to get a natural feel by playing on the Akai's pads — you get 16 levels of velocity. I did the drum programming for Barry White's comeback album years ago, on a tune called 'Come On.' When the video came on TV, there was a live drummer playing my drum programming! I want my loops to sound like a real drummer. Unfortunately, you have to quantize in a lot of cases, just so that everything else locks up to it. But I try to go for as loose a feel as I can possibly get.

"I generally start with a two-bar phrase, because it's nice and tight. Your stability's there, your timing's there, and you get to fine-tune your rhythm without waiting for that extra two bars to come around. I'll put in the hi-hat now, doing things that a drummer would do, that a drum machine guy wouldn't necessarily do. Right here in front of the Akai, I'll just play the pads, and create and manipulate the sounds of the snares and other drum sounds inside the unit itself. I'll tweak or pitch-shift them so they're close to happening within the loop."

BEAT 3: LOCK IT DOWN

"So I've got a nice little drum sequence as a starting point. All the samples reside in the MPC2000. Then I save my sequence as a MIDI file to a floppy disk, put the disk in my Mac, and open it in Logic. Now the MPC doesn't trigger sounds when I hit it — it just sits there as a drum module. I've got my loop laid out in Logic, and what was once a two-bar phrase, at the simple click of a mouse becomes a four-bar phrase. Now I add whatever turnaround I want to, and I can start taking the samples and moving them around in this new arrangement.

"Sometimes it'll sound a little bit different when I open the loop up in Logic, but if it's a tasty accident, I'll go with it. I'll overdub MIDI tracks and new audio, adding vocals or instruments. There are no rules at all when I do this. It's truly whatever feels good. When you're making records with guys like Jam and Lewis, unless specifically requested, you don't want to use samples of somebody else's stuff, because there are funding issues that come into play. If there's a particular vibe I'm trying to create, I'll just create it myself, or bring in a singer or player.

"I try to match the key of the most prominent sample, and this may involve offsetting the tuning of the samples. I'll tweak the timing, too. If I record my own bass sample, maybe I'll trigger it eight clicks before everything else, which sets it off just a little bit. I'll slide things around to get the feel I'm looking for; I'll try it ahead of the beat, or I'll lay it back. If I'm having trouble making the bass line work, I'll cut it in two and mess with just one part of it. We want it to lock down, and one of the oldest tricks in the book is to take a problem sample, cut it in two, and make the two pieces work individually."

June 1997
CHEMICAL BROTHERS

Is vinyl your main source for loops and samples?
Yeah. I mean, we'll hear things, sample it, play around with it, and start adding our own stuff to it. A lot of it is actually me playing guitar and bass on the record. And then some tracks, like the last two, are written around a guitar and a sitar, which I played, and then we made a loop out of. But generally, I like the sound you get when you sample things from all different contexts and put them together. You end up with a sound that you can't get any other way. You're sampling from eight completely different sources, and they've all been treated differently, and you put them all together.

BEAT 4: MAKE THE ARRANGEMENTS

"This loop is the basis for my whole track, so I'm going to spend as much time as I need to make these parts work together. Once I've got what I want, I may load up a different kit in the MPC2000 to see what the loop sounds like triggering a different set of sounds. If it's great, maybe I'll use that as a breakdown, or as the basis for the chorus.

"This is what the R&B and hip-hop thing is all about: creating this kind of a vibe, carefully, one sound at a time. Then someone will be able to sing over it, or you can bring in a keyboard player who lays down just the right Rhodes thing, and pretty soon you've got this arrangement that's just off the hook, it's a great song, all based on your locked-down loop.

"The reason that I can whip this stuff out without creating melodies or chords — it's the samples. What I like to do, though, is to bring in real players and produce something that shows musical ability. That'll really make the track happen. But all this stuff here is the foundation."

As a longtime fan of Acid and working with loops, Doug Beck has some choice insights on customizing soundware loops to fit your musical identity.

April 2001

Advanced Loop Editing
Tips and tricks for better audio loops

Audio loops have become an integral part of the production process over the past few years. Sample CDs and downloadable loops are more popular than ever, and their ever-increasing variety indicates that the market is picking up steam. Loops are here to stay.

While many users of the technology are quick to tout the benefits of loop-based production, more could be said about the challenging aspects of working with loops. As someone who has spent literally thousands of hours creating, editing, and tweaking audio loops, I think it's safe to say that I've encountered just about every one of those challenges! Granted, audio editing tools have come a very long way in recent years, and fortunately many of the problems I experienced early on have become a thing of the past. But to get the maximum benefit from any professional audio editing program, it might be worth your while to try a few of the loop-editing techniques I discovered along the way. In the hope of saving you some time, not to mention the frustration I endured, here is the article I wish I'd read back then.

CLEAN LOOP POINTS FOR SYNTH & BASS LOOPS

With synth and bass loops in particular, I often run into difficulty getting a "clean" loop point; that is, getting the loop to repeat without any click or pop. Sustained synth bass phrases can be especially tricky to loop, and other synth phrases share this characteristic as well. I found that drawing small crossfades between the loops sometimes did the trick, but not always. Eventually I discovered a simple but effective solution: Zoom all the way in on the wave, select a small sliver of audio at the very end, and apply the "fade out" function to smooth out the end of the sample. The result: No more pop or click. Simple and effective.

MAXIMIZE YOUR CONTENT

You get what you pay for with most products — and audio content is no exception. Whether you invest in a high-quality sample CD, download content from the

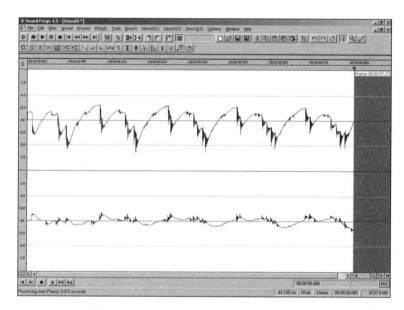

Figure 4-5
Here I've zoomed in on the end of a loop. The right channel (lower wave) ends below the blue center line; as the file loops, this will cause a click or pop.

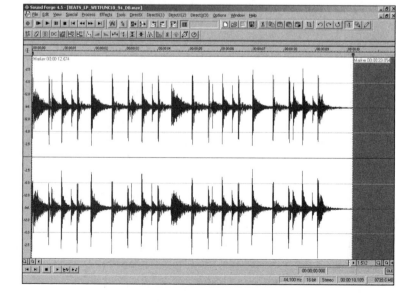

Figure 4-6
A typical drum loop waveform.

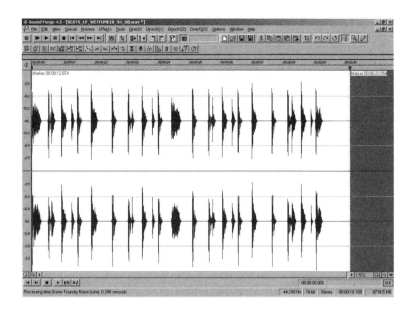

Figure 4-7
This shows how the file looks after a gate effect is applied.

Internet, or take some extra time to create your own source material, you can take some simple steps to maximize your production budget and squeeze the most juice out of your loops.

Gates. Most professional editing tools have a simple, adjustable gate feature that can be used to great effect, especially with drum and percussion loops. If your original loop is dripping with reverb, increasing the sensitivity of the gate and shortening the speed at which it closes can give the loop a much drier, tighter sound without fundamentally altering the phrase or the instrumentation. Increasing the sensitivity even more and toying with the gate speed or threshold can cause certain notes or even instruments to drop out entirely — a result that can fundamentally change the sound and feel of the loop. You might also consider using your newly gated loop solely to trigger the opening of the gate. You can then process other loops and pieces of audio through the gate in real time. All of these gating techniques can be applied to an audio signal in software or using any outboard gate/compressor module.

Regions. My editor of choice (Sound Forge) has an "auto region" function that places markers in the loop at the transients. From there, chopping the loop into smaller regions and rearranging them is a piece of cake. New loop patterns instantly emerge, fills and transitions are easily constructed, and all retain the tone and instrumentation of the original loop. I save any promising pattern to a new file, and I continue rearranging and saving regions until I have a nice stockpile. In this way, any good audio editing tool can be transformed into a virtual loop factory, and a single sample can yield megabytes and megabytes of great new source material. (Programs such as Propellerhead's ReCycle also perform this function very well.)

Music production is, at its best, a harmonious marriage of art and technology. But as music-making technology continues to expand in leaps and bounds, we are certain to

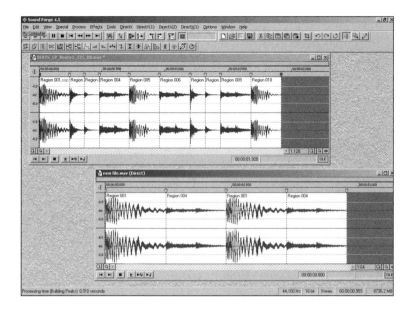

Figure 4-8
Here I've applied region markers to the transients of the top file (booty1). By pasting regions 1 and 4 together in a new file I've created a totally new loop. I can experiment with different combinations to create variations of the original file.

encounter new issues and problems to work out. This is, after all, the nature of the beast. One thing is sure to be a constant, though. In the end, it really doesn't matter what's in your studio or loaded on your laptop. What counts are your ideas, and making sure you're getting the most out of what you have.

Sometimes your favorite part of a sample or loop is a discrete sonic element within a mix. Greg Rule is no stranger to that phenomenon, and has a few tips for extracting or highlighting a desired sound within mixed audio.

February 2002
Taming the Wild Loop
Ways to "remix" pre-mixed material

There's no shortage of excellent drum loop CDs on the market today, and in a wide range of formats. Take Discrete Drums. What makes that title particularly attractive is its multitrack formatting. If you like a particular loop, but want to turn down the snare, for example, Discrete Drums gives you control over the separate tracks: kick, snare, toms, overheads, etc.

But what do you do when you're working with a pre-mixed stereo loop and you need to make adjustments to the individual components within it?

Recently I was working on a remix, and was experimenting with a drum/percussion loop in the verse. The loop was working out well, but the snare was mixed way too loud for the song. There are several ways to approach this problem. I'll walk you through a few of them below.

June 1998
ARMAND VAN HELDEN

When you sample, what's your primary source material?
Everything I get, all my source stuff, is from diggin' in my [record] crates. Every single track I do.
How much editing do you do to your samples?
It depends. Now, like in hip-hop, you can just loop Steely Dan and make the biggest record. That's happening right now. Hip-hop's easy. If you get the right loop, like all the Premieres and Puffys of the world, it's worth gold. But it's getting that right loop, and it's what you do to it. What I'm saying is in all the other stuff I do, like in the house stuff and these type of things, I don't loop hardly anything [instead sequencing note-for-note]. The only loops I have are at the end of a song to make an effect.

SOLUTION 1: EQ OR FILTERING

If the components of the loop are frequency-isolated enough, you can use a notch filter or parametric EQ to reduce the level of a specific offensive frequency. The best-case scenario for this technique is when the kick drums are residing alone in the low-frequency range, the snares are in the middle, and the cymbals are up on top. In Figure 4-9, I've reduced the 4kHz band by 5dB, thus mellowing a very piercing snare.

If, on the other hand, the snare contains too many high and/or low overtones, EQing or filtering the snare frequencies might adversely affect other instruments in the loop as well. Whatever the case, it isn't a bad idea to start with this "quick and dirty" technique and see if it yields the results you desire. If not, move on to the next solution:

Figure 4-9
In some cases, a notch filter or parametric EQ can tame a loud instrument within a pre-mixed loop, such as a piercing snare drum in this example.

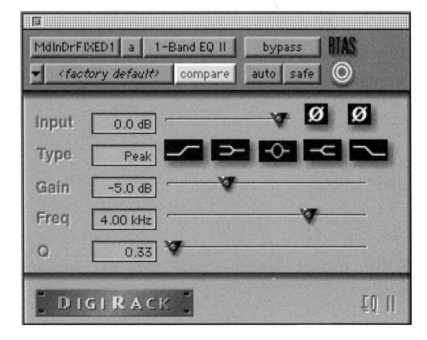

SOLUTION 2: VOLUME AUTOMATION

Make sure your loop is properly truncated and locked to a tempo grid. (All major sequencer/recorders offer a grid feature, in which a tempo is designated and audio regions are "snapped" to its subdivided grid.)

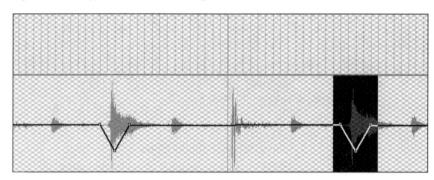

Figure 4-10
Volume automation is particularly effective for manipulating pre-mixed material. In this example, each snare hit is being reduced by 5dB.

Select the volume automation feature and draw a volume "dip" over the first snare hit. (Figure 4-10 shows Pro Tools' rubberband-style timeline superimposed over the audio track.) Now play that portion of the audio and listen to the mix. Is the snare still too loud? If so, draw a deeper dip. Once the snare is sitting properly in the mix, proceed to the next step.

Select the volume automation data, copy it, paste it over the next snare hit, and repeat. This is where grid mode can save the day, as it takes the guesswork out of the pasting process. Just snap the cursor to the grid line before each snare hit, then click with the mouse and paste. Once you've pasted several times, you can select a larger region and paste it as many times as necessary. This assumes that all snare hits have consistent dynamics and placement. If not, you might need to automate each hit individually.

Figure 4-11
In this example, all kicks have been stripped out of the loop and moved onto a separate track, as have snares. This provides greater mix control, and opens the door to more creative processing opportunities.

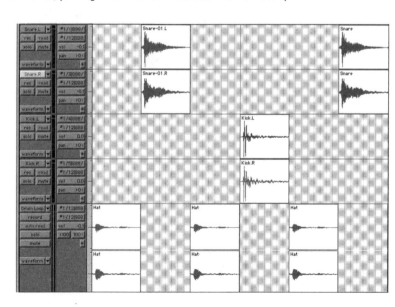

Note: This technique might not work well if you're using loops that have sustained or ambient material, such as ride cymbals. If so, try increasing the grid resolution (or turn it off entirely) and draw the volume dips extra tight to minimize the ducking effect.

June 1997

SNEAKER PIMPS ON SAMPLING

If you're ever stuck debating with someone who has an aversion to sampling, enlist Liam Howe to fight on your side: "You have the choice to sample and take any bits that you want, taking those out of context. That's the prerogative of the post-modern musician, to be able to interpret other people's work in an entirely different way. You can take just a single word from a song and remix it, and that's the only fragment that you keep. People who deny the importance of samples, I think, are being slightly too purist, traditional about the way that music is progressing through culture."

SOLUTION 3: SLICE AND SPLIT

For even finer control, you can slice a loop into individual hits and separate the similar components onto their own tracks; one for kicks, one for snares, and so on (see Figure 4-11). In other words, slice out all of the kick drums and move them to their own track. Then do the same for snares, and so on. Most major apps offer some type of "strip silence" feature, which may be able to automatically separate the elements for you.

Once the slice groups are assigned to their own tracks, you can adjust the track volumes independently with the volume faders. This allows you to apply EQ and specific effects to each track as well.

Note: Just like the volume automation technique mentioned above, this approach will yield varying degrees of success based on the material you're working with. If a crash cymbal overlaps the first few kick and snare hits, for example, the slicing technique will likely produce an undesired chopped effect. Experimentation is the key.

I hope these techniques will help you manipulate your loops to a finer degree. And by all means — don't stop with simple volume edits! Try shuffling the hit slices around. Add effects to certain slices. Take those stock loops and make them your own.

While most modern DAWs include some sort of integrated tempo-matching and time-stretching features, not everyone has the cash for the latest musical doodads. If you're working with an older program, Craig Anderton has some tips for getting your loops in sync.

July 2001

Tempo Matching in the Real World
When did you want to hear it?

When doing a remix, you're usually given a song's essential elements in a multitrack format. This allows you to do things like (for example) extracting a vocal from a hit song and wrapping a new accompaniment track around it.

But what happens if there's only a two-track mix from which you can work? Oddly enough, this happened to me three times in the last week. First was a remix assignment for a pop tune that was cut in the early '80s. It needed not only remixing, but also some cleanup and fixing, and all that was available was the stereo master mix.

At the same time, I had just started work on another movie soundtrack. The opening scenes had been cut to a music library selection, and now the producers had a problem: They liked the tune's basic approach, but felt it lacked punch. Cool sounds were also needed to go along with hit points. Again, I was given a two-track mix and asked to augment it.

Finally, I was reviving one of my techno tunes from 1983 that was in desperate need of an updated drum sound. The master was long gone, so of course all I had was, once more, a two-track mix.

Mission impossible? Not at all. Here's how to deal with this type of situation.

E-Z TEMPO MATCHING

Because these assignments required adding loops as well as audio recorded to standard hard disk tracks, I booted up Sony Acid. However, other programs (Pro Tools, Cubase, Digital Performer, Logic, Cakewalk Sonar, etc.) will work.

The first task: Match the program's tempo to the existing audio. The following procedure works if the music was cut to a click track and has a constant tempo.

■ Trim the two-track music to be remixed so it starts exactly on the downbeat. If the song doesn't start on a downbeat, then split the file in two. Save the section prior to the downbeat as a separate file that you can reattach later.
■ Import the two-track into Acid as a one-shot sample.
■ Bring a click reference track into Acid. I generally use a four-on-the-floor kick drum loop.
■ Extend the click reference for the length of the song.
■ Start playback and note whether the click leads or lags the original song's tempo. If the click falls behind, speed up the tempo. If the click moves ahead, slow down the tempo.
■ Keep fine-tuning the tempo until the beats match as closely as possible.
■ Zoom in on the original track's audio; you should be able to recognize the downbeats by seeing peaks. Compare this to the reference signal (see Figure 4-12).
■ Fine-tune the tempo further if you need to so the peaks line up exactly.

Figure 4-12
The reference kick in the lower track lags the obvious downbeat in the original song (upper track). Assuming the two are lined up at the beginning of the song but have drifted apart by the point we're looking at here, the solution is to speed up the tempo slightly.

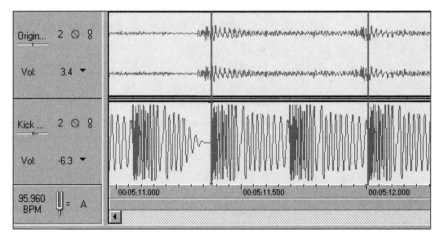

- Move further along the song, tweaking tempo as needed so the downbeats line up for the original and reference signals, until you reach the end.
- Play from the beginning, and the click reference should chug along perfectly in time with your original song's beat.

Acid can resolve tempo to a thousandth of a BPM, which turned out to be a good thing. For the movie theme, which was nominally at 96 BPM, a setting of 95.995 allowed the click to remain perfectly in sync for more than eight minutes. From there, it was a simple matter to fold in some loops, record a few parts on the hard disk tracks, and mix the whole thing down.

TOUGH TEMPO MATCHING

But what if the original song has tempo fluctuations? If they're not extreme, the procedure below should do the job. I used it with my pop tune remix, as there were just enough tempo changes to make life difficult. The solution was much more time-consuming than the method mentioned above, but it still worked. [*Editor's note: Today, the whole process could be accomplished much more easily in Ableton Live using Live's warp markers.*]

- Cut the original piece into one- or two-measure segments. Save each segment as its own file. (Include useful info in the file name, such as "V2_0708.WAV." This would indicate the seventh and eighth measures of the second verse.)
- Now bring each segment into Acid on its own track, in the correct order (see Figure 4-13). [*Editor's note: Prior to version 6, Acid was unable to place different audio segments in a single track.*]

Figure 4-13
The original tune to be remixed has been cut into one-measure pieces, each of which has been brought into a successive track in Acid (above these are some added drum loops).

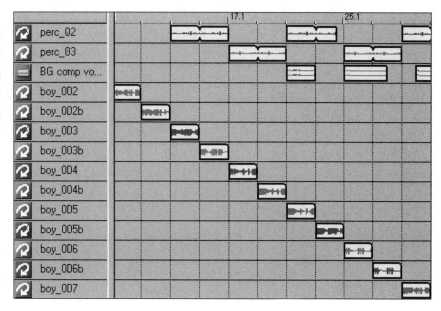

- Adjust the overall tempo so that the gaps and overlaps between segments are minimized. Some segments might fall a bit short, others might spill over the measure line. If the variance is minute, the listener may not notice any gap or spillover. If the variance is extreme for some of the measures, then it may be necessary to use a software tool like Prosoniq Time Factory to shorten or lengthen individual segments as needed.
- If at some point in the song the measures fall consistently short of the tempo, then the tempo needs to speed up a bit. If they consistently spill over into the next measure, then the tempo needs to slow down. Insert tempo change commands as necessary to keep the measure timings as consistent as possible.

EXTREME TEMPO CHANGES

If the tempo changes are really extreme, adding digital audio loops or additional tracks to the basic song may prove to be impractical. In this case, using a MIDI/audio sequencer to add MIDI parts can provide the ideal solution.

As with the previous techniques, first bring the track to be augmented/remixed into the program, again trimmed to a downbeat. Depending on your sequencer, there may be a tap tempo option or a master tempo track. If you have a good sense of time and

January 1997

THE DUST BROTHERS

The Dust Brothers —John King and Mike Simpson — have been key producers, some might say visionaries, in styles ranging from hip-hop to rock. One of their most significant productions, the legendary Beastie Boys' *Paul's Boutique* record, virtually defined how sampling influenced music production in the ensuing years. Here's what they had to say about it.

What roles were each of you playing in the process when you started out?
Simpson: We were both experimenting. Initially, the first gear we had was the [Roland] S-10, and we didn't even have the sequencer worked out. I had an Oberheim DX drum machine that I'd bought in high school, and I was using the analog triggers. I'd program a kick drum on the one on the DX, and send the analog trigger to the S-10 to make a loop. I could do one loop at a time, and since we had the 4-track I could put one loop on there and then get another loop going. Even when we did get into sequencing we were still limited by the amount of

sampling time we had on the S-10. Then when we got the [E-mu] Emax we were still limited by the rudimentary nature of the sequencing program. But it was fun in a lot of ways. A lot of the tracks that became [the Beastie Boys'] *Paul's Boutique* arose from things we'd put together on the 4-track.

***Paul's Boutique** is considered by many hip-hop fans and critics to be a landmark album. Tell us about it.*
Simpson: For us, it was the culmination of about two and a half years of being in the studio 16 hours a day, seven days a week.
King: Intense experimenting, playing, and learning.
Simpson: But that record was all about having fun. It was such a dream come true to work with the Beastie Boys.
How did you get the gig?
Simpson: The Beastie Boys just happened to walk into the studio where we were working. They weren't even thinking about making a record at the time. They were looking for a party. [*Laughs.*] They heard the tracks we were working on, and were like, "This stuff is really cool. What

can follow the tempo variations, using the tap tempo command will usually be the most expeditious way to follow the song's tempo. Otherwise, you'll need to adjust the master track tempo by trial and error until the sequence tempo variations match those in the original song.

Now add your parts using MIDI instruments. Because this doesn't involve digital audio, extreme or rapidly varying tempo changes won't warp the pitch, as can happen when digital audio tries to follow tempo changes. MIDI parts will seamlessly track any tempo changes without causing pitch problems.

Of course, it's vastly easier to do a remix when you're given separate tracks from a multitrack. But when all you have is a two-track, one of these solutions might save the day.

While hip-hop and mash-ups are the most-obvious-examples, sampling other people's recordings is also a tried and true way to create an instantly familiar and infectious remix track. For better or worse, sampling has become a thorny issue in today's increasingly litigious musical world. So we'll round out this chapter with a primer on navigating the stormy waters of sample licens-

are you guys doing with this?" We said we were planning to release them as instrumentals, and they were like, "We'd love to rap on this stuff. Maybe we could work together." And so they went back to New York, and we put a tape together for them. It took a couple of weeks for them to get the tape, and meanwhile we were sitting by the phone, sweating. Then one Sunday night they called us: "We're flying out tonight on the red-eye. Book studio time. Let's start making a record."

When the project started, did you build on your pre-existing tapes, or start over from scratch?

King: We used the songs.

Simpson: We transferred a lot of the old stuff to 16-track from 4-track. I mean, we still had it all; all the loops were still programmed. They were backed up, programmed in the computer, and saved.

On your Web site, there's a long list of all the samples you used on Paul's Boutique *and had cleared legally. What's your take on the state of sample clearance these days?*

Simpson: I have a love/hate relationship with samples. I rely on them as a source of inspiration, and the sound you get from samples you just can't get anywhere else. I'm happy to pay for the use of samples, but I think there's a line where it becomes unfair, and there's a line where it just becomes obscene. We've found that the publishers are so incredibly difficult to deal with on the sampling issue. And usually the person who's negotiating isn't a musician. They're a business person and they can't distinguish between a sample occurring once in a five-minute song versus something that gets looped and forms the basis of the entire track. It's like, "We own the copyright so if you use our stuff, we get 50 percent." And we're like, "You don't understand. We sampled other people to a much greater extent on the same song, and we only had to give them. . . ."

We really feel like we're creating new works, and a lot of people who are out there sampling, especially in the rap world, aren't creating new works. They're basically putting new lyrics to another person's song. We want the publishers to acknowledge that, hey, we've done something new with this. We're willing to pay, but let's make it fair.

ing. Rich Stim is a San Francisco attorney and the author of several books, including Music Law: *How to Run Your Band's Business* (Nolo Press). This feature originally appeared in the April 1999 issue of *Keyboard*, but Stim rewrote it specially for this book to keep readers up to date with the changing legal landscape.

April 1999
Sample Clearance
How to secure the permissions you need

For musicians and songwriters there are many dangers involved in unauthorized sampling — but don't tell that to Brian Burton, a.k.a. DJ Danger Mouse, whose career as a music producer was launched through the illegal use of samples. In 2004 Burton created *The Grey Album*, a mash-up of the Beatles' *White Album* and Jay-Z's *Black Album*. He pressed 3,000 copies of *The Grey Album* and distributed them to indie music sources.

EMI, the owner of rights to the Beatles album, learned of the project and quickly squelched it by sending a cease-and-desist letter. "EMI is absolutely in favor of music sampling," an EMI spokesperson told the press. "There's a very well-established way to get sampling and [Burton] did not participate."

Burton complied with the EMI order and stopped distribution of the recording. But fans uploaded the album to the Internet, where it became a worldwide sensation. Since EMI never pursued Burton after he agreed to stop, he suffered no serious legal consequences. And *The Grey Album* led to a slew of producing opportunities as well as recognition in *Rolling Stone* and *The New York Times*.

Sampling, however, has not been as kind to other artists. Consider the makers of the film *I Got the Hook-Up*, who were sued because a two-second sample (a three-note riff) from George Clinton's "Get Off Your Ass and Jam" (sampled by N.W.A. in their song "100 Miles and Runnin'") appeared in the film. Although many listeners could not even discern the sample in the mix, a federal court ruled that *any* sampling from a recording amounts to copyright infringement and found the filmmakers liable for infringement and financial penalties. Ouch!

Should you make use of samples from someone else's copyrighted music? How does the average working musician decide what to do?

In a nutshell, you should *always* seek clearance for use of a recognizable sample when you are signed to a recording contract, when you're releasing your own album or single commercially, or when preparing music for a commercial client — for example, for a videogame, advertisement, commercially released film, or the like. If you don't get permission under these circumstances, you could get sued, your record label or client could get sued, and you might be prevented from distributing your music to the public at all.

As a practical matter, if you're only selling recordings at shows and don't expect to press more than 1,000 copies of a record, you run less risk for uncleared samples, because it's unlikely that the owner of the source recording will ever learn of your samples. If they do learn of it, they may not be inclined to pursue you unless they sense you have deep pockets (legal slang for people with substantial assets).

However, always keep in mind that if your recording becomes popular and becomes a staple of clubs, or on the radio, or a major download sensation, you'll likely have to deal with the issue of clearance. And unfortunately, using uncleared samples can be dangerous to your financial health. Artists have been forced to pay sums in the range of $100,000 as settlement for the uncleared use of samples (and often must give up substantial music publishing royalties as well).

You're also probably familiar with the Catch-22 of sample clearance: In order to get a signed sample clearance agreement, you'll have to provide the owners of the sample (a music publisher and record company) with a recording that shows how much of the source you intend to use, and how you intend to use it. So you'll likely be doing your recording first, with no permission. If you then find that you can't get permission, a lot of hard work will have gone to waste. (FYI, in the event that you intend to proceed without clearance, you should be familiar with some legal principles which I'll explain a little later.)

So what should you know about getting permission to use samples?

The process of getting permission from the owners of the sampled music is referred to as "sample clearance." When you sample music from a pop recording, you'll need two clearances: one from the copyright owner of the song, who is usually a music publisher, and the other from the copyright owner of the master tapes, which is usually a record company. In general, clearance is required only if you're planning to make copies of your music and distribute the copies to the public, not for sampling at home. If you're only using samples in your live performance, you probably don't need to bother with clearance unless your act is drawing the type of attention that would awaken a copyright owner as to your use. (In any case, most venues have blanket licenses with performing rights societies such as ASCAP and BMI and these licenses may cover the sampled music as well.)

The costs for clearance are negotiable, and there are no standard fees. However, as a general rule the music publisher usually wants an up-front "advance" payment (which, unfortunately, could be anywhere between $5,000 and $10,000) plus a percentage of the song income (anywhere between 15% and 50%). The owner of the master recording will also want an up-front payment (usually at least $1,000) plus a "rollover." A rollover is a payment made when a certain number of copies have been sold. Sometimes, instead of a rollover, the owner of the master may want a portion of future record royalties (although sampling consultants advise against this practice).

Sample rates have become so steep that it's often difficult for small independent labels to acquire clearances. An independent artist with a recording budget of $20,000 may, for example, have to pay $10,000 on up-front payments for two or three samples.

In some ways, sample clearance has become easier than it was ten years ago, and in some ways it has become more difficult. Some labels and publishers have begun to make it easier for artists to acquire rights by providing online sample clearance procedures and by permitting the emailing of the proposed use. But a bigger issue—mergers and acquisitions within the music industry—has slowed down the licensing process.

"It's become harder to clear samples," says Cathy Carapella of Diamond Time, Ltd., a clearance service in New York (www.diamondtime.net), "because there are fewer people handling the same amount of requests. People are dropping like flies [in the music business] … and often there's one person handling the clearances that two or three people used to do. Nowadays, it's just much more difficult to get the attention of a licensing executive."

FIND THE COPYRIGHT OWNERS

The first step in obtaining permission is to locate the copyright owner(s) of both the song and the master recording. The song and the master recording will often be owned by different entities, and you need permission from both of them. Since it's always easiest to find the music publisher, you should start there. The best way to locate a publisher is through performing rights organizations such as BMI, ASCAP, and SESAC. These groups collect money on behalf of songwriters for radio, TV, and other public performances of songs. (In Canada, the performing rights organization is SOCAN.) You may be able to obtain similar information from the Harry Fox Agency.

You can locate the key information on the Internet by visiting the performing rights society websites and determining which organization controls rights for the source song. That will lead you to the music publisher.

Some detective work may be required. BMI's searchable database includes more than 20 entries, for instance, for songs titled "Yesterday." If you can't locate the song you're looking for online, try phoning the performing rights organizations and ask for the "song indexing" department. Once you have the publisher's name and address, phone or write the publisher to determine if they will grant clearance for the source music. Many publishers, unfortunately, have a policy not to grant permission for sampling.

If the publisher can't lead you to the owner of the master recording, you can check online record stores or the Phonolog directory at your local record shop to find the record company that is currently releasing the source music. Major labels have special departments to handle sample clearance. For example, masters owned by Warner Bros., Elektra, and Atlantic are handled by Warner Special Products. Locating master owners may prove troublesome — record companies may fold or sell their copyrights to other companies. In addition, rights in masters may revert to the original artists after a number of years. In that case, you may have to use the assistance of a sampling consultant.

- ■ **Use a Clearance Expert.** For an hourly fee, sampling consultants can guide you through the clearance process. Consultants like Cathy Carapella of Diamond Time can save you time and money because they're familiar with the procedures, costs, and key people who license rights at the major music publishing and record companies.
- ■ **Plan Ahead.** "The biggest mistakes [in sampling clearance] are not planning far enough ahead and not having enough alternatives if a sample is rejected," says a representative of EMI Music. "Sometimes it can take months to get all of the approvals." Many copyright owners (for example, the Beatles) have a no-sampling policy. If the sample request isn't approved, be prepared to replace the sample with something else.

You also need to plan ahead on your end, says Carapella. She strongly recommends that before beginning the clearance process, "get all your songwriting info up front. Really think about who owns what percentage of the new work. I have a couple of deals that have been slowed down because the songwriters still haven't figured out their splits. You have to get that stuff straightened out up front."

■ **Re-Create the Sample.** Some artists have avoided paying part of the sampling clearance fee by re-recording the sampled section. How does this work? Let's say you want to use a six-second sample from "Green Onions." Instead of sampling the original recording, you play the parts yourself and re-record the music to sound exactly like the original. In that case you have not infringed the master recording. (Due to a quirk in copyright law, you can only infringe a master recording if you actually copy it — not if you imitate it). You will not need to seek permission from the master owner, and need pay no fees. You will, however, still need to seek permission from the music publisher of "Green Onions."

■ **Show Them the Money.** If you're an independent or unsigned artist, you may be able to overcome the "never heard of you" syndrome by offering to make the payment up front. If you show them that you can write the check to pay the advance, they'll be more inclined to deal with clearance.

■ **Find Sample-Friendly Copyright Owners.** Some copyright owners are willing to clear samples — so much so that they encourage the process. Copyright owners of songs by the Average White Band and the Gap Band have in the past pro-actively sought to promote their music for sampling.

■ **Contact the Artist or Songwriter Directly.** If you run into problems with a music publisher or owner of a master, you may have better luck contacting the artist directly. This works if the artist still has some say or control in what gets cleared. For example, Shirley Manson of Garbage wanted to use the line, "You're the talk of the town," at the end of a song. Lawyers for the band ordered her to drop it, but Shirley called up Chrissie Hynde, who sent the following letter to Garbage's attorneys: "I, Chrissie Hynde, hereby allow the rock band Garbage to sample my songs, my words, and indeed my very ass." (Of course, this only works if the musician or songwriter controls the copyrights—not a third-party music publisher or label.)

■ **Try the Creative Commons License.** A newer more enlightened method of obtaining sampling clearance is available through the Creative Commons, an organization that proposes an alternative to traditional copyright thinking. Musicians can post their music under a Creative Commons license and permit others to take and transform pieces of the music for sampling purposes (but not for advertising). Check out their website (www.creativecommons.org) for more details.

OPERATING WITHOUT CLEARANCE

As noted, if you are using an uncleared sample, you can lower your risks by making it unrecognizable, by not using the sample as the groove or hook, and by burying it in the mix. And of course, don't use the title of the source music in the title of your song. Under the copyright law, you may be in the clear in the following situations:

■ **If your use of the sample doesn't infringe or is considered inconsequential.** Unfortunately, the current state of sampling law is not so clear that we can chart a noninfringing course for you. As noted earlier, a federal court ruled that the use of *any* sampled recording — even as little as two seconds — was an infringement. Although many legal experts think the ruling went too far and was improper under copyright law (including the Recording Industry Association of America, who stated in legal papers that the decision is "unprecedented and unsustainable"), this ruling is law … at least in Michigan, Tennessee, Ohio, and Kentucky, where this court has jurisdiction. (In other states, it's not yet clear in early 2006 whether this "zero-tolerance" policy applies.)

Certainly if the master recording clearance is not an issue, you may only be permitted to use certain elements of a song without permission. For example, when the Beastie Boys recorded the song "Pass the Mic," they repeated a six-second sample from a song entitled "Choir" from an album by the award-winning flautist James Newton, Jr. The sample consisted of a three-note pattern, *C, D*-flat, *C*. Newton simultaneously sang and played these notes, a method known as vocalization. The Beastie Boys obtained permission to use the sample from ECM, the label that owned the sound recording copyright, but they did not get permission from Newton, the owner of the musical composition copyright. Newton sued. In 2002, a federal judge ruled that the three-note pattern from "Choir" was not, by itself, a protectible composition and that permission from Newton was not necessary. In other words, the three-note pattern, even though it included Newton's rare vocalization skills, was not original enough to merit a payment. It was labeled *de minimis* (too small to matter).

■ **If your use of the sample qualifies as a fair use.** Fair use is the legal right to copy a portion of a copyrighted work without permission because your use is for a limited purpose, such as for educational use in a classroom or to comment upon, criticize, or parody the work being sampled. For example, the rap group 2 Live Crew's use of the musical tag and the opening lyric line from Roy Orbison's "Oh Pretty Woman" was considered to be a fair use because it was limited (they only used the riff once) and it was for purposes of parody. (Keep in mind that 2 Live Crew did not include a sample from the Orbison master recording.)

There's a widespread myth in the sampling community that "less than two seconds is fair use." Don't believe it. What a judge and jury will feel is fair use depends on a number of factors other than the length of the sample. Generally, when reviewing fair use questions, courts are looking for three things: (1) that you did not take a substantial amount of the original work; (2) that you transformed the material in some way; and (3) that you did not cause significant financial harm to the copyright owner.

What kind of financial harm might sampling cause? It could cause the loss of income from other artists who might want to use the sample but were discouraged because you sampled it first. Or what you consider a "parody" might be so close to the original that substantial numbers of music lovers buy it *instead* of the original.

In principle, it's good to know these defenses, but the obvious difficulty with all of them is that they are *defenses*. The time you'll use them is when someone is coming after you. There is no predictable way to guarantee that you'll win your court case based on these defenses (assuming you can even afford to hire attorneys to fight the case). Of course, in some cases, this fact can give rise to a form of legal blackmail: The fear of a lawsuit may outweigh any benefits of winning the legal battle, so you may prefer not to use a sample even if the usage would have been ruled permissible.

You'll find yourself on safer legal ground if you seek permission. This is especially true if you're signed to a record label and your record contract puts the burden of sample clearance on your shoulders. Your contract probably contains an indemnity clause, which means that if you and the record company are sued, you must pay the record company's legal costs. Ouch!

USING SAMPLES WITH COMMERCIAL CLIENTS

There's an extra wrinkle if you use a sample for purposes of selling a product (for example, in a Volkswagen ad) and the sampled artist is identifiable. In cases like this, you also need to get the source artist's consent. That's because the ad creates the impression of an endorsement. Without the consent, the source artist could sue for what is known as the violation of the "right of publicity." (The same would be true if you imitated the source artist's voice without sampling it.) So when you use a sample for an advertising agency or other commercial client, be aware that a third type of clearance or "release" may be necessary.

What about sample CDs — recordings that contain sounds and riffs specifically sold to be used in samplers? Most sample discs are "pre-cleared," which means that by buying the disc, you're automatically granted permission for music usage without the payment of any further fees. (Note: The permitted use of pre-cleared samples may vary from one disc to another. Don't assume you can use the sample in whatever way you like: Review the documentation that comes with the CD for any license information. If you find that your purchase of the disc doesn't grant the rights you need, contact the soundware manufacturer to see if you're eligible for a refund.)

Most companies that make sample discs grant the user a "nonexclusive license" to use the samples. A "license" is a grant of permission to do something (*i.e.*, use the sample in your composition). "Nonexclusive" means that you're not the only person who can use the samples. All buyers of these sample discs share the right to use them. You're *not* buying the right to redistribute the samples, however, only the right to use them in musical works.

The fact that the license is nonexclusive can make a difference if you're composing music on behalf of a client — for example, creating music for commercials. The issue is "ownability," says Rick Lyon of New York's Lyon Music, who has scored spots and TV themes for the likes of ABC, MCI, Volvo, and ESPN. "'Ownability' is the Holy Grail of advertising," says Lyon. "It helps ensure uniqueness in the marketplace. That's why brands work so hard to control the creative ele-

IT'S THE DILITHIUM CRYSTALS, CAPTAIN!

Want to sample the dialog from a movie or TV show? Start by contacting the production company that owns the film. They may be able to grant the clearance themselves. If a separate clearance is needed from the author of the screenplay (or the underlying novel on which the film is based), the production company should be able to tell you how to find the copyright owner(s). A good place to start searching for movie production companies is the Internet Movie Database (www.imdb.com). If the segment you have sampled also includes music, you'll need to obtain separate clearances from the music publisher and the owner of the sound recording.

ments of their identities. Clients want to be sure that a riff featured in their new campaign isn't going to appear in another spot for someone else. We're talking about the sanctity of brand image, with millions of dollars at stake." Since the composer doesn't own exclusive rights to the pre-cleared sample, he or she will probably be unable to sell the requested rights to the client.

Even with these legal issues aside, the greater concern is whether you're going to aggravate a client. So beware of using a pre-cleared sample as an important element of an ad campaign. Anyone who buys the same sample disc has the potential to dilute your campaign and may raise legal and business risks for you.

FOREWARNED IS FOREARMED

Using samples in your recordings doesn't have to be dangerous. As long as you're aware of your legal responsibility, and acquire the appropriate clearances, sampling can be as safe as it is inspiring.

The Sample Clearance Agreement
Get it in writing

If you're not signed to a major label (whose legal department may be able to assist in sample clearance), you should consider using the services of a music attorney or sampling clearance expert to review clearance agreements. You can keep the cost of these services to a minimum by familiarizing yourself with the common provisions in these agreements. If you're comfortable with music business negotiations and savvy about legal agreements, you can handle the work yourself. Some legal self-help books provide examples of sample clearance contracts.

Sample clearance contracts are almost always provided by the copyright owners of the source music: one from the music publisher, the other from the owner of the master recording (although occasionally one company owns both and it's all in one agreement). Below is an outline and explanation for common sample clearance agreement provisions.

SAMPLE CLEARANCE AGREEMENT PROVISIONS

Introduction to Agreement. The introductory section (sometimes referred to as the "whereas" section) defines the parties (the people who will sign the agreement). In both types of agreements, the owner of the source music is referred to as the licensor and the person seeking to use the material (you or your record label) is the licensee.

Definitions. Most agreements contain a "definitions" section that establishes the parties' respective rights to the original source recording and the new recording (the one in which the sample is included) and identifies the source song and the artist who originally performed the source song. In music publishing clearance agreements, these terms may be "Source Composition" and "New Composition." In master clearance agreements it could be "Source Recording" and "New Recording."

Approved Usage. You will have to furnish a copy of your new composition to the owner of the source copyright. The "quantity" of use (that is, how often the source sample is used and how it is featured) is often referred to as the "approved usage." This provision establishes that you cannot create another version that uses more of the source sample than is used in the version you first furnished to the owner of the sample.

Grant of Rights. This provision is what officially allows you to use the sample on recordings and for promotional videos. Usually this section includes a statement, "This grant shall be binding upon Licensee's assigns and sublicensees," which means that if you get a record deal or transfer ownership, the sample can still be used.

Territory. This section will indicate where you can use the sample. It would be best for you to obtain worldwide rights. However, if the company you are dealing with only has rights in certain countries, then your agreement will be limited to that "territory," and if you intend to sell in other territories you'll have to acquire rights there, as well.

Payments. As explained earlier, fees for sampling can vary. Although it may be possible to acquire rights for a flat fee (that is, a one-time payment), music publishers and master owners usually want an up-front payment plus additional payments. These payments are always based on unit sales regardless of the configuration of your recording (that is, CD, cassette, etc.). Music publishers will want a percentage of your mechanical rights income (payments made each time your new song is manufactured — currently 9.1 cents per copy). They'll also want the same percentage of performance rights income — payments from BMI and ASCAP when the song is played on the radio, TV, or other public performances. The music publisher will want you to notify the performing rights society of the amount of each party's song income. (The performing rights society pays each party the performing rights income separately.) This is done by filling out clearance forms provided by the performing rights society.

June 1997
CHEMICAL BROTHERS

Back in their heyday, the Chemical Brothers had it easy. Here's a glimpse into their approach to sampling, before everything *really* changed.

Much continues to be said about the legalities of sampling from other artists. What's your view on this issue?
Our approach, especially on this record, is to disguise it. We like the idea of the sample culture. In the late '80s you had those records where people were just barefaced stealing, things like De La Soul and stuff. I thought it was quite a liberating thing. I really liked it. You could sit these things next to each other, and people knew what they were. But you can't do that now, really. So the main thing is to take a source sound and make it something else that it wasn't. You start with a sound that you generally know, and think is cool, and then you move it somewhere else. And we cut it up so small. If you play the things [we've sampled] to the people who played them, they wouldn't be able to tell it was them. That's an exciting thing. I like the feeling of having a recorded sound, and in essence, you're recording it again. You know, someone took it that far, and now you're taking it somewhere completely different. And when you start mixing up different things, you end up with things that you'd never think of. It's a good way of working.

If the owner of the master wants ongoing payments, these are usually made in the form described in the first part of this article as "rollovers." Each time a certain sales number is reached, another payment is made. Sampling consultants discourage paying the master owner a percentage of your record royalties.

Copyright Registration. When you apply for copyright registration for your song or for your recording, you are required to declare the use of the source sample in your application. Many sample owners include a special provision in the clearance agreement requiring this action.

Credit. A credit provision requires that you include a credit indicating the source music (and other information). Not all companies insist on receiving a credit.

Warranties. Warranties are legal promises. The licensor should promise they own the source music or recording. You may have to promise that you own the original music in your new composition and that you will not do anything to harm the rights of the copyright owners.

Commercial Release. Usually the music publisher and the master owner of the source recording want copies of your recording to verify the sample usage.

General. Like all agreements, sampling agreements usually contain language referred to as boilerplate (or miscellaneous provisions). Usually these provisions establish that the agreement is the final version and that any further modification must be in writing. These provisions may also establish which state law governs or where or how disputes are to be resolved. Occasionally there may be a provision that provides that the winner in any lawsuit between you and the copyright owner will receive attorneys' fees.

Since all agreements are different, you may not find all of these provisions in every clearance agreement, or you may find the provisions merged or in a different order. When reviewing an agreement, it's always wise to make a photocopy so you can write comments, underline sections that are troublesome, or highlight provisions you don't understand. If you're using the services of an attorney, you'll find that this practice will save time and money.

WHERE TO LEARN MORE

- www.copyright.gov: Copyright information and forms from the Library of Congress.
- http://creativecommons.org: Creative Commons information, including a search engine for freely licensed materials and instructions for publishing your work under a Creative Commons license.
- www.harryfox.com: A leading licensing agency.

Chapter 5
SOUND DESIGN

The term *sound design* covers a lot of ground, and so does this chapter. From synthesizer programming to exotic effects processing, these articles and features focus on a wide variety of approaches to realizing the sounds that are in your head, whether they're retro classics or utterly unique.

If you're using hardware synths, you're going to end up dealing with direct audio outputs, whether real-time — in parallel with your other tracks — or recorded directly into your DAW. Craig Anderton explains a few ways to enhance your hardware-based tracks. Keep in mind that many of these tricks are equally applicable to software synths as well.

May 2000
Tips for Recording Synths Direct
Nifty tricks for capturing a better sound

Recording direct is the simplest way to record synthesizers, drum machines, and other electronic instruments. But while going direct may not seem as complicated as setting up mics, there are subtleties to the process that must be taken into account. For example, a direct-recorded synth can sound unnatural because it lacks any ambience. This can be particularly obvious when the synth is mixed with sounds that were miked.

CREATING AMBIENCE

In the real acoustic world, our ears are used to hearing evolving, complex acoustical waveforms that are very unlike synth waveforms (especially the "freeze-dried" sound of sample-playback machines). We can get away with using sample-playback synths, though, because our ears care mostly about a sound's attack. We identify an instrument based on its attack.

The lack of subtle complexity in a sound is a sure tip-off that we're listening to something unnatural. I'm not just talking about simulations of acoustic instruments; I believe one reason why people like analog synths is because their inherent drift and small component mismatches make for a more interesting, dynamically changing sound. Here are some ways to add more character to dry or otherwise less-than-interesting synth sounds.

- Mix two or three very short delays (20–50ms, no feedback) in the background. Delays this short add comb filtering effects that alter the frequency response in a complex way, just like the reflections in a real room.
- Synthesize an acoustic environment using "two-stage" reverb processing. While tracking, patch your synth through a reverb unit set to a small dark room with very few (if any) first reflections. This

will provide a bit of acoustic depth. Then run the synth tracks along with the other instruments you've recorded through a main hall reverb during mixdown. This will help all of the tracks mesh together a lot better.

- Borrow your guitar player's multi-effects. These units are specifically designed to alter an instrument's character. Processes such as tube-generated distortion, speaker emulation, and graphic equalization are not always found in a keyboard's internal signal processors. It's amazing how a little distortion can dress up the sound of any synthesizer. In fact, tube distortion in itself is a sophisticated type of signal processing that combines compression, non-linear response, and high-frequency response alterations. Tubes are ideal for taking some of the "edge" off digital synths, particularly FM types.
- Mic a real amp, and mix it in with the direct waveform. Split the direct signal into a tube guitar amp and mic it. When you add this underneath the main synth track, you'll hear some ambience and a slight edge of distortion that augments the direct sound.
- Mic the mechanical noise of your synth's keys as you play the part (sometimes a contact mic works best). Mix this *very* subtly in the background — just noticeable enough to give a low-level aural "cue." Amazingly, this can fool the ear into thinking that the

July 2001
SQUAREPUSHER

I love gear and programming. There's a buzz to it. Like a real logical buzz. It's like reading a map and finding out where you're gonna go. It's really masculine.

Although I love wringing whatever I can get out of a piece of equipment, I don't want to be stuck. I don't want to start repeating myself because I can't do any more with it. People stay with the same gear, and they stagnate 'cause they're not moving their sound forward. The other example is people who buy so much new stuff, especially with all these new software synths coming out, that they never use most of it. I'm somewhere in the middle. I'll get everything I can out of something, but the minute I have, it's on to the next thing.

What are some of your favorites?
At the moment, the Eventide DSP 4000 Orville, which is a DSP 4000 on steroids. As far as software goes, I've gotten the most out of [Native Instruments] Reaktor so far. I make my own software for Reaktor. I'm bang into it. The Akai S6000 is the thing I use for all the chopping up. I'll manually chop all the breaks in the Akai. I've got an old DX rackmount, a TX81Z, and a [Yamaha] FS1R. The sound sources are dead basic, really. It's the sampler that does most of the work.

The Eventide handles all the real-time DSP. A lot of the sounds are made and then resampled. I've actually built synths in the Eventide. They're the fattest synths! So rude, so digital. It's really juice. I'm bang into it. I make a lot of sounds on that.

"GoPlastic" is the first record I've done with gear that anyone would look at and say, "Yeah, that's quite good." The first record and everything else I've done was made on bullshit, rubbish equipment. Nobody would even glance at that stuff.

I see production and engineering as input as well as composition and sound design. It's the whole thing rolled into one. Once you've got to that level, everything blurs. Production is part of composition, which is part of engineering, which is part of sound design. It's all a big spiral.

synth sound is more "real." This technique works especially well with Hammond, Clavinet, and Wurlitzer electric piano patches.

- Impedance-matching transformers, or direct boxes that use transformers, are also signal processors. Transformers add a bit of warmth to the sound, in part due to midrange "ringing" that slightly emphasizes the lower mids. Paradoxically, a $12 adapter from Radio Shack might give more of the effect you want than a top-of-the-line Jensen transformer, which gives a more uncolored sound.

- To make a synthesized sound stand out in a mix, add a little bit of a pitch transient using an oscillator's pitch envelope. One of my favorite examples: program a choir patch using two oscillators. Now apply a pitch envelope to one oscillator that falls down to proper pitch over about 50 ms, and a second pitch envelope to the second oscillator that rises to the proper pitch over about the same time period. Set the depth for a subtle effect. This creates a more interesting transient sound that draws the ear and makes the sound *seem* louder. Remove the pitch envelopes, and the voices appear to drop further back in the mix, even without a level change.

- To get a really wide stereo field without resorting to ambience processing, try programming a synth's "combi" mode (also called performance, multi, etc.) with several versions of the same program. Restrict the note range of each combi, then pan each range to a different place in the stereo field. For example, set program 1's note range to C1–B1 and pan the output hard left. Program 2 should cover C2–B2 and be panned slightly left of center. Make Program 3's note range C3–B3 and pan it slightly right of center, with program 4 panned hard right range and set to C4–C5. (This trick doesn't chew up polyphony, because the ranges don't overlap.)

MORE SIGNAL, LESS NOISE

In addition to ambience issues, recording direct shows up every detail of a synth's sound, including noise and hiss. Here are some ways to keep noise to a minimum when going direct.

- Set your instrument's master volume control to maximum. In most devices this control affects the digital (not analog) stages, so turning things up squeezes the maximum range out of the unit's digital-to-analog converter(s). If distortion occurs, lower the level elsewhere in the synth (*e.g.*, change an output level parameter, or lower an amplitude envelope's maximum level).

- Older synthesizers often generate some background hiss at all times. While standard noise gates will help take care of this, downward expansion devices (*e.g.*, the Rocktron Hush) do a more natural-sounding job. If neither form of noise reduction is available, then try the pre-emphasis/de-emphasis trick: When recording, boost the highs on the synth (usually by changing to a waveform with more harmonics and/or increasing the filter cutoff frequency or envelope amount). On playback, use your mixer's equalizers to roll off a bit of the top end to compensate. This will make the hiss less obvious as well.

- Most synths have several level adjustments: mixes for individual oscillators, the envelope levels controlling DCAs, final output mixer, onboard signal processing levels, etc. For maximum dynamic range and minimum distortion, these must be tweaked with the same care with which you set ("gain-stage") the preamp, submaster, master, etc. controls on a mixer. Generally, you want maximum levels early in the signal chain. So set the oscillator levels to the maximum possible, short of causing distortion in subsequent stages, such as filters.

■ With samplers, you can often use the instrument's onboard filtering to reduce noise. The trick is to modulate the filter with an envelope so the maximum high-frequency response occurs during the attack, and then, during the sustain or decay, the filter closes down to reduce noise. This can really help clean up otherwise marginal samples.

■ Ground loops are another problem with going direct, as you may have multiple grounds finding their way back to the main power ground. While discussing ground loop removal is beyond the scope of this article, one sure fix is to use a synth with optical outputs (S/PDIF or ADAT lightpipe). Since there's no ground connection with digital audio I/O, there's no chance of getting a ground loop.

With the possible exceptions of EQ, delay, and compression, I think it's safe to say that filtering is the most prevalent method of transforming and molding sounds of all kinds — synthesized or otherwise. If you're unfamiliar with how filters can be used in a remix, Joey Donatello's primer on effects is a great way to get your feet wet.

September 1998
Filters 101
The lowdown on sculpting tone

Filters have become an indispensable part of dance music production. Whether they're used to whack certain frequencies from an overly tubby bass track or to give a dull synth pad or vocal some extra color and personality, filters can drastically change the sound of your music.

What is a filter? On its most basic level, a filter is a circuit or digital algorithm that can remove specific frequencies from a sound while letting other frequencies pass through to

November 2000
JIMMY JAM

How deep do you get into programming and editing your synth sounds?
I don't really alter the presets a whole lot, because I figure if people are getting paid to program great presets, then they'd better be great presets. There's been so many synths that have come out, and I go through the presets and they suck. But everybody says, "Yeah, but if you get in there and program...." I don't want to get in there. I don't have time to get in there. I just want to call up sounds. I might modify something a little bit, but there are people who get paid to come up with great sounds, and if they can't come up with great sounds on it, what am I gonna do that's better? I don't even want to deal with it.

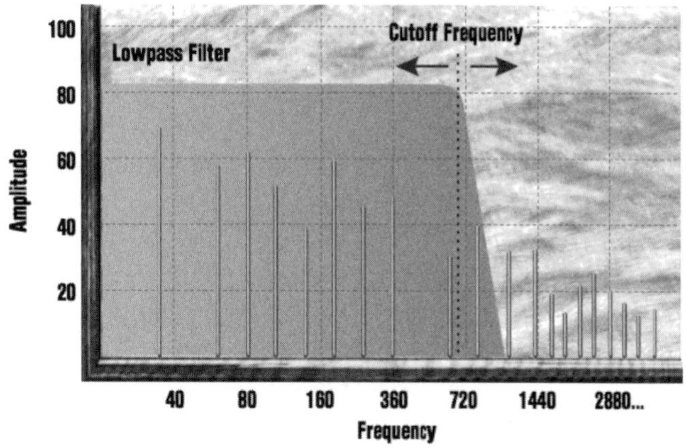

Figure 5-1

The frequency response of a lowpass filter. The cutoff frequency determines which frequencies will stay and which will go. In this case, the frequencies above the dotted line will be cut.

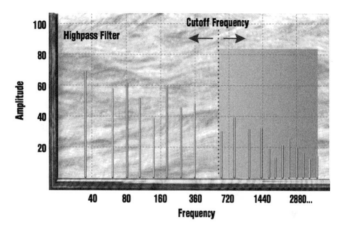

Figure 5-2

The frequency response of a highpass filter. Here, frequencies below the cutoff are suppressed.

the output. There are many different types of filters, but since this is an introductory piece let's cover just a couple.

The two most common filter types are lowpass (see Figure 5-1) and highpass (see Figure 5-2).

A lowpass filter lets the low frequencies pass through, removing or "filtering out" the high frequencies. A highpass filter does the opposite, cutting the lows and letting the high frequencies pass. Filters come in various packages; you'll find them built into samplers and synth modules, and also as stand-alone units. Since stand-alone filters don't generate sound themselves, you'll need to feed external audio signal into them. Any type of audio will do (vocals, guitars, synths, samples, you name it). Just patch your source into the filter's audio input, run another cable from the filter's audio output to a mixer, and start twisting those knobs. Let's try a few experiments.

Using a sampler, load a sample that you'd like to filter. Next, locate the filter section in the sampler's edit menu, and select lowpass. If you're not sure how to do this, refer to your manual. The menus and features will vary from sampler to sampler, but the basic concept is the same. Set the cutoff frequency control to its highest value. That's your starting point.

With the sample playing, bring the adjustment down little by little, and listen to the way it affects the sound. Since we're using a lowpass filter, the high end will start to disappear. The lower the setting, the more the high frequencies will go away.

If you don't hear the filtering, check to make sure the filter is switched on. Also make sure the signal from an envelope generator isn't pushing the cutoff frequency upward. To hear the filter in action, start by turning off any envelope modulation of the filter.

Once you get the hang of it, you can try adding resonance (also called Q). Resonance emphasizes the frequencies around the cutoff frequency, causing those frequencies to ring or even whistle depending on the setting. Start by setting the cutoff frequency low enough that part of the sound is being filtered. Then set the Q value to its lowest point and slowly raise it. In many cases you should hear a nasal type of sound. The higher the Q, the more nasal or peaky the sound will be. Experiment with various settings for the cutoff frequency and the Q.

If you're using a MIDI sequencer, you can record, edit, and play back the filter changes (providing your MIDI instrument can transmit and receive parameter control data). Try this: Connect a synthesizer to a MIDI sequencer (MIDI in to out, and vice versa). Record-enable a new sequencer track. Make sure the patch you're using has a filter parameter or two mapped to either the mod wheel or any other programmable knob or slider on the synth's front panel. (Your manual will tell you how to do this.) Record a two-bar riff into the sequencer, copy it a few times, and then overdub onto the track while simultaneously turning the mod wheel or knobs. After you record, you should see lots of MIDI data in your edit window. Now play back the track and listen to what you recorded. You should hear the filter opening and closing in a musical way.

November 1999
DAVID FRANK

One of the most notable synth hooks in "Genie in a Bottle" is the verse pizzicato/pad morph. "It's made up of two parts," Frank explains, "a pizzicato riff that leads into a synth swell. The swell started as a basic brassy synth sound on the Nord, but then I started fiddling with the frequency cutoff knob. They aren't exactly timed rhythms," he says of the filter sweeps. "I just kept recording it into Logic until I thought the feel was right." Frank sequenced the bass line with the TR-Rack, while a Roland JP-8000 was used for the big chorus synth stabs. "One of the things I like most about the track is one of its most simple elements: the piano part in the chorus. It's up in the high end of the piano, and it reminds me of a '50s kind of thing. The same part is played in the bridge, but it's down in the middle range."

Here's another fun thing to try on your next track: Sample a whole chunk of music — a loop with drums, bass, and all. Take the sample and make a copy of it. Apply a highpass filter to the original and a lowpass filter to the copy. Tinker with the cutoff frequencies of both until you end up with an all-high-frequency sample (the original) and an all-low-frequency one (the copy); there shouldn't be any noticeable low-frequency elements in the original, just high end, and vice versa. Route each sample to a separate channel on your mixer. This is when the fun begins. For certain sections of the song, mute one of the samples. Experiment with muting and unmuting each at various points in the song, bringing both into the mix together for the chorus, or whenever maximum beef is needed. Don't forget to apply Q for added expression.

Try filters on individual tracks, too — drums, vocals, bass, whatever. You can really add new attitude to an otherwise generic track just by cranking the filter up and down at strategic moments in a song. And when you start messing with the Q, fahgeddaboutit.

Now that you have a grasp of the fundamentals of filtering, let's dig a little deeper into how you can use filters in slightly more complex ways. The next piece is from a Dance Mix column I wrote.

January 2001
Creative Filtering for Remixers
Wow your friends

Over the years, I've been inundated with questions about various effects that are popular in modern electronica. The interesting thing about these queries is that the answer is almost invariably: Use a filter! Filters have been a mainstay in synthesizer programming since its inception. Most of those boingy, spring-loaded patches and boww-boww basses are the result of lowpass resonant filters applied to a variety of waveforms and samples.

With the advent of filter plug-ins for today's audio/MIDI sequencing applications, remixers have the tools to apply classic synth programming techniques to vocals, recorded instruments, or even entire tracks. This approach allows for some wild tricks, ranging from making a track sound like it's coming from outside the club and slowly entering the acoustic space to the classic "radio" vocals in recent tracks from Madonna and Christina Aguilera. Good stuff.

Another way to achieve these effects — without plug-ins — is by exploring the filtering options available within your sampler. You could also purchase dedicated hardware like Korg's Kaoss Pad, Boss's EF-303, or Electrix's Filter Factory and Filter Queen. There are also synths with audio inputs that allow external audio to be filtered. All are terrific tools and well worth the money if you plan to apply these effects directly to instruments, tape tracks, or in a live setting. It's also worth noting that Yamaha's classic (and ubiquitous) SPX1000 multi-effects processor includes integrated resonant filters — but these are buried deep in the processor's submenu structure. Time to crack open those manuals, kids.

LOWPASS
One effect in particular has become so popular lately that it's bordering on cliché. This effect consists of a track — or even an entire mix — starting out muffled and slowly transforming into full-bandwidth audio. I've heard this sound described as an "underwater" effect, an EQ sweep, or "that neighbor's stereo through the wall trick." It's really a lowpass filter applied to a track or set of samples. The secret to making this effect work dynamically is to slowly raise or lower the cutoff frequency — usually via MIDI automation — to gradually make the sound brighter or darker. Increasing the resonance on the filter adds an overtone that follows the filter sweep, providing a more electronic, synthesized sound.

Another nifty lowpass filter trick can be accomplished by applying an envelope follower to the filter cutoff frequency. What an envelope follower does is increase or decrease the cutoff frequency of the filter depending on the volume of the signal. This approach can be used to recreate classic wah-wah effects on clean guitar parts or add a slick, synthy effect to drum or music loops. Prosoniq's freeware North Pole VST plug-in (see Figure 5-3) includes an envelope follower in addition to its resonant lowpass filter, making it especially useful for this type of sound.

HIGHPASS

Highpass filtering produces an entirely different set of effects that are also useful for remixing. Because they eliminate the low frequencies from a signal, these filters are terrific for emulating the sound of a tinny radio speaker or telephone. Gradually lowering the cutoff frequency returns low frequencies to the signal, giving the effect of a track morphing from thin to phat. Try this on a complete mix, either during the intro, during a breakdown, or on a scan for fadeouts later. It's quite dramatic when done right.

MULTI-FILTERING

A more advanced — and very handy — approach to filtering audio consists of applying different types of filters to music and drum loops within a mix. For instance, mixing two drum loops that contain competing kick drum patterns can muddy the groove. By isolating the drum loop with the offending kick pattern and applying a highpass filter to it, you can effectively delete most of the kick while retaining the hi-hats and snare. Conversely, if a loop has shrill or awkward snare hits and cymbal crashes, these can be minimized with a lowpass filter, keeping the lows intact. I use this approach all the time on breakbeat tracks, though it sometimes requires a little effort to get the resulting blend just right. As always, use your hips as well as your ears to find the perfect combination.

Figure 5-3
North Pole is a freeware filter plug-in for VST-compatible sequencers that features resonant lowpass and bandpass options along with envelope following, distortion, and echo. Check it out at www.prosoniq.com.

The above techniques should provide a solid starting point for you to begin your own experiments. It's also worthwhile to Google the terms *filter* and *VST* or *AU* to discover the myriad third-party options for plug-in-based filtering, as several newer products — like Antares' sophisticated Filter plug-in and U-He Audio Software's Filterscape — go beyond the basics of high- and lowpass filtering into more exotic realms like comb filters (terrific for phase- and flange-type effects) and bandpass filtering (another useful tool for wah-wah-type effects). The secret to blazing new trails is taking chances, and filters are a wonderful way to get expressive results from even the most mundane performances.

> **The coolest thing about effects processing is that there are no real "rules" as long as your tracks remain audible and sensibly mixed. Even a bit of distortion here and there can help pump up a track, so I'm not going to disallow the ever-popular option of clipping, as long as it works in the mix. Here are a few ways to use effects that you may not have thought of yet.**

November 2001
Off the Beaten Path
More tips from the bag o' tricks

One of the secrets to innovative mixing is to take standard processors and use them for things that they may not have been intended to do. This is where your creativity comes in. Anyone who ever built a fort out of a discarded refrigerator box will immediately relate to this strategy. In this section, we'll focus on using common effects in uncommon ways.

DE-ESSING

Most musicians think de-essing is about as exciting as a new set of hedge trimmers. Not so, grasshopper. While de-essing is indisssssspensssable for silencing sibilance, its usefulness extends far beyond vocal touch-ups. Ever find an old drum loop with distorted and screechy snares and cymbals that didn't mix well? Slap a de-esser on it and tweak until the highs are in line. Ever come across an instrument riff that was too harsh, but only during certain passages? Again, one solution is a de-esser.

The way a de-esser works is by compressing a limited range of frequencies, typically a slice of the highs between 7kHz and 12kHz. Most de-essers can be fine-tuned to more specific ranges, so you can zero in on offending frequencies and restrain them, rather than eliminating them with an EQ. And therein lies the beauty of this approach. In the above examples, you won't kill the highs, just rein them in a bit when they get out of control.

STATIC FLANGING

Most remixers are familiar with the whooshing sound of a flanger. Flanging is a terrific way to add animation to individual tracks — or even a complete mix, during transitions. But a less common approach to this type of processing, static flanging, can deliver equally interesting results that can be tuned to the key of a track.

You don't even need a flanger to create this effect. All that's required is a mono or stereo delay with feedback. Select a track — drum or percussion loops often sound especially cool — and begin by shortening the delay to 1 millisecond (or a fraction thereof, if your processor supports it) and increase the feedback to just under the maximum amount. When you hear a distinct pitch superimposed on the original signal, you're there. At this point, the effect should sound like a flanger minus the modulation. The next step is tuning the delay time so the pitch of the feedback tone is aligned with the song. Shorter delay times raise the pitch, longer delays lower it. Note: If your delay won't let you adjust the time in under 1ms increments, you'll have trouble tuning the effect.

Static flanging is also a nifty way to add a metallic sheen to spoken or sung vocals. The trick here is to make sure the vocals are sufficiently compressed so the added frequencies don't overwhelm the mix. Try applying compression before and after the delay, then decide which approach sounds better in context.

GATED REVERB
Yeah, yeah ... the infamous Phil Collins drum sound of the '80s. But it's still handy for gargantuan toms and handclaps, as well as industrial percussion. If you haven't tried it on crunchy lead synth riffs, though, you're missing half the fun.

Take a distorted and/or sync swept lead sound and bathe it in gated reverb and you'll get a mammoth sound that will rock a breakdown like nobody's business. As a starting point, use huge room sizes, gate time between 100ms and 500ms, and maximum diffusion, then compress the results.

Warning: Emits showers of sparks. Light fuse, then get away.

VOCODING
Vocoders have traditionally been used to create robot voices and for sweetening background vocals, but there's so much more to this effect than simply messing around with a singer's voice.

A vocoder is essentially a series of bandpass filters, each assigned to a narrow frequency spectrum and auto-triggered by audio input in the various ranges. The carrier input handles the audio to be processed, and the modulator input provides the content that will shape the signal. The human voice makes a dramatic modulator, and sounds with a wide range of frequencies (like sawtooth waves) provide terrific material for sculpting, which is the classic approach to using this tool.

Instead of vocals, try using drums or even entire multitrack music samples as modulation fodder. Or, for more rhythmic exotica, you can use a multi-instrument groove as a carrier signal and modulate that with vocals. Better yet, try a dynamic hard-synced and modulated sawtooth-based riff. The results can range from subtle to totally over-the-top, so spend some time exploring your options.

BANDPASS FILTERING
Nearly everyone working in modern dance music has heard — or experimented with — highpass and lowpass filtering for creatively warping elements in a mix. But for many, bandpass filtering still remains a mystery, and that's too bad.

Lowpass and highpass filters work by attenuating the highs or lows of a signal, respectively. Bandpass filters attenuate both ends of the frequency spectrum simultaneously, allowing a range of frequencies in the middle to pass. The sound can have a strong, resonant quality if the range is narrow, or a sweeping EQ-like quality when the range is wider.

Bandpass filters are the source of classic wah guitar effects and can be used on nearly any instrument to excellent effect. An obvious choice would be a clean rhythm guitar track, but don't forget hard synth leads, EPs, and distorted guitars. Vocals can also benefit, gaining a freak tremolo if the bandpass cutoff frequency can be modulated with a tempo-based LFO. Drums are great fodder too. Try processing individual percussion elements, as well as the whole shebang.

If you have a bandpass filter handy, chances are you have a band-reject (notch) filter, too. Try using notch filtering on a pad, with a slow triangle LFO modulating cutoff frequency. This adds a phaser-like swirl to pads, strings, or any other sustained instrument. It's subtle but effective for ambient chordal passages. Tip: With notch filtering, the effect is more dramatic if the resonance/bandwidth parameter is set to a low value rather than a high one.

It's been over 100 years since ragtime was first denounced as the Devil's music because of its brutal and captivating rhythms, so we may as well admit that beats are here to stay. Synthesizers have numerous features with which you can program your own rhythms, and bubbling, burbling, bouncing synths are a time-tested way to keep a groove flowing. As long as everything's in sync, go for it. Below, Jim Aikin describes a bunch of ways to make your mixes percolate.

March 2003
Rhythm Injection
High-octane synthesizer fuel for your creative fire

Timing is everything. And in music, "timing" means rhythm. In school, they'll tell you music consists of melody, harmony, rhythm, and tone color. What they may not tell you is that rhythm is the foundation for everything else.

With an array of the latest technology at our fingertips, we have several ways to generate crowd-pleasing rhythms. Sampled loops, of course, get a lot of press. But they're not the only game in town. In this article we'll look at some other tools for injecting riveting doses of rhythm into your music, things you can do with a synthesizer and a bit of creativity.

The clever lads and lasses who create factory synth presets can offer some potent inspiration. If you've played just about any of the current generation of synths, you've had the experience: You choose a patch, slam your hands down on the keyboard, and find yourself in possession of a killer rhythm pattern. It rocks along and sets your pulse racing. All you need to do is sync the tempo to your song, and you're good to go.

But what if that factory patch isn't quite right for your track? Maybe it's too buzzy, and you need to tame the tone. Maybe the tone is perfect, but the rhythm doesn't sit well with your drum track. Or maybe the sound itself is perfect, but you can't figure out how to lock it to your groove. Time to break out the manual.

Rhythmic synth patches, you'll quickly discover, are more complex than any other type; they're a sound programmer's Mt. Everest, and a swamp in which the novice can quickly founder. But in truth, programming a rhythmic patch, or editing someone else's, isn't too difficult, once you've grasped a few basic principles. In this article we'll lay out the various pieces of the puzzle and show how they fit together. We'll also show how to dissect and customize an existing patch (see "Break It Down" later in this article).

Covering the specific features of all of the synths that can do rhythmic patches would fill a book. From time to time I'll illustrate the concepts by referring to items of hardware and software you may own, or not. By poring through the manual, you should be able to figure out how to apply these ideas in your own instrument. Be warned, though: Every instrument has its own cool features, as well as its own limitations. You may discover that your instrument will do esoteric things not discussed here, or, contrariwise, that it flat-out won't do some of the things you'd like it to. Chances are, though, it will do a lot.

Figure 5-4
The envelope shape on the right, as seen in Emagic SoundDiver Virus editor/librarian software for the Access Virus, has an instant attack, medium-fast decay, and a low sustain level. This type of envelope is often used for TB-303-style filter tones; varying the decay time or envelope amount while an arpeggiator or sequencer plays a repeating line will give the line an expressive shape.

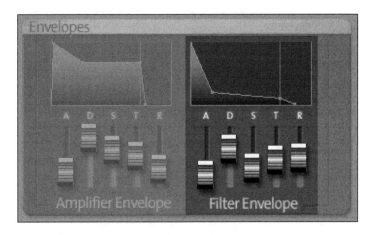

We're going to be talking about modulation. But this type of modulation doesn't necessarily come from the mod wheel. In fact, it probably won't. "Modulation" is a general term that means the tone is being changed (modulated) in some way. We'll look at various sources for modulation signals, such as LFOs and envelopes, and at various destinations, such as filter cutoff frequency. Put them all together, and you have a lively, animated tone, but it may or may not be a rhythmic tone. The source of the rhythm may be an arpeggiator or step sequencer, for instance.

Since everything relates to everything else in the world of rhythmic patches, we'll have to throw around a few terms, such as "LFO," before we define them. Hang in there: All will become clear.

One thing we won't get into is the question of what makes a cool rhythm, as opposed to a lame one. It's a subjective question, and differs from genre to genre. You probably have some ideas of your own on the subject. If not, I'd encourage you to listen to your favorite

CDs and dissect exactly what's going on in the rhythm tracks. Transcribing some rhythms with a pencil and score paper can be an incredibly useful exercise.

Even if you have a great tone and a great rhythm, it may not sync up with the tempo of your song. So we need to start by discussing the all-important concept of synchronization.

SYNC

Most synths allow various parameters to be synchronized to the instrument's own internal clock, or to an external source of MIDI clock signals. MIDI clock is used to lock the tempo of two or more tempo-based devices, such as sequencers. To use MIDI clock, you need to make one device the clock source (also known as the master), and transmit the MIDI clock signals from the master to all of the other devices that you want to sync.

This can mean sending the clock messages down a physical MIDI cable, for instance, from a computer-based sequencer to a hardware synth. If you're running a software synth as a plug-in inside a sequencer, the sequencer should automatically send clock signals to the plug-in.

Whether you're using hardware or software, you need to instruct the receiving device to sync to the incoming clock signals. In a hardware synth, you'd typically do this by going to the global, master, or utility area and choosing "MIDI" as the clock source rather than "internal." A synth whose clock source is set to internal will usually follow its own tempo, cheerfully ignoring any clock signals it receives. On some synths, you can sync the speed of each LFO or other parameter to MIDI clock individually, but on other synths, external sync may be an all-or-nothing proposition. Check your owner's manual for details.

A MIDI clock message is transmitted 24 times for every quarter-note. The technical term is "ppq," which stands for pulses per quarter-note. MIDI clock runs at 24 ppq, no matter what clock resolution the transmitting device is set to. Your sequencer may have an internal resolution of 960 ppq, for instance, but in that case, it will transmit one MIDI clock message for every 40 internal clock ticks.

If you speed up the tempo on the master, the clock messages will get closer together, and if you slow down the tempo, they'll get further apart. The receiving synth synchronizes its operation to the MIDI clock simply by counting the messages. For instance, if an LFO is set to sync to sixteenth-notes, it will start a new LFO cycle every six clock pulses (because there are four sixteenth-notes in a quarter-note, and 4 x 6 = 24).

In many synths, MIDI clock sync is not implemented as well as it could be. Here's the catch: When synced, your LFO will cycle nicely at the same tempo as your sequencer, but there's no guarantee that all of the LFO cycles won't start a little too early or a little too late in relation to where the sequencer thinks the beat is. MIDI defines not only clock, but start, stop, and continue messages. It would be nice if all the MIDI-syncable LFOs in the world were designed so they'd start a new cycle on receipt of a start message, but most of them don't. The result is, the rhythm pattern coming out of your synth may sound different each time you start your sequencer to play the song, even though the two devices are in sync.

The way to solve this problem is simple, though not elegant: You can record the audio output of your synth (playing at the correct tempo) into the sequencer as an audio track.

Do as many takes as you need to, until you get one where the LFO cycles line up the way you want them to. Once you've captured the synth's rhythm pattern, you can treat it like any other audio loop: Synchronization is no longer needed, and the synth itself can be switched off.

You can use this method when you're in a hurry, or even with a synth that doesn't offer any type of synchronization. Turning the synth's own tempo knob and then recording an audio track is often easier than setting up sync.

MODULATION DESTINATIONS

When a patch is pulsing and percolating, it's because the tone color is being modulated. The most often used modulation destinations are filter cutoff frequency, oscillator wave-form, distortion, loudness, and of course pitch. The attack, decay, and release times of envelopes are also useful destinations in some circumstances, as are the oscillator and filter mix. We'll look at each of these in turn.

First, though, a cool effect I've been experimenting with lately is sending a sound that already has rhythm through a synced stereo delay line. Almost any patch gets bigger and more interesting when you do this. With a ping-pong delay setting, you can hear the dry sound in the center of the stereo field, an echo on the left after an eighth-note, and an echo on the right after a quarter-note. A few highly programmable synths even let you send the outputs of individual oscillators within a patch to specific effects. Routing one oscillator to a synced delay can be extremely cool, because the echoes coming from the delay won't have the same tone color as the dry sound.

Filter cutoff frequency. The filter is what shapes and tames the raw tone of the oscil-lators. Assuming the patch is using a lowpass filter, as the cutoff frequency opens up, more oscillator tone pours through, and the sound gets bigger and brighter. Conversely, with a highpass filter, raising the cutoff frequency will eliminate everything except the high, buzzy overtones.

There are two ways to modulate filter cutoff. You can either modulate the cutoff direct-ly, or you can increase and decrease the amount of the filter envelope. In some patches, these two methods will sound similar, but in others they'll be radically different. If the envelope is set to a fast attack, medium-fast decay, and a low sustain level, increasing the envelope amount will add spiky peaks to the attack portions of the notes, but it won't change the overall tone color. Modulating the cutoff directly, on the other hand, will add or subtract brightness throughout the tone. The attack peaks will be boosted along with everything else.

Modulating filter resonance is somewhat less useful, but if the filter is being swept in a rhythmic way by an envelope or LFO, adding a bit of extra resonance to the peaks or val-leys of the sweep may help the tone cut through.

Pitch. If your synth has looping multistage envelopes, you'll be able to create a pitch "sequence" that will play for as long as you hold a note by modulating pitch from an enve-lope. Better yet, the sequence will start reliably at the beginning of each new note, and will transpose automatically up and down the keyboard. Play a chord, and the whole chord will march through the same sequence in lockstep.

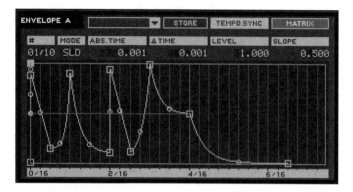

Even if your envelope generators aren't up to the challenge, there are still things you can do with pitch modulation. Try setting a couple of LFOs to square waves, sync the LFOs to the tempo, and set them to different rhythm values, perhaps quarter-notes and sixteenths. Next, adjust the amount of LFO modulation being sent to the oscillators so both LFOs produce in-tune intervals, such as a perfect fifth and a minor third. This will give you a pattern with four pitches that outline a minor 7th chord. Many other harmonic patterns are possible, especially when you hold down two keys at once.

The most common way to modulate pitch is with an arpeggiator. We'll have more to say about this later in the article.

Tone color. Leaving aside the filter, most synths offer several ways to modulate tone color. The easiest, though not the most interesting, method is to crossfade back and forth between the tones of two oscillators or two filters. If one oscillator is set to a thin pulse wave while the other is producing a muted sawtooth, for instance, the tone will alternately thin out and thicken up as the modulation rises and falls. Adding the output of a ring modulator to the mix will take your rhythm pattern still further.

Some synths allow a distortion effect to be modulated. Fattening up the distortion at one spot in a rhythm pattern is a great way to add an accent.

If you're using an analog-type synth, you'll probably be able to set up waveform modulation in the oscillators. Pulse width modulation, which is the classic type, can add a definite edge to the tone of a square/pulse wave. If your synth allows you to apply FM (frequency modulation) from one oscillator to the other, increasing and decreasing the amount of FM can goose the tone and cause it to jump in interesting directions. Some oscillators provide other types of waveform modulation: You may be able to sweep through the waveforms in a wavetable, for instance, or even jump back and forth between waveforms under LFO control.

If one oscillator is synced to another (this is entirely different from MIDI clock sync), sweeping the pitch of the synced oscillator with an LFO or a looping envelope can produce some beautiful metallic overtones. In effect, you're not modulating pitch, you're modulating tone color.

Envelope segments. Envelopes are used for various things, but mainly to change the amplitude (loudness) and filter cutoff (tone color) of notes. An envelope is usually applied

104 **THE REMIXER'S BIBLE**

over the duration of a note, so envelope-segment modulation makes most sense when the source of the modulation is something outside of the synth voice. Sequencers, for instance, often let you control the envelope decay or release over the course of a whole phrase by assigning the envelope parameter to a MIDI controller.

Modulating envelope attack will change the notes from hard-edged to mushy. If the modulation is set too high, some or all of the notes may disappear, because the envelope won't have time to open up before the note ends.

Modulating the release time of a filter envelope won't have any audible effect unless the amplitude envelope also has a long release time. In effect, a short amplitude envelope release time overrides a long filter envelope release time, because you won't hear the filter envelope release: the amplitude envelope will cut it off. Modulating the amplitude envelope's release will change an arpeggiated or sequenced pattern from choppy (short release) to smooth and legato (long release).

Depending on how the envelope's sustain level is set and how long the gate time is, modulating decay time may sound similar to modulating release time. Also, note that modulating the filter envelope's segments will have no effect unless the envelope is actively driving the filter.

Loudness. The general term for the modulation of the output amplitude (loudness) is tremolo. A sawtooth wave coming from an LFO is a useful source of tremolo, but square waves work well too. Using a square wave to switch the sound between full amplitude and zero (silence) will give you rhythm-based slicing or chopping. You may be able to do this either in the synth itself, or in an effects device. Doing it in the synth is interesting because each voice in a chord can be slicing in and out on its own, giving you a sort of pseudo-arpeggiator effect. When the slicing is done in an effects device, all of the voices in a chord will cut in and out together.

MODULATION SOURCES

We've already mentioned the two most important modulation sources, LFOs and envelopes. Each of them has a few features you'll need to get familiar with if you want to make rhythmic patches. An external MIDI sequencer is another great source of rhythmic modulation. Arpeggiators and step sequencers are also important modulation sources, so important that they deserve a section all their own (see below).

LFOs. Setting up an LFO so it syncs with the rhythm and modulates some interesting destination is only the start of the fun. First, your synth probably has two or more LFOs. By setting each of them to different rhythmic subdivisions, such as eighth-notes and sixteenths, and then assigning them each to a different destination, you can come up with much more complex and interesting rhythms.

Some LFOs can't be synced to an external clock. You may have to use your ears to find an LFO rate that works musically. If the LFO's frequency is shown in Hz, however, you can use a bit of math to find the right setting. To get the correct Hz value for one beat at the current tempo, divide the bpm by 60. For instance, at 138 bpm, an LFO will produce one cycle per beat when set to 138/60, or 2.3Hz. To get the LFO to lock to a longer or shorter rhythm value, multiply or divide this figure as needed: The LFO will take four beats to sweep through one complete cycle if it's set to 2.3 divided by 4, or 0.575Hz.

In discussing synchronization, I mentioned the difficulty of getting an LFO to start its wave cycle reliably on the beat. There's a workaround, however: Most LFOs can be switched to a mode in which they start a new wave cycle each time a new note starts. (This may be called retrigger mode, as opposed to free-run mode. Check the manual.) As long as you play the notes exactly on the beat, the LFOs will give you reliable rhythms. On the other hand, you can start some notes in a chord on an offbeat, which will generate syncopated rhythms. For this to work, the LFOs have to be in poly mode. Some LFOs can be switched between poly and mono operation: In mono mode, the LFOs for all of the voices in the chord will be locked together. Both modes are useful, depending on what you're trying to achieve.

Sine and triangle wave LFOs are usually used for vibrato, but you'll find that the sawtooth and square wave settings are more useful for rhythms. Your LFOs may also have a phase parameter. This controls the point in the waveform at which the LFO starts when you play a new note. Shifting the phase of an LFO by 90 or 180 degrees (1/4 or 1/2 of its complete cycle) can cause a dramatic change in the rhythm pattern.

Your synth will probably let you control LFO depth from the mod wheel. After setting this up, push the mod wheel up during a long note to add more powerful pulses to the tone.

Envelopes. If your synth is equipped with humble ADSR envelopes, they may not be too useful for adding color to rhythmic patches. This is because the envelope will fire once per note and then just sit there. Multi-stage envelopes like those in Figure 5-5 are useful, though, even when they don't loop. If they will loop, so much the better. Higher peaks will add stronger accents to the rhythm. Editing the envelopes to get the rhythm you want is not guaranteed to be easy, but some envelopes of this type have rhythmic grids already set up for editing.

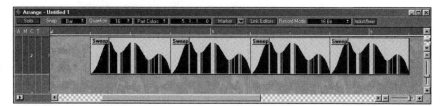

Figure 5-6
A 2-bar controller sweep (in Steinberg Cubase), block-copied four times so it repeats.

Sequencers. A humble MIDI sequencer is a great source of rhythmic modulation. All you have to do is record a controller move and then block-copy it for as long as you want the modulation to repeat. One-measure and 2-measure blocks work well. Your synth may let you record controller data from the front panel, for instance, by turning the filter cutoff knob while the sequencer is in record mode. After recording the move, you can use the sequencer's pencil tool to shape it as desired, then block-copy the shape, as shown in Figure 5-6.

If you're using a synth whose knobs won't transmit MIDI, you may be able to draw the data in the sequencer and then assign the correct MIDI controller number to the synth parameter you want to modulate. Image-Line FL Studio takes this concept an intriguing step fur-

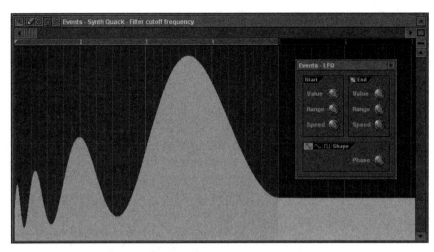

Figure 5-7
Controller sweeps can be programmed in Image-Line FL Studio using an LFO utility. Here, I've selected a 4-bar range. The sweep shown, which is adjusted with the controls in the dialog box at right, will play each time the pattern is inserted in the song.

ther: The program's graphic controller edit window (see Figure 5-7) has an LFO utility that lets you create controller sweeps by turning knobs.

Check your synth's manual to find out how to assign MIDI controller data to the parameters you want to modulate. Some synths have fixed MIDI controller assignments, and some let you assign each knob to whatever controller number you'd prefer.

ARPEGGIATORS

An arpeggiator is a device that looks at the notes you're playing on the keyboard, most likely a chord you're holding, and spreads the notes out into a repeating arpeggio. The word "arpeggio" comes from the Italian word for harp, because the spread-out strumming of a chord on a harp was a classic effect in symphonic writing.

In the early days of commercial synthesizers, an arpeggiator was a pretty boring device: Up, down, repeat until nauseated. Today's arpeggiators are a lot more interesting. Each synth, if it has an arpeggiator at all, has its own variation on the theme. Some synths have multiple arpeggiators, which can be synced to one another and layered to produce complex rhythm patterns. (Instruments from E-mu, Novation, and Access are in this category.) Some have user-programmable memory banks, in which you can save your own setups. Many of them store arpeggiator parameters with individual synth programs, so each program you call up can be ready to spill out its own complex rhythm. Some let you include rests, velocity accent patterns, and pitch transpositions in the arpeggio. Some come with fancy, funky guitar-picking patterns to which the term "arpeggiator" barely applies.

Fancy arpeggiator patterns have been a staple on Yamaha synths for years now. The Motif, for instance, has 256 factory patterns and 128 user-programmable patterns. Some of the factory patterns don't even play notes, they're strictly for generating controller sweeps. User patterns are recorded in the Motif as sequencer tracks and then copied into the arpeggiator, which means you can use the sequencer's edit facilities, such as quantization, to polish your arpeggios.

Like other devices mentioned in this article, arpeggiators can either be synced to incoming MIDI clock or serve as the master clock source. When the arpeggiator is serving as the master clock, you can sync internal LFOs and other modules to it, and also transmit MIDI clock to another device such as a sequencer.

Some arpeggiators have a switch for choosing whether to transmit the notes of the arpeggio via MIDI. Transmitting the notes can be useful, as you can record them in a sequencer and then edit them to taste (or simply line up the pattern with the bar lines). Once the notes are in the sequencer, you'll need to turn the arpeggiator off. If you don't, the synth will try to arpeggiate the notes it receives from the sequencer, which are already arpeggiated. The results tend to be unpredictable.

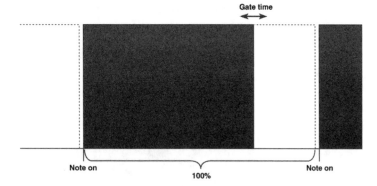

Figure 5-8
Most arpeggiators give you control over the gate time (the length of the notes). By controlling gate time interactively from a knob, you can shape the phrases coming from the arpeggiator.

When evaluating a synth that has an arpeggiator, take a look at the arpeggiator's front-panel controls. A tempo knob is useful. Even more useful, if you're syncing the arpeggiator to something else, is a gate time knob. The gate time is the length of the separate notes in the arpeggio (Figure 5-8). By massaging the gate time while the arpeggio plays, you can give the music a more exciting shape. This works best if the envelope release time is short. If it's long, changes in gate time won't be very audible, because the long release will fill the gaps between notes.

For that matter, almost any knob on the front panel can be a potent resource for tweaking while the arpeggiator is running. Changing the filter cutoff frequency and/or the filter envelope amount during a pattern is a classic effect. Tweaking the amplitude envelope's attack and release times can change a spiky arpeggio into a soft blur of harmonic motion. And by boosting the input level or regeneration of a delay line that's synced to the same tempo as the arpeggiator, you can turn a dry one-note line into a vivid chord pattern.

While exploring your arpeggiator's features, you'll probably discover other musical resources. Most arpeggiators can be latched, for instance. (Latching is also called "hold.") When the arpeggiator is latched, once it starts playing an arpeggio it will keep playing it, even if your hands have left the keyboard. This lets you play a solo over the arpeggio, or simply apply both hands to the knobs.

One trick used in some of the fancier arpeggiators is to send the pattern of notes to a drum/percussion layout on the keyboard. When you hear powerhouse beats coming from synths like the Korg Triton, this is the most likely source. If the arpeggiator (or the keyboard) has a transpose knob or parameter, you may be able to change the sound of the beat drastically by shifting it up or down in half-steps. Some of the transpositions will be comic, but some may prove inspiring.

Step sequencers. The more programmable an arpeggiator is, the closer it comes to being a step sequencer or phrase sequencer. With a phrase sequencer, you can trigger a whole phrase, possibly even including multiple MIDI channels and several different sounds, with a single keypress. If you tap the key a little late, the whole phrase will be late, so some dexterity is required. Phrase sequencers are typically found on synths (from Korg, Roland, and Yamaha, for instance) that also have standard multitrack sequencers. There will probably be a utility with which you can grab the music in one or more sequencer tracks and turn it into a triggerable phrase.

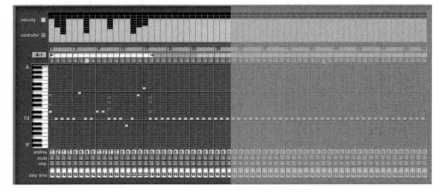

Figure 5-9
The arpeggiator/step-sequencer programming screen in VirSyn Tera. Each step can be given its own velocity and controller data using the strip along the top. Moving the small rectangles up or down changes the transposition of a given step, and outlined boxes show where the step will play a chord rather than a single note. Rhythms are programmed in the rows along the bottom, and the "arpkey" setting controls which note in a held chord will be used if the software is in arpeggiator mode. The grid is interactive: You can change a pattern while it's cycling.

Today's step sequencers have a mixed heritage. On one hand, they're descended from the analog sequencers of the '60s and '70s. Analog sequencers typically had a few rows of knobs, and the sequencer's clock stepped through the knobs over and over, sending out control voltages at each step. An analog sequencer is very interactive, because you can turn the knobs while it's playing. Step sequencers are also closely related to drum machines. Hardware-based step sequencers are no longer common, but Roland's MC series and other hardware units include step sequencers along with their own internal synths. And software-based "virtual rack systems" like Propellerhead Reason and Image-Line FL Studio specialize in step-sequenced rhythms. The arpeggiator in FL Studio turns single notes into arpeggiated chords, and lets you choose from a long menu of chord types. VirSyn Tera uses a single grid (see Figure 5-9) for programming both its step sequencer and its arpeggiator.

The Korg Wavestation, which was introduced in 1990, pioneered a related technique called wave sequencing. Instead of playing one sampled waveform for the entire duration of each note, a Wavestation oscillator could cycle through a series of unrelated waveforms, producing a shifting frequency contour, a drum beat, or a percolating combination of the two. I'm not aware of any current hardware synths that will do wave sequencing, but used Wavestations in good condition are still available, and Korg has released a software version whose sound and features are identical to the original. Another option would be Native Instruments Reaktor, where you can build your own wave sequencing synth (or just about any other kind) in software, if you have some creative vision and some patience.

BREAK IT DOWN

If you want to edit a complex rhythm-based patch, but you're struggling to figure out how it was put together, strip it down in a systematic way. The basic steps work like this:

1. Is the arpeggiator running? If so, switch it off and play the patch. Then switch it back on, and compare the two sounds.

2. Bypass any effects processors. As before, compare the sound with and without effects. The composite rhythm may be coming from a combination of arpeggiation and a delay effect. If so, listen to the delay without the arpeggio, and then the arpeggio without the delay.

3. Check the modulation routings to see what the LFOs are doing. After switching off the arpeggiator and delay, trim the LFO modulation routings, one at a time, down to zero. By now the patch should be getting pretty naked.

4. After setting the LFOs back to their original values, turn the oscillator outputs down to zero, one after another. By isolating a single oscillator, you can hear the contribution it's making to the sound.

5. Figure out what's modulating the filter. Is it an LFO? A multi-stage envelope? Try turning the filter modulations down to zero and listen to the patch. If there's more than one filter, repeat the process for each of them.

6. Take a look at the envelope generators. Are they looping during each note?

By analyzing a few complex factory patches in this way, you can get a handle on exactly what your synth is capable of.

Now that you have the essentials of the rhythm method in place, let's look at ways to creatively edit your samples and loops to get rhythmic effects that would be hard to obtain otherwise. Greg Rule spells out the specifics of loop slicing in this 2002 Dance Mix column.

March 2002
Creative Slice & Dice
Arpeggiation without an arpeggiator

Whether it's NIN-like machine rock, Kraftwerkian techno, or you-name-it electronic music, there's nothing quite like a pulsing, percolating synth track to inject adrenaline into a song. Many of us have synths with built-in arpeggiators, and that's a great way to get a bubbling, animated track going. There are also synths with auto-pattern generators, such as the one built into Roland's JP-8000, that can be used to achieve similar results. And Korg's

Electribe-R is an example of a groovebox that allows you to gate external audio for cool sliced effects. But if you don't have an instrument with features such as these, you can still give your tracks an arpeggiated feel using a software recorder/sequencer such as Pro Tools, Digital Performer, Cubase, Logic, or Sonar.

Here's how:

- Assuming you've worked out a chord progression, select a sustained sound (strings, pads, Rhodes, etc.) and record a few bars. The goal is to get a track that sustains smoothly from chord to chord. It can be a static sound or something that moves (filter sweeps, etc.), but just make sure the amplitude doesn't drop too much from start to finish (see Figure 5-10).
- Once the part is recorded, listen to it and make sure you're happy with the performance. It doesn't have to be spot-on perfect; as long as there are no major clams, you should be ready for the next step.
- Activate grid mode and select the grid resolution of your choice. For this lesson, let's start with sixteenth-notes.
- Select every other sixteenth-note chunk on the grid and delete, thus creating a series of note slices that are locked rhythmically to the grid (see Figure 5-11). Now listen to the result: Your smooth pad has transformed into a choppy pulse. Fun, eh?

September 2003

MASTERS OF EBM (ELECTRONIC BODY MUSIC) AND INDUSTRIAL

To bring you the real story of what makes the modern EBM and industrial scene so vital, we assembled a roundtable of artists to discuss its past, present, and future: Stephan Groth, known also as Grothesk, the mastermind behind the Norwegian outfit Apoptygma Berzerk; cEvin Key from Canada's Skinny Puppy; Joakim Montelius of the Swedish band Covenant; Daniel Myer from the German trio Haujobb; Ronan Harris of VNV Nation (hailing from London, VNV stands for "Victory Not Vengeance"); and Patrick Codenys and Daniel Bressanutti from the groundbreaking Belgian band Front 242. All of these artists generously agreed to share some delicious details about how they go about fusing fury with electronics. Let's crank it up.

Our readers are always looking for new, innovative ways to distress and mangle their sounds. Can you describe one of your favorite tricks for processing or composing new textures?

Stephan Groth: I use a lot of bit-shifting and distortion. I think the trick is to know your equipment. Even though it's a drag, read the manuals — probably not a very popular thing to say. Find out what a piece of gear can do, and try out all possibilities.

cEvin Key: Personally, I like to try various methods in the recording chain including tube EQ, specialized outboard FX, and quality compression. I then like to take the end result once it's recorded, then tear it apart with a variety of plug-ins and edits with new FX, all automated with Logic Audio.

Joakim Montelius: We're big fans of vocoders. Using the same sound as carrier and modulator can give great results. Crappy time-stretching — like the one on the Akai S950 — is great for weird modulation. Digital distortion (not modeling, but overdriving digital signals) has a more aggressive, nasty, and piercing sound to it. So has bit-reduction and low-resolution sam-

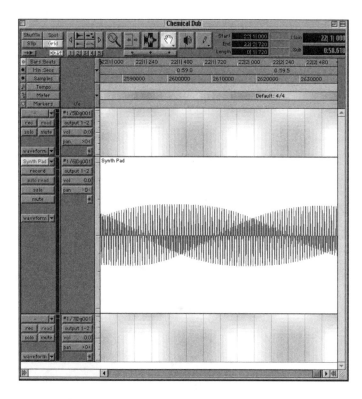

Figure 5-10
The original waveform
before slicing.

pling, when you get aliasing and crude waveforms with big gaps for that lovely digital hardcore harshness.

The important thing is to keep the sound usable, to mix the trashed sound with the original to retain some texture and harmonics. Otherwise you end up with just noise. That may be good and well, but if you want it to work musically, it's usually a good trick to mix the sounds. Compressors are great tools for manipulating beats. A properly abused compressor can completely alter a rhythm, highlighting or changing the focus in very creative ways.

Daniel Bressanutti: Playing with a real modular synthesizer is my favorite trick for getting innovative sounds.

Ronan Harris: Maybe it's my age, but I love analog. I tend to find a lot of pro sounds are too clean; they lack any dimension. They make nice building blocks. I like to do things like run digital tracks or sounds from the computer through a triggered modular system and some effects, give them character, and record them back in.

Even in the computer domain you can do this with synth designs in [Native Instruments] Reaktor. I love putting sounds through effects that feed and saturate other effects that in turn feed back to somewhere earlier in the loop and create incredible sounds. If it's not that, then it's finding the weirdest plug-ins I can and processing all sorts of things through them to see what works and what doesn't. Ordinary mixing boards can't do what you can do with a computer. I'm also going retro these days by taking clean sounds and resampling them on an old sampler which has a character all its own. It's subtle, but it works.

Daniel Myer: I love the Frohmage plug-in from Ohmboys. It's some kind of filter distortion thing. I also like the Waldorf D-Pole. Usually I loop a beat and let the arrangement play, then I record the beat while I play with the knobs of Frohmage or the Waldorf. Afterwards, I cut the pieces that I like and start a new song.

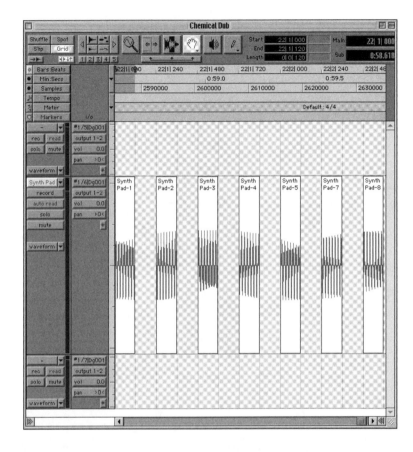

Figure 5-11
Waveform with every other
sixteenth-note chopped out.
(Note the gridlines above
and below the track.)

November 2001
BT

On *Emotional Technology*, the world of unreal note values becomes much more real, and not only with stutter edits. "I made up a new technique, nano-correcting, in which I correct to unreal note values. The coolest thing is with sound effects. For 'Last Moment of Clarity,' we had the guitar parts looping on the monitor while we all took a break. I went outside into the rain with a Minidisc recorder, and recorded this thunderstorm with the guitar loop bleeding through from inside the house, and I recorded the sound of all that as I walked into the house. What you hear is being out in the rain to moving into the studio. Then I did an FFT analysis of the Minidisc and an FFT of the original track in Kyma, and I did Spectral Morphing between the two. Then I took the beginning of the rain track and time-corrected the rain-drops so they were falling exactly at 256th-note level.

"The cool thing about nano-correcting is that your ears are really drawn to the symmetry of the sound. When you go into unreal note values, anything smaller than 64th-notes, your brain stops telling you that what you're hearing is a repeated slice of sound. What it starts telling you is that it's a tone. But your mind still perceives the symmetry of it. So if you have a jumbled mass of 128th-notes, it just sounds like some splurchy, organic sound. But if you time-correct them, it starts taking on symmetrical patterns. And your brain is drawn to it, even subliminally. You start to perceive it as organized sound, but your brain doesn't understand how it's understanding. It's my favorite thing in the world."

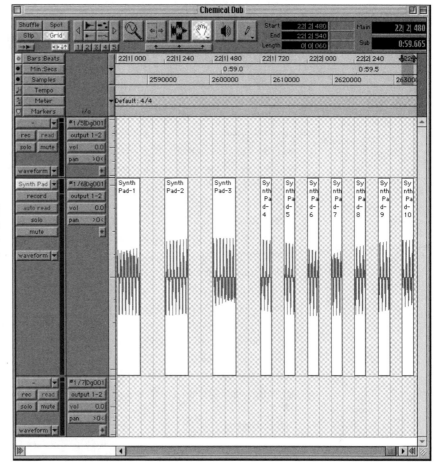

Figure 5-12
Waveform with sixteenth-notes and 32nd-notes sliced out.

■ If you hear undesirable click/pops at the splice points, zoom in and draw tiny fades at the beginnings and/or ends of the offending pieces. And remember to listen to the track in the context of the overall mix before getting too anal about the fades. In many cases I'll leave the clicks in, as they add a desirable percussive effect to the song.

■ The sixteenth-note example above is just to get you started. Experiment with other note values and rhythmic patterns as well. Figure 5-12 shows a mixed sixteenth- and 32nd-note pattern. Approach it as you would a drum track.

■ Finally, experiment by retuning certain slices within the pattern. I like to select a few notes and change their pitches an octave higher or lower with a pitch-shift plug-in, which yields a classic arpeggiated sound.

As simple as this technique is, I'm surprised more producers don't take advantage of it. It's amazing how you can turn a bland track into a blockbuster by chopping it up in strategic ways. So get out those virtual scissors and snip, snip, snip.

Some dance genres — like trance and deep house — favor a polished, smooth sound. Others revolve around the rough edges. Here are a few tips from Rob Hoffman for adding audio aggression to your music.

July 2003
Lo-Fi Junkie
Outboard tools for sandblasting your tracks

Let's talk about some dirty lo-fi effects, including filtering, distortion, extreme EQ, and pummeling amounts of compression. You've heard these types of sounds in all kinds of music from dance to country, from pop to rock. Some of the younger artists I work with actually call filtering the "Genie in a Bottle" effect, referring to the vocal filtering effect created by producer David Frank on Christina Aguilera's pop hit by the same name. They have no idea that Sir George Martin was experimenting with filtering and compression on the Beatles almost 40 years ago. Today there are myriad software plug-ins that you can use to create these effects. In fact, the trend certainly seems to be the shrinking of studios as they bail on their racks of outboard gear in favor of compact plug-in alternatives. Plug-ins are great, I'm all for them. But everybody's got them and sometimes it's just too easy to instantiate a plug-in and leave it set on the "Telephone" preset. I believe outboard gear leaves much more room for experimentation, happy accidents, and unique sounds that few others have access to. Once you have a great song and arrangement, it's all about the ear candy — those unique sounds that grab listeners' attention and keep them coming back for more.

STOMPBOXES
Probably the cheapest and easiest way to get into prime lo-fi territory is guitar footpedals. They're available everywhere, and it seems there is an infinite variety. Boutique pedal builders introduce new models almost monthly. I picked up my "Roadkill" distortion pedal from the local guitarmart for a measly $19.95. Yeah, it sounds terrible, but that's a good thing. I send drum sounds through it from my Akai MPC-2000 and it instantly evokes Björk-like distorted percussion *á la* Homogenic.

My favorite pedals for crunch and filter effects are built by a company called Z.Vex (www.zvex.com). Zachary Vex definitely has an ear for odd and extreme sounds. Primarily designed for guitar, his pedals are anything but subtle. Loops just love going through the Machine, and the Fuzz Factory is probably the most versatile distortion pedal I've ever used. Both the Seekwah and Oohwah offer some crazy alternatives to auto-wah or your run-of-the-mill filter effects by including a step sequencer with individually controllable filter cutoff frequencies for each step and an overall speed control. The Octane and Woolly Mammoth can warp your synth patches into an unbelievable low-end frenzy. Yeah, they work on guitars too; just don't let your guitar-playing friends borrow them or you may never get them back.

GUITAR AMPS

While we're in guitarland, let's not forget about guitar amps. I love feeding audio signals out of my DAW back into little practice amps. There are so many opportunities to muck up your original audio source. Try EQing the send to the amp, adjust the EQ and drive at the amp, use a good microphone, try a crappy microphone, and try different mic pre and EQ combinations, plus maybe some extreme compression. The variations are endless. Matching levels can be a bit of a challenge, but luckily there are pedals that can do that as well. The Reamp by John Cunniberti (www.reamp.com) is one such tool, as is the Little Labs PCP Distro box (www.littlelabs.com).

When in doubt you can feed the pedals via a bus or aux send. Start with the level all the way down and slowly bring up the send until you hear something you like. Be careful — I've blown up a few speakers this way and fried a couple of pedals. For example, I love the MXR Dynacomp for drum compression, but it can't take too much level. There will definitely be some noise, but if we wanted pristine audio we wouldn't be feeding our tracks through guitar pedals, now, would we?

TAPE

Got an old 4- or 8-track Portastudio lying around? How about a boombox with a built-in microphone? Record a loop or even the whole track to cassette, then re-record it into your DAW from the cassette. Sometimes the hiss and grunge from the cassette add that little bit of spice a track needs, or sometimes all that noise forces you to EQ things radically differently than if you had a nice clean source from CD. A very long time ago, back when I was a starving music student, a friend of mine gave me an audiocassette copy of a very popular loop CD. It was a terrible copy, but I used it to death, EQing it relentlessly to get rid of the hiss and to bump up the low end. Those tracks always had a cool vibe even though I was using a loop source that quite a few people had. (For the sake of the copyright-conscious, I should mention that I have since bought legitimate copies of that sample CD in three different formats.)

When I used to assist for engineer for Bruce Swedien we would often record live bass to an Ampex ATR-102 1/2" 2-track machine, then sample those bits into the Akai MPC-60 (did I just date myself?). Hardly lo-fi, but what a cool vibe the bass had coming off that half-inch and being sampled by the 12-bit MPC. For you history buffs, it was the same 1/2" tape machine that Bruce mixed Michael Jackson's *Thriller* to.

If you're one of the few people who haven't thrown their console away, try feeding signals down multiple channels. I once fed a bass through three channels of an SSL (direct out to line in) with every knob turned on full. It was pretty distorted, but unlike any other bass sound I've ever heard. Obviously you don't need an SSL, but try it out on your console. You might find something useful. Follow that up with some crazy compression such as the Nuke function on a Distressor and you're into distortion heaven. Of course, if you have access to an SSL, the talkback compressor is the ultimate in squash.

INPUTS AND FILTERS

Another favorite effect of mine is the audio input of an analog synth. Overdriving these inputs can lead to some interesting sounds. The Minimoog and Korg MS-20 are two of my all-time favorites for this, but we can get into those types of sounds much cheaper today via the Moogerfooger MF101 and Frostwave Resonator pedals. Some other great options with quite a bit more controllability would be the Sherman Filterbank and Mutronics Mutator. You can hear some great examples of the Mutator on Peter Gabriel's *Up* — Peter credits the Mutator in the liner notes for each song it's used on, so you can listen for it. A couple of years ago I wrote about Electrix effects and how much I use them. The company is no longer in business, but the effects are still in my rack and are very affordable on the used market.

Of course the ultimate audio tweak tool is the modular synth. The beauty of modular synths is that you can start small, say just a power supply and a filter module, and add on as your needs expand. Modular synth manufacturers make some pretty esoteric modules beyond the common filter and ring modulators. Doepfer makes some affordable packages, as does MOTM. For the adventurous footpedal connoisseur and modular fan, Lovetone's footpedals offer patch points for CV input and other audio control functions. They sound amazing, but due to their limited availability, they're becoming more and more expensive on the used market.

In this day of the all-in-one DAW, I think it's even more important to think outside the box. Search your studio and house for unique sound sources and manipulation techniques. Look for bargains as musicians unload their outboard gear and synths for the latest and greatest software plug-ins. Who knows, you might find tomorrow's trendsetter, this decade's TB-303. In your quest for new sounds, I caution you to keep the volume low until you know what you've created. Otherwise you'll be searching for speaker parts across the room.

February 2000
NINE INCH NAILS

Charlie Clouser contributed his fair share of strange noises and loops to *The Fragile* as well. "We did rely heavily on processing on this record," he reveals, "because there were so many new tools around. A few years ago our choices were limited to basically running stuff through the filter input of the Minimoog or putting it into the Eventide H3000. Those were the two main choices in those days. Now there are piles of plug-ins and crazy processing tools. We used the TC Electronic Fireworx effects unit a lot, which has some interesting filters and such. We also did a lot of passing audio through the filter inputs on the Access Virus module and the Roland JP-8080."

Case in point: "The pulsing synth-type line that runs throughout 'Into the Void' is Trent playing guitar through the MicroWave XT's filter inputs, and the big, heavy sub-bass sounds that come in on the song 'The Great Below' are, I think, Quasimidi Rave-O-Lution through the filter bank on the JP-8080," says Charlie. "There are also a lot of ambient drones on the 'The Great Below' and 'The Way Out Is Through' which are, I believe, a ReBirth bass sequence running on a Macintosh passing through the filter inputs on the JP-8080. So there was a lot of starting with one thing and ending up with a completely unrecognizable result by basically removing 99% of the audio from a sound, and just winding up with a delicate little squeaky noise when the original was a screeching, squalling sequence."

One of the greatest things about music — all music, not just dance tracks — lies in the fact that, like fashion, styles are cyclical. The adage "everything old is new again" seems to apply especially to dancefloor trends. If you're looking to add some classic textures to your next house opus, here are some pointers from yours truly on nailing those sounds of yesteryear.

November & December 2002
Retro Grooves
Getting old-school tracks from a modern rig

Modern house music covers a vast array of subgenres and styles, from progressive to tribal and beyond. Two flavors that seem to remain popular regardless of current fashion are deep house (which has been around for over a decade in various forms) and funky French house. Both styles rely heavily on the classic disco and soul sounds of the '70s and early '80s. So how do you get the authentic sounds of these genres with a modern rig?

BASS
While synth bass has been around for decades, most vintage disco and soul tracks relied on the organic flavors of electric bass guitar. Your first choice for getting this sound should be an actual human being, preferably someone with some chops. If you don't know a good bass player, check out one of the "live" bass loop CDs on the market. Using bass lines from CD's sometimes requires a bit of hand editing to adjust the pitch and timing to fit your track, so a copy of Propellerhead's ReCycle, Sony Acid, or Ableton Live will come in handy when you're integrating a bass guitar loop with your mix.

If you can't afford to pick up a loop library or hire a bass player, there's another option: Carefully program a synth to sound like a real bass, and then play the part yourself. The secret lies in learning to riff like a real bassist, which is no small task. If you study old disco and soul tracks, you'll begin to understand some of the nuances of the idiom. Accenting certain notes by playing them up an octave with a staccato feel, or restraining the range of the overall part to just a few adjacent notes are common techniques used by bassists. If you really want to get your inspiration from the source, check out vintage tracks by Bootsy Collins (P-Funk) and Chic, or pick up a few disco compilations.

Then there's the bass sound itself. It's crucial to choose the sound carefully, as more than a few sampled basses found in workstations sound nothing like bass guitar when played in a sequence (unless your idea of a bass guitar is the *Seinfeld* theme). Generally speaking, fingered bass patches come closest to approximating that classic disco sound. Additionally, Reason users should check out Subtractor's "Bass Guitar" patch. This is by far one of the best synth bass patches I've used. Played correctly, it's quite convincing and can sit beautifully in a mix.

I've also had good results with Minimoog-style patches created with Steinberg's Model E. Start with a single triangle-wave oscillator in the 32' or 16' range and turn the cutoff down until you're hearing just the fundamental with a bit of buzz (this helps simulate the finger/string sound of a real bass). Then add another triangle-wave oscillator one octave higher at about 60–80 percent of the original oscillator's volume (adding the prominent second harmonic of many bass guitars). Sometimes detuning the second triangle wave slightly will enhance the character. The envelope should have an immediate attack, short decay, 80–90 percent sustain level, and a short release. Add a touch of envelope mod to the filter to enhance the attack-decay aspects of the patch.

If you've done this correctly — and it may take a bit of tweaking, depending on your synth — you should hear a muted bass sound that's almost too bland. If you find the sound is too boomy, back off on the first oscillator and add a tiny touch of resonance, as this will often reduce the bass content slightly if the synth is modeled accurately. Note that some analog models include a "fat" filter mode that effectively negates the thinning of the low end. Try to stick with "classic" filter mode when applying this trick. Alternatively, a touch of highpass filtering will tame the excessive lows that often compete with kick drums in a mix. On its own, this bass patch still sounds like a synth. But if you play it idiomatically with a slammin' drum groove and mix it correctly, you can get darn close to what a real bass guitar would sound like. Experiment!

Figure 5-13
Applied Acoustics' Lounge Lizard can emulate electric pianos from Rhodes to Wurly and includes classic effects such as phaser, wah, and delay.

ELECTRIC PIANO

Rhodes and Wurly sounds are a fantastic way to add soul to a track. Most modern workstations include some form of Rhodes sample, but the quality and authenticity varies. Emagic's EVP88 and -73 VST are stellar emulations of these classic instruments, and Applied Acoustics' Lounge Lizard is developing a following among vintage key aficionados.

Savvy producers realize that the secret sauce is in recreating the recording techniques of the '70s. Keep in mind that effects processing options back then were quite limited by today's standards. The most commonly used effect for electric pianos was the integrated tremolo found in the Rhodes suitcase and Wurlitzer 200A. In addition to tremolo, the sound was often enhanced by slightly overdriving the console preamps, which gave the instrument a bit more warmth.

Another signature Rhodes effect of the '70s was phasing. A perfect example of this processing technique is the piano comp in Steely Dan's "Peg." The main effect consisted of a slow phase with a fair amount of resonance/feedback, which gave the sound a softly animated quality that worked beautifully in context.

Most modern multieffects processors include some sort of phaser algorithm. There are several fantastic freeware VST plug-ins such as SmartElectronix's SupaPhaser (a must-have, in my book) and GreenOak's Phaserifier. There are quite a few pedals that offer phasing, and most can be had for under $75 if you shop around.

And don't forget chorusing. Depending where you insert it, chorusing can thicken and warm up an electric piano track or add some animation and widen the stereo image. Try placing a chorus at the end of the signal chain — after the tremolo, overdrive, and phaser — for a truly wet and classic sound.

August 2002
MOBY

"Some electronic musicians are really obsessed with creating new, interesting, remarkably experimental sounds, and I admire people who do that. But my goal is just to make emotional music. So I'm not too concerned with inventing new sounds, since I already have sounds that I like. Honestly, I tend to use the same sounds over and over. If you listen to most of the strings on *18*, it's the same synth I've always used to make records, the SY22.

"The same thing goes for my piano sounds. Ritchie Bittner is the guy who built my studio. He heard *Play*, and he asked me how I recorded the piano. When I told him it was just my old E-mu Proformance half-rack module, he was so disappointed. He thought it was a grand piano that I had miked. I said, 'How do I have room to have a grand piano in this studio?' It's a simple choice: A half-rack synth module that sounds like a beautiful piano, or a full grand piano with all the mics. I use the Proformance for 90% of my piano sounds; that's what you hear on *18* as well. Sometimes I'll layer it with a Rhodes patch from my SY85, with a little vibrato, like on 'In My Heart' and 'At Least We Tried.'"

Strings are a big element of the sonic landscape of Moby's sonic world, and *18* is no exception. Lush, warm, and expansive on "We Are All Made of Stars," they're ethereal and transparent on "Sleep Alone," and gritty and heavily vibratoed on "Great Escape." His secret? Not some patented string library, just his trusty SY22, Roland JV-5080, and Triton, respectively. "The SY22," he says, "I turned it on 12 years ago, and it's been doing the same sound ever since."

GUITAR

I cannot urge readers strongly enough to go out there and find a real flesh-and-blood guitarist. Even in tracks that consist exclusively of synths and drum loops, the addition of a real guitar riff will often make a mix sound completely authentic. Here in Austin, I do quite a bit of work with Adam Whaley from the Morrows. He plays in a wide range of styles, and is a loop generator if ever there was one. Regardless of where you live, it's definitely worth scouting your area for a great player.

If you can't find a player with the chops you need for your dance tracks, you should definitely check out the soundware out there. There are some fantastic libraries available for about $100 each. I like Big Fish Audio's *Guitar Studio*, to name one, as it includes a wide variety of styles at a fair price — though the funk focus is on wah-wah guitar, not the chicken-scratch disco riffing popularized by Nile Rodgers in his work with Chic. Another of my favorite guitar libraries is Zero-G's *Funk Guitar*, which features a slew of soulful guitar riffs, including the sexy wah chords from Busta Rhymes's "What's It Gonna Be."

When it comes to producing classic disco riffs, an ever-so-slightly overdriven sound is your best bet. But if processing is needed, the most common disco and funk guitar effects are wah-wah and phasing.

Wah-wah can be applied to almost any guitar sample to give it a hyper-funky chocodelic appeal á la Barry White or Isaac Hayes' "Theme from *Shaft*." It can even sound great on distorted leads, though that's not really a vintage disco/funk effect. Still, wahed-out leads have been used on more than a few Parliament and Isley Brothers songs, so experimentation is worthwhile.

Phasing sounds particularly good on single-note rhythmic guitar licks, and served as the basis for several Bar-Kays, Slave, and Brothers Johnson tracks, notably "Strawberry Letter 23." I've added phasers to several synths' "muted guitar" patches and achieved results that sound fine in the context of a mix.

If you're looking for a slightly more '80s rhythm guitar flavor, try adding a touch of chorusing. Depending on how your effect is set up, it could add that cheesy Rockman sound. But one producer's Velveeta is another's brie.

Figure 5-14
The Hohner Clavinet was a key instrument in '70s funk keyboard arsenals.

CLAVINET

Clav can provide a unique texture that's been underutilized in the modern dance music scene until very recently. If you've never heard a real Hohner Clavinet, check out old Stevie Wonder records — notably "Superstition" —— for a taste of what the real thing sounds like. Billy Preston's clav work on "Outa-Space" is another terrific example.

Leading the charge for bringing back the Clavinet's percussive, guitar-like sound is Thunderpuss, whose killer new remix for Whitney Houston's "Whatchulookinat" spotlights some very tasty licks.

Clav textures sound great using the guitar processing techniques described above, especially with a bit of overdrive and wah-wah. Most synths have some sort of Clavinet patch, and E-mu's Proteus/Vintage Keys patches are standouts. So dig through your rig and see what you find.

STRINGS

Orchestral strings are another essential ingredient for the disco sound. There are several approaches for using strings in a dance mix; some quick and easy, some more challenging.

By far, the easiest trick to adding some disco gloss to your arrangement is simply adding a high string drone to certain sections of your song. Find a note — either the tonic or a related note in the song's key — that sounds right when sustained over the entire chord progression. Add this note over the choruses or other sections that need highlighting. For

June 1997
CHEMICAL BROTHERS

You guys have become masters at murdering sounds.
Yeah. We don't make clinical machine music, even though I'm a great fan of bands like Kraftwerk and such where everything is so precise. I really like that. But one of the major things we've done from the beginning is use rough guitar effects. We've got quite a large collection of Electro-Harmonix pedals and stuff like that. They always put a bit of a bite into things, which you don't really get from your new, latest Roland effects unit type thing. I think when people were making effects and pedals back then, there was a wild edge to what they were doing. I think it was more experimental.

Is there one particular pedal that gets the most service?
The [Electro-Harmonix] Bass Microsynth, which is quite a fierce pedal. And we use the Frequency Analyzer a lot, which has got the wildest filter I've ever heard. It's the most extreme thing. I was reading some literature about it the other day, and it was meant to be used on brass. I can't imagine any horn player playing through it. If you put a bass through it, or drums, it just sounds wild.

additional drama, take the part up an octave for the final choruses of your track.

String soundware is plentiful these days. You can easily spend a small fortune on exquisitely recorded and articulated sample libraries for streaming samplers such as GigaStudio or HALion and achieve truly remarkable results, but this might be overkill for a club mix. On the other hand, Reason ships with the Orkester soundbank, which is more than adequate for most dance tracks. The trick with using string soundware is in getting the articulation right. Many disco producers employed full orchestras for their sound (Barry White's Love Unlimited Orchestra was unparalleled in this area), and the subtleties and phrasing of string runs and falls are hard to duplicate via standard keyboard technique. Fortunately, the Orkester soundbank covers these bases with a full complement of sampled string articulations, so the disco essentials are well represented in Reason.

Other instruments that also should be considered in the quest for the retro sound are acoustic piano (of course), Hammond B-3, and various percussion elements such as tambourines, shakers, claves, etc. Still, when it comes to disco and funk, the most valuable assets in your rig are your ears — and access to classic recordings as a source of inspiration. Analyzing the original performances may surprise you, so get out there and listen.

A few years into the 21st century, it's become apparent that the '80s were one of the most fertile and profoundly innovative periods of electronic music. Due, no doubt, in large part to the mainstream proliferation of British electropop and German experimentalism, the spiky sounds of early analog synths became part and parcel of the vocabulary of electronica. Nowadays, modern remixers have put their own spin on integrating these textures into styles ranging from electroclash to nu-wave. Something old, something new, something borrowed, something blue....

May 2003
Electroclash of the Titans, Part 2
The key to that '80s sound

A few chapters back we covered the essentials of '80s drum machine sounds. Now that you've had a chance to experiment with bitchin' beatbox rhythms, it's time to add some gnarly keyboard textures.

One thing to keep in mind when creating '80s sounds is that the synths that started the electro movement were bare-bones by today's standards. Since analog technology was quite expensive in those days, many of the most popular synths of the era offered only a fraction of the features available in today's polysynths and plug-ins.

The architecture for most of these stripped-down synths was fundamentally the same: one or two oscillators, perhaps a sub-oscillator that tracked the main oscillator with a square wave one or two octaves lower than the original pitch, a simple resonant lowpass filter, an LFO, and one or two ADSR envelopes for controlling the filter and amplifier circuits.

The key to recapturing the '80s sounds is to understand the limitations of the era's technology. If you want that sound, you won't find it by exploiting the matrix modulation features and multiple filter paths in modern synths. The essence lies in moderation, grasshopper.

Figure 5-15
The hardest thing about coming up with great single-oscillator patches is resisting the urge to engage additional oscillators. In Apple Logic 7, you can easily come up with the patch we describe using the ES2 soft synth. Here's what that patch looks like.

For example, spiky Kraftwerk textures are often best recreated with a single oscillator (square, pulse, or saw — no sampled exotica, please), followed by a simple lowpass filter. Set the ADSR for quick attack, rapid decay, no sustain, and fast release. Once the patch is set up in this manner, start tinkering with the filter. Be sure to try various resonance settings in conjunction with envelope modulation of cutoff frequency — the key to those classic '80s rubbery bass sounds.

For long filter-swept patches, try taking the above sound and raising the resonance and envelope decay to higher settings, then lower the cutoff frequency while increasing the amount of envelope modulation applied to the filter. "We Are the Robots," indeed!

Now that you're on your way, here are some rules of thumb when designing retro patches:

When creating dual-oscillator textures, don't just diddle with fine detuning of the oscillators' pitches in the same octave range. Instead, keep the fine-tuning at zero while experimenting with different octave ranges and/or interval-based tunings. Better yet, familiarize yourself with the harmonic series, then set the second oscillator's pitch to a specific harmonic of the primary oscillator. By adjusting the mix of the two oscillators, you can dramatically affect the overall timbre of the patch without resorting to sampled waveforms.

For truly authentic retro filtering, stick to lowpass filters, but go wild with the resonance. Most of the classic synths didn't have notch and bandpass modes, so while those are fantastic for exotic textures, they are often out of character for modern electro-pop excursions.

If your synth supports it, experiment with inverted envelope modulation of filter cutoff. Back in the day, we didn't have 64-stage tempo-synced envelopes, so we had to get creative with inverse modulation. When using inverted envelopes, it's important to set the filter cutoff a bit higher than you'd normally expect, as the inverted envelope mod amount will now subtract from the cutoff setting.

The groovy thing about old-school programming techniques is that they don't require the latest plug-in doodads. The simple synths that come standard with today's software sequencers are more than ample for all but the trickiest '80s riffs. Apple Logic's array of integrated synths is fabulous for electroclash bass, pad, and lead sounds. Cubase SX's A1 and Sonar's DreamStation are almost too powerful for these types of patches, and Reason is probably more than you'll ever need for recreating the sound of the New Romantic era.

As for processing techniques, it remains crucial to stick with the basics. Digital reverbs didn't reach the mainstream until — get this — 1983! Prior to that, even a single, non-programmable modulated delay would set you back at least $300. You kids have it so easy.

Accordingly, the classic synth effects of the era are: echo/delay, flanger, phaser, and chorus. Applying distortion will definitely give your tracks a more modern edge, but in the '80s we wouldn't dare mess around with our pristine spiky textures.

I'll leave you with a classic processing trick that launched a few New Romantic tracks for bands like Japan and Duran Duran:

Start with a spiky bass sound with immediate attack and a quick decay-to-zero. Use two sawtooth or pulse oscillators set an octave apart. Open the filter fairly wide and don't add too much resonance. Now sequence a simple one-measure sixteenth-note bass line at around 130 bpm. Repeat a single note, alternating octaves every third note like so: C1-C1-C2-C2-C1-C1-C2-C2, etc.

Once you have this loop chugging along, insert a flanger on the channel (or use an effects send, your call). Keep the rate fairly slow, but crank up the depth and feedback. Adjust the wet/dry mix to taste. If you've done everything right, you should have a part that resembles the intro to Duran's "Hold Back the Rain" or any number of classic Giorgio Moroder joints.

Ultimately, if you want to ride the Retronica wave, you'll need to study the old masters. Japan, Kraftwerk, OMD, Human League, Simple Minds (pre-Breakfast Club), and Heaven17 are good places to start your research. Check out "The Model," "Spacelab," and "The Robots" (don't forget to roll the R!) from Kraftwerk's *The Man-Machine*, and the Cars' *The Cars* and *Candy-O*. So get crackin' ... and pray the hairstyles don't come back too.

Daniel Fisher is a professor at Boston's prestigious Berklee College (trivia fans take note, BT is an alumnus) and a member of the aptly named tribute band Pink Voyd. Here's a grab bag of synth tricks that includes something for everyone.

June 2003
Best of Synth Tricks
All-purpose pointers for patch programming

Here are some pointers to keep in mind as you learn the inner workings of your synths and samplers. Think of this as sort of a "Top 10" list.

1. Learn how to back up and restore your patches. You'd be surprised by how many people never save the factory and custom patches so they can be retrieved later on. Until your sounds are safely backed up, you'll be less likely to experiment.

2. Create a "Blank" patch that has all of the parameters set to normal values so you can dial in different ROM or RAM samples and not have to undo any unusual settings. (Some synths already come with a blank or "initialized" patch, but it may have settings you don't want.)

3. Every time you make a change to a patch, save it to the next memory location with a higher number or letter at the end of the patch name. This way, you can always go back a step or two to see if your patch is getting better or worse. If you've made a backup of all your patches you won't have to worry about deciding which patches to overwrite every time you want to save a new tweak.

4. Adjust every editable parameter in a patch and listen to what happens. You'll not only learn a lot about your synth, you may even stumble onto some happy accidents worthy of being saved.

5. If your synth allows it, try using slightly more than a whole-step of upward pitchbend. This will help guitar-like bends sound more realistic. If possible, try an even greater downward pitchbend range like a fourth, fifth, or octave. Using extreme downward pitchbend with samples creates the effect of slowing a record down to a complete stop.

6. When setting the depths of your typical control sources (velocity, mod wheel, aftertouch, etc.), set the minimum and maximum amount for each as you play the keyboard. The idea is to make the instrument respond more naturally for your performance style.

7. If you have extra real-time performance controllers that aren't being used (knobs, sliders, ribbons, foot controllers), set them up to create extreme changes such as wild vibrato, panning, tremolo, or filter sweeps. Better yet, assign two different destinations to one controller. See if you can find a depth amount for each des-

October 2005
TOM STEPHAN, A.K.A. SUPERCHUMBO

I sometimes use a reverse reverb to add intensity to a build-up just before the track kicks back in. We just record one beat of the whole track when it kicks in and send that through a really long reverb. Reverse that file and place it so that it leads up to the kick. Then I had the idea to stick it through the Vari-Fi plug-in. This plug-in simulates vinyl. It takes an audio file and makes it sound either like a vinyl spindown or startup. If you put the reverse reverb sound through the Vari-Fi vinyl startup sound it's amazing. It sounds like the whole track is lifted off the ground and brought back to life.

tination such that, when you move the controller all the way, it generates a very complex but intriguing effect. This way you can move the controller around in real time and know that you have a very cool way to end it. This also works for modulating effect parameters.

8. To give high-fidelity sounds a gritty "telephone" edge, apply a bandpass filter with a bit of resonance, then sweep the cutoff frequency until the sound has enough bark without sounding too muddy or shrill.

9. Set LFO rates and arpeggiator speeds to match the delay times of the built-in effects. If your synth allows it, synchronize the LFO rates, arpeggiator speeds, and delay times to MIDI clock. This is key to creating modern electronic grooves.

10. And most important, to be prepared for when the creative bug bites, have your synth set up and ready to go, with your previous work already saved, and your keyboard plugged in with headphones or speakers ready to go. Every second spent setting up drains away the initial energy that could be spent on creating new sonic masterpieces.

One style of music that hasn't yet been covered in depth in this tome is old-school hip-hop. While many of the tips in the other chapters of this book are especially applicable to creating the icy, lockstep textures of modern hip-hop and R&B, the nuances of classic hip-hop have infused other dance genres, such as trip-hop, illbient, and lounge. Accordingly, Michael Bradford's comprehensive tutorial on the elements of hip-hop is especially applicable to understanding the nuances of those genres.

Bradford is an engineer, producer, and programmer based in Los Angeles. He has worked with Terence Trent D'arby, Kid Rock, and Madonna, and with film composer Paul Buckmaster.

September 1999
Enter the Temple of Hip-Hop
Production techniques that capture the vibe

Hip-hop. The very mention of this music elicits an immediate response ranging from absolute love and devotion to the common complaint, "That's not real music." Groups like EPMD, Public Enemy, Run-DMC, and Grandmaster Flash And The Furious Five were there at the early stages of rap's emergence, but many considered those groups' appeal strictly urban. These days, however, regardless of where you stand on the subject, it's hard to deny the pervasiveness of the hip-hop sound and its influence on even the "poppiest" of pop music.

You'll notice people using the terms "rap" and "hip-hop" interchangeably, which is fine. But it might help to know that hip-hop actually describes not just a type of music, but a complete lifestyle with its own clothes, clubs, and culture. Rap (which predates the hip-hop scene and in a literal sense is nothing more than speak-singing) was an important part of the growth of hip-hop, but it's not all there is to it.

The loops and production techniques that originated with hip-hop are now heard in every kind of music. And exciting, emerging combinations of rap and rock are coming from long-time practitioners of the craft like Kid Rock, who has been doing it for ten years, and the recent collaboration between Trent Reznor and Dr. Dre.

The sounds and beats of hip-hop were easy to detect even in Reznor's earliest efforts. Nine Inch Nails used 808-style drums and old-school beats going all the way back to their first album in 1989, *Pretty Hate Machine* (TVT). And let's not forget Beck and Garbage, two acts that use the loops, drums, and sampling techniques of hip-hop in equal measure with their other influences. Whether you like rap or not, the sound, style, and beats of hip-hop have become as much a part of contemporary music as guitars and synthesizers.

We're going to talk about some techniques that will enable you to make convincing-sounding and -feeling tracks. But whether you're a programmer/engineer, a budding producer, or an aspiring artist looking to work some hip-hop into your sound, remember that the most important thing is to "keep it real." It has to sound like the real thing, and it has to feel like the real thing, even if it's being mixed into a rock or pop record.

In the early days, hip-hop was not a style created by rich rock stars with unlimited resources and fully equipped dream studios. Much like punk, it truly began as the music

November 2001
BT ON BEATS

In *Keyboard*'s 2001 cover feature, Brian Transeau delivers the details on how he creates his trademark stutter edits and sample-accurate layered grooves.

I see a number of laptops and tower Macs with TDM hardware, a PC, and a Kyma system. What program do you primarily work in?
Regardless of where I might start an idea, everything lives in Logic. To me Pro Tools feels like you're working with a tape deck, and Logic feels like you're writing a song.

With Pro Tools I have to assign what bar one is. I don't want to have to define bar one, you know? I don't want to have to repeat objects — I want to turn on a loop. I like to get a break going, loop it, maybe grab a guitar and start making a track.

That said, I think Beat Detective [for Pro Tools] is the most amazing algorithm for time-correction. It won't give you the sound that I get by time-expanding the ass-ends of drum hits and trimming them to the beat, or the sound of the EQing I do — it's not for that. What I've found Beat Detective works best at is live instruments. For example, I recorded a

traditional Northern Indian ensemble (tabla, tamboura, sitar, that sort of thing) for *Zoolander*, and Beat Detective was great for getting them all time-corrected. Sometimes Beat Detective has a hard time assigning the downbeats in the right place. It'll push things off by a sixteenth- or 32nd-note, so what I do is first use Beat Detective to find just the downbeats of the bars, then search for quarter-notes, then sixteenth-notes or whatever.

Do you have a preference for creating your stutters — do you prefer stuttering the whole mix or just bits of a loop?
It depends. Since I've started doing more film music I've started thinking in terms of stems [separate audio files of subgrouped instruments and effects]. Now when I do mixes I print everything to the stems — I've done all my compression and EQ with AudioSuite plug-ins usually before I apply my other TDM effects, like Echo Farm, Pitch Blender, or whatever, but I print all of that. Then I'll do the stutters and maybe I'll just chop up four stems.

For movies I usually hand in 16-wide [stems], so eight stereo pairs of rendered, EQ'd, compressed, effected, nor-

of the streets — even though more of hip-hop's consumers now live in the suburbs and its stars can afford the same lifestyles that their pop counterparts enjoy.

You can succeed with basic tools as long as you also possess a love for the music. But you do need two important things: an ear for the sound and a feel for the vibe. This means that you'll want to listen to as much hip-hop as you can, even if you only plan to produce a few sessions by others, or incorporate elements of the style into your own music. It's the only way you'll be able to know whether your tracks are real enough to compete on the street. It doesn't cost a lot to make good-sounding tracks, but it will cost you your cred if the tracks are wack.

If you're still with me, let's enter the temple. Shoes off, please.

VIBE

First, turn off your keyboards, drum machines, and computers. You'll need only your mind and ears for this part. Put on a good hip-hop record. Vinyl is preferable for the full effect, but CDs or cassettes work well, too. Listen. Although most pop music production goes for a clean high-tech sound, hip-hop records are raw and decidedly unpolished. Listen some more and you'll begin to recognize the *feel* of a hip-hop record — the most important part. Let's try to tackle this seemingly intangible concept.

malized audio tracks, then all we do is throw the stuff up in the surround speakers. If you put the faders up at unity, it's the mix how I want it to be.

Same thing when I get to that post stage of a track or arrangement and I'm starting to do some really tricked-out stuff in Kyma and other programs. I save the stems as stereo AIFF or WAV files and put them on every one of my computers and do the most esoteric shit with the files, then re-import them back into the main Logic session. From there I'll do stutter treatments on the effected stems.

So if a particular phrase or syllable had a cool treatment or effect, you'd bring that back in and replace the original bit with the processed material?
Right. I did that for the *NSYNC track, "Pop." I did 40 treatments of the vocal. I did one pass through the [Roland] VP-330 vocoder, another pass through a cheesy little ring mod box I have, another two passes through the TC FireWorx, I did a pass through the Sherman Filter Bank, a bunch of passes through Kyma, a pass through an Echoplex, and a guitar amp. I brought all that back in, lined everything

back up, and auditioned everything. So maybe I'd be listening and go, "Whoa. On the *and* of three up to four there's some dope shit." I'd take just the part I want, cut it, crossfade into it from the main vocal track, and crossfade right back out. I do a lot of that kind of work. That's the final stage of making a piece of music for me.

It's almost like there are two hemispheres to creativity. One side is the emotional, creative side. A good example is what I've done with Peter Gabriel. He and I will have dinner and talk about something, the news or whatever might happen to inspire us. The way he talks is like poetry. One of us might say something and it'll be like, "That's amazing what you just said. It would make a cool line for a song." We'll forget about our dinner and go straight into the studio to start working on a new track. That's the initial creative rush where you formulate an idea or an emotion that you're trying to articulate through music. The other side is more lab coat, you know? Taking that idea and making it congeal into something that is palatable for a listener and sonically interesting for me.

A lot of what you feel in hip-hop is invigorated by the sound that you hear. Lo-fi, which we'll discuss more below, isn't just an effect to get your attention — it really has a cultural significance that extends back to the sounds, sights, and smells of urban life. Hip-hop's grainy aural texture and sparse sonic spectrum are metaphors for this, but they're offset by (in most cases) a very laid-back, behind-the-beat approach informed by older jazz and R&B. As a matter of fact, unlike a typical rock or pop musician, a hip-hopper will tend to *slow down* to increase intensity.

Contrary to popular myth, though, the beats are not the most important thing in hip-hop. The drum rhythms tend to be straight-ahead because what's really vital is the story. The beat is there to provide a solid foundation for the storyteller (most often a rapper) to get their point across. When the rhythm swings, it just swings a little bit, rather than the car-icature-like dotted-rhythm "happy swing" that betrays many hip-hop dilettantes.

Are you getting it? Think grain, groove, and vibe.

THE SOUND

A lot of the sound of hip-hop comes from sampling — particularly from sampling vinyl — to get beats, riffs, and hooks. This is changing to a degree, as more producers are creating new tracks or recreating grooves from the ground up, but the sampled sound is often retained.

The earliest hip-hop records, in the early '80s, were made with samplers like the Ensoniq Mirage and the Akai S950, and drum machine/samplers like the Akai MPC60 and the E-mu SP-1200. These and other products of the day sampled mostly at 8- or 12-bit, and this low resolution is key to the grungy hip-hop sound. You can try finding one of these machines on the used market, but you can also get the sound with a new sampler, computer recording software, a drum machine, or even tape. (After all, the Mellotron and Chamberlin, the first "sample" players, used tapes instead of RAM.) Don't fear: There are tons of current tools and techniques that allow you to rough up your samples!

Lo-fi. How low can you go? Whether you're using a sampler or software, lower reso-lution will get you closer to the raw sound of hip-hop. Lo-fi can mean a lot of things, but in this context the topic can be split into bit resolution (8-bit, 16-bit, etc.) and sample rates (22.05kHz, 44.1kHz, etc.). You'll usually want to start by reducing the bit resolution, since that often creates the most drastic change. But lowering the sample rate can also add some nice fuzz. If you're actually sampling into a hardware machine at a lower rate, it will give you extra memory to boot.

If you can't get low-res by using an actual 8-bit sampler, don't worry; newer models often have powerful options for getting some funk into the sound. If you have a *resampling* fea-ture, you're in luck. Resampling allows you to take a sound that's already in the machine and internally "resample" it with different settings. For hip-hop music, you'll usually be reduc-ing a sample's bit resolution from 16-bit to 8- or 12-bit, and its sample rate from 44.1 or 48kHz to 22.05kHz or lower.

Resampling while the music plays has the advantage of letting you take separate drum hits being played in a sequence and record the groove as a single sample loop. This may take some extra RAM, but will save polyphony (since you're now only using two voices for a stereo loop).

There are other ways to get the lo-fi vibe. More recent products such as Roland's SP series have extremely cool features that allow you to get grungy, in some cases adjusting the level of "dirt" in real time. And then there's a universe of software programs and plug-ins to choose from.

Filters. Going back to the vinyl analogy, another part of the sound of classic loops is the limited frequency range of older records. Most samplers have filters that you can employ to achieve a similar effect. For example, the e6400 has a very impressive complement of filters, including hi- and lowpass, notch filters, and various types of EQ, plus flangers and phasers to give you more of a "warped" sound. With your sampler or a plug-in equivalent, try the lowpass filter. It takes away the highs and gives the sample an "older" sound. This is the sound of old speakers with blown tweeters. It's the sound of block parties and boomboxes turned up to 11. To get more of an old transistor radio effect, try the highpass filter. This takes out the lows and gives a thinner sound.

Now for real fun: If you can, map your keyboard's modulation wheel to the filter's cutoff frequency, and "play" the filter in real time with the song — pulsing on certain beats, doing sweeps into transitions, that kind of thing. Better still, you can map the resonance of the filter to the mod wheel, and the filter frequency to the pitch wheel, giving you a range of frequency manipulation, while the center position of the pitch wheel represents your initial frequency setting. I can do this with my E-mu e6400, because it can route MIDI controllers to these and other parameters.

Distortion. Let's not forget the other important component of the street sound. If you listen to a boombox at maximum volume, or go to an underground club, the sound you'll hear is the distortion that comes when speakers and components are pushed to the limit. Sometimes distortion is applied to the overall mix, or it may be selectively applied to a vocal track to achieve a chaotic "bullhorn" effect. You can achieve this sound several ways, running the entire mix through a fuzz box, tube preamp, or a plug-in like Line 6's Amp Farm or Apple Logic's Guitar Amp Pro.

DRUMS

The most popular elements of the hip-hop drum sound are deep kicks, long booming sub-kicks, tight snares, dry claps, and in-your-face hi-hats. You can easily buy samples or use modules, but why not have some fun? Get a cheap drum kit, put up a room mic, a kick drum mic, and a mic over the hi-hat/snare area. Play some basic beats with the recorder running. This allows you to get the old-school drum sound, but with new beats. Chop it up using your sampler, or use ReCycle to get individual drum samples that you can then sequence into new beats. Ideally, you'll use a mix of samples and modules to give you a mix of sounds.

If you're using modules like E-mu's Planet Phatt or the Alesis DM series, you may find that although they have a very clean sound, they sometimes lack a certain raw punch. On some tracks that I worked on with Kid Rock and DJ Kracker, we sampled Planet Phatt drum sounds into an MPC60, giving us the best of both worlds — access to hundreds of great sounds, and the instant grit that comes from the low-tech sampler in the MPC60. Plus, we could then create beats with the MPC's sequencer. Instant funk!

One DJ told me he didn't know why I bother creating original drum loops and samples, since there are so many records to bite. My reply was, "Where do you think those records came from?" Musicians played on all of those records. Remember that people sample those records for the sound, so if you can recreate the sound, you'll be more valuable to a wider range of artists — especially those who want the sounds and techniques of hip-hop applied to their original music. I also play guitar and bass in addition to drums and keyboards, but if you don't, then get some friends over and jam. You'll create that live vibe, too. Run a DAT while you're jamming, and you could end up with a sample CD's worth of original loops for the cost of pizza and beer.

Of course, you can always sample beats and grooves off of records, but you're running a huge legal risk unless you're taking literally one kick, one snare, and one hi-hat, and then making new patterns (even then, you may have to pay the piper if some astute person figures out the source of the sample). [*Editor's note: Also, sampling records creates licensing hassles, as explained in Chapter 4.*] Some DJs and producers pride themselves on sampling records and then modifying the samples until you can't easily recognize their source, but try getting your writing and engineering chops together. It's the way things are going anyway, and you'll be able to get the vintage sound while still applying your own creativity to the rhythm.

If you're having trouble getting "that" sound, try adding some vinyl noise to your loops. Some plug-in effects will do this, or you could drop the needle and sample the "silent" space between tracks. There are tons of sample CDs with the authentic vibe already built in. (The Vinylistics series, distributed by Big Fish Audio, is a popular choice.)

BEATS

How do you get a great beat? Well, I'm afraid you're on your own on this one. You simply can't fake the funk — beats are as individualistic as the people who program them. However, if you want some great examples, check out Track Masters, Jermaine Dupri, Premier, Timbaland, and pioneers like Rick Rubin and Dr. Dre. There are many more monsters out there; this is just a start.

What I can tell you is that the best beats are deceptively simple (Timbaland being an exception), and make you feel like moving. If your beat doesn't get heads rockin', try again. Like the great R&B drummers who have been sampled countless times, the feel is more important than the technique. Overly complex beats just don't work in this music, because the rapper's rhythms are often so complex. When you listen to old records from people like James Brown and Parliament, notice that what makes a record funky is the fact that the beats are simple, leaving room for the other instruments to provide syncopation.

Also listen to old-school drummers like Bernard "Pretty" Purdie, Yogi Thornton, and Steve Gadd, not to mention rock drummers like John Bonham. Check out the Meters and Neville Brothers records, Little Feat, and the Motown and Stax catalogs as well. Then try to create your own versions and process them with the techniques discussed in this book.

VOCALS

One popular approach to recording vocals is to go for a very dry sound. Hip-hop is often created on a budget, and there's not always the luxury of extensive outboard gear. If the vocalist is doing a rap, try a dynamic mic like the Shure SM57. It can be handheld (most MCs are used to holding their mikes, even in the studio), it has low handling noise, and can take a lot of level up close. It also has a nice proximity effect — the closer you get, the bassier the sound.

For singers, a condenser is always a good choice. Since these mikes are more sensitive, they can't take the up-close treatment, but they are better at capturing the nuances of a singer's performance. If you have a large or ambient room, you can also get the benefit of the natural "slap" of the space that you're working in. Personally, I use an SM57 as my favorite low-cost dynamic mic, and the Røde NT/2 as my low-cost condenser. Expensive mic preamps are great, but remember that many hit records are also made with nothing more exotic than the built-in preamps on Mackie mixers.

These are guidelines — experiment and use your ears as the final judge. Although most singers like condensers, Stevie Wonder made many of his classic records with an Electro-Voice RE20, and the great vocalist Anita Baker often uses a Shure SM57. These are both dynamic microphones, so if you can, try several mikes, because no two singers are alike.

No matter what style of music you do, if you're the producer or the engineer, it's important that you get the vocalist as comfortable as possible, or nothing will happen. The voice is the only truly one-of-a-kind instrument, and the quality of the sound and the performance of the vocalist can be influenced by the recording environment, both positively and negatively. So be prepared. Get a good vocal sound by working with the mic yourself or with a tech before the vocalist arrives. Most rappers, in particular, don't write their rhymes until the track is almost finished, and some just come in and "freestyle" on the spot. So it's up to you to be ready when they are.

The voice is a fragile thing, so a great vocal sound with a bit of ambience boosts confidence, both in their performance and in you and your skills as a recordist. Turn the lights down, have water (not ice-cold . . . tightens the throat), tea, and lemon slices around, and please keep extra people to an absolute minimum unless the vocalist wants it otherwise (most don't). The vibe is all-important. No musician should have to just fake their way through a performance, but a vocalist really can't. Make them comfortable, stay in record, and get out of the way . . . and you'll keep your job. I was once on a session with a big-name female singer, doing drum programming for some of the writing sessions for her most recent album. An engineer changed mikes in mid-session in an attempt to impress her with his "superior" knowledge. Her response was, "We don't need a new mic, we need a new engineer." Dead man, coming through.

November 2000
JIMMY JAM

Tell us about the Janet Jackson single "Doesn't Really Matter." How did you approach that song?

It sounds very sequenced, doesn't it? But I think the only thing we actually sequenced was the one little main part that doubles the melody, a vibes sound. What happened was, Alex, my drum programmer, was in town and we did the initial track. I told Janet I'd give it to her as it was and she could write to it, but she requested that we fill it out a little more. By then Alex had left town and I said, "I ain't hookin' up nothing. I'm just gonna play the stuff." Even though it has a very sequenced sound to it, it was mostly played live to tape.

MIXING

If you haven't already figured it out from what I've been saying, the overall sound of hip-hop is dry, slightly live, and heavy on the bass. This means that a minimum of effects are necessary. If your samples are tight and you have a well-recorded vocal, you'll find that mixing can be the most fun part of the session. If you've listened to some good hip-hop to tune your ears before mixing, chances are you're hearing the vocal with a bit of slap, the kick and snare way up front, and a very prominent bass (guitar or synth). Everything else becomes part of the overall texture, but doesn't disturb the groove.

Overall, hip-hop tracks are rather sparse, and this lean sound is another key to getting an authentic sound. If you add too much decoration it becomes more "pop" and will be considered "soft."

Rappers often double certain key words, either by themselves on another track, or they have a second rapper do the doubles. This technique comes from live rap, and so the double should be very prominent and sound distinctly different from the "lead" rapper. Sometimes, the double is timed to be more like an echo of the original line or word.

The most common effects in this style of music are gated reverb (for that live sound), distortion on certain vocal tracks, reversed snare hits, and slapback echo. Go to a hip-hop club and notice the live ambience. The idea is to recreate that club sound on your record.

If there is a sung hook, this is usually treated with some reverb and delay. I also like to patch in an Aphex Aural Exciter to give some sparkle to this "radio-friendly" element. This is also available as a plug-in for Pro Tools.

Some adventurous types are using vocoders on the vocals, and the old guitar "talk box" as well. These add a rock edge to a track, and can also hint at a more electro influence. You hear the vocoder up front and center on the Beastie Boys' "Intergalactic," to point out one example.

And let's not leave out compression. You can hit the compressor pretty hard in hip-hop, which makes a track sound more present and up-front. It can also be used to squash a too-clean sound into something a little more raw-sounding. Radio stations use a lot of compression in their broadcast to keep levels even, but the effect of this is a raw, aggressive sound. It can also be used to great effect on your mixes. It's especially useful on drums and to get those bass guitars and synths sounding nice and fat.

Most important, once you begin your mix, listen critically to hear whether your track turns you on in the same way that any big hip-hop album does. When I say listen critically, I mean it. A&R men are very busy, and very focused on what they want from a track. If they don't like it, it's off to the circular file, so be objective. Criticize your work as if it weren't your own. Treat your favorite records as your competition. If you can do this, your tracks will end up being listened to. If you let your weak spots slide, believe me, the A&R man won't. And there are very few second chances in the record business.

MORE LOW — END THEORY

Hip-hop recordings are well known for their heavy low end. This can be achieved by simply adding EQ to the overall mix (I often find that 250Hz is the "magic" frequency to pump up), plus using sounds with plenty of low beef, such as the classic 808 drum sounds. If you don't have an 808, there are plenty of sample CDs available, plus my personal favorite, Propellerhead ReBirth software [*Editor's note: ReBirth is now available as a free download from www.rebirthmuseum.com.*] This great application runs on both Mac and Windows systems, plus there are many "mods" available that change the sounds but keep the basic operating interface, which has the appearance of an 808 plus two [Roland] TB-303s, a mixer, delay, and distortion.

Another approach is to pump the mix through some big speakers and use a microphone to re-record it. Back in the '90s, I worked with Terence Trent D'arby on a song for the soundtrack of the film *The Fan*. The entire original track minus vocals was pumped into a large room and re-recorded with a basic condenser mic onto another track, and then the new track was mixed in judiciously.

You can do the same thing by putting a speaker into a bathroom or staircase and recording it. The combination of low end and ambience is what makes this sound work, unlike EQ alone. You can add extra EQ to the low end and then patch in a touch of reverb with a gated effect. Whichever technique you try, the overall result should be a boomier and more "live"-sounding low end, much like the hyped-up car stereos that you hear in SUVs on the street. That's why they often call it a "Jeep" mix.

PEACE

There you have it. We've covered a lot of ground, but the main thing I'd like you to remember is that hip-hop is a music with a vibe and culture all its own. The way to make better tracks is to listen and to keep practicing. Go for the feel; this is not about chops. And best of all, it doesn't require buckets of money and a state-of-the-art facility. It just needs you and your heart.

Thanks for dropping by the Temple of Hip-Hop. You are always welcome.

Chapter 6
VOCALS

Unless you specialize in instrumentals or dub remixes, vocals are going to be the centerpiece of your remixes. There are many different components to crafting a killer vocal track, from arranging and comping the various vocals to time-stretching or compressing and exotic editing techniques that will make your track stand out in a set.

Let's begin with Rob McGaughey's deep insights into building the foundation for a good vocal.

September 1999
Editing Vocal Tracks
Creating the perfect comp

Getting the perfect take from a performer can be a real challenge for a recording engineer. Not only are there the technical issues such as microphone selection, level settings, and appropriate processing to deal with, but you also need to be concerned with the musical quality of the performance itself. Nowhere is this more of a concern than when tracking vocals. Is the performer on pitch? [*Editor's note: Today, Antares Auto-Tune or Celemony Melodyne can fix bad pitch.*] How's their tone? Can you understand the words? How's the phrasing? The list of concerns goes on and on.

One way to address these questions is to use the editing tools at your disposal to perfect a good performance. I'm not suggesting that editing can (or should) take the place of a decent performance, but using your tools to enhance a track can be an effective way to make a good performance even better. The worst case is that you'll find yourself basically creating a performance from the ground up. More commonly you'll be fixing a word here and there, perhaps cleaning up a flubbed phrase or fixing the occasional out-of-tune note. There's a side bonus to working this way: Once your performer knows that the pressure to deliver one perfect take has been removed, he or she will often relax and give you better, more consistent tracks to work with — a decided advantage.

Many products on the market offer waveform editing and/or volume automation appropriate for this kind of work. Digital audio sequencers and hard disk recording systems include editing capabilities. A number of self-contained digital recorder/mixers also offer this functionality. These are extremely powerful tools if you know how to get the most out of them. Here are a few tips targeted at editing vocal tracks, although they can be applied to instrumental tracks as well.

GETTING STARTED

The first step is to create a composite vocal track that contains the best overall performance. This process consists of recording multiple takes of a part and then editing (cutting/copying/pasting) the best verse, chorus, phrases, words, and/or syllables together onto a new track to create the best-sounding performance pos-

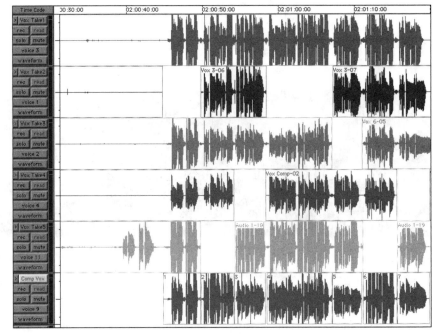

Figure 6-1
Comping together a track from various vocal takes. In this case, the bottom track has been assembled from pieces of the top five tracks. You can see where sections have been cut and dragged down to the bottom track.

sible (see Figure 6-1). As you're listening to the various recorded tracks, trying to select the best performance for each segment, pay particular attention to pitch, energy, timbre, and performance quality. These are often difficult or impossible to fix later (although there are some good pitch-correction utilities available). Audio problems such as clicks and pops are easier to fix than musical imperfections; the main goal at this point is to put together a good performance.

Copy and paste editing is an art form that can seem difficult and incredibly time-consuming at first, but the more you do it the faster you'll get. Eventually you'll be able to make edits by looking at waveforms without even listening to them — always use your ears as the final quality check, though. Some suggestions:

■ Where possible, perform edits starting and ending at silent spots in the track.
■ If you can't edit at a silent point, and you have the ability to zoom in on a track down to the sample level, be sure to start and end edits at zero crossings. (A zero crossing is the

Figure 6-2
If you must edit in the middle of a waveform (rather than at a silence), try to place the edit in/out points at zero crossings — the points where the waveform crosses the center line from positive to negative or vice versa.

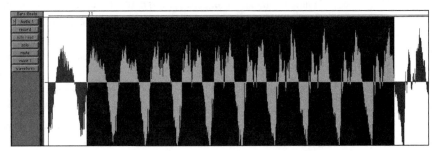

Figure 6-3
Your audio editor's crossfade function can help smooth over rough edit points by fading out one segment while fading another in.

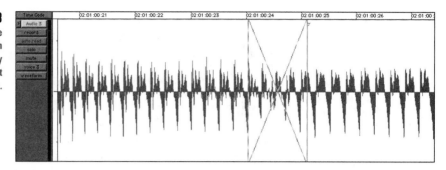

Figure 6-4
If your audio editor doesn't support crossfades, you can accomplish much the same thing using automation. The lower track's fade-out is offset slightly from the corresponding fade-in above it to avoid a noticeable volume drop where the two curves overlap.

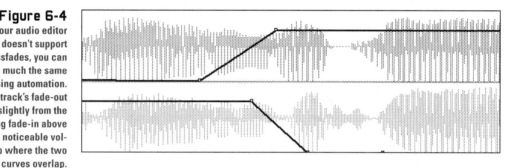

point where the waveform crosses the center line on the waveform display from positive to negative, or vice versa; see Figure 6-2.) This will prevent clicks when two audio segments are pasted together.

■ If you'll be copy/pasting phrases together end-to-end, it can be helpful to edit on a beat. This will help preserve the original timing/groove and can also help you keep track of where things go as you're moving audio segments around.

■ Sometimes, no matter how carefully you copy and paste, you'll still hear the edit points in a track. In these cases, crossfading can be used to make the edits less noticeable. A crossfade is where you fade out one segment while fading in another (see Figure 6-3). When you're working with tight edits inside a phrase, the crossfades can be extremely short — as little as a few milliseconds. Many digital audio editors offer crossfading as a feature and some even do this automatically when you cut/paste audio. If your editor doesn't have this feature but does have volume automation, then you can do the same thing using complementary volume curves across two tracks (see Figure 6-4).

CLEAN-UP & DYNAMICS

Once the ultimate composite track is created, I like to start cleaning things up at the macro level and then work down to the details as I go. I start by editing out breathing and other extraneous noises in the dead spaces between phrases. You can use volume automation or actually cut (delete) the dead space to accomplish this task. I prefer to use volume automation, as you can fade in and out so as to be less abrupt (see Figure 6-5). Even if you're editing out extremely low-level noise, an abrupt edit may be noticeable when played back against

Figure 6-5

Using automation to control dynamics and to clean up the spaces between phrases. Note that the garbage between the phrases hasn't been completely cut out; letting a bit of it slip through in the background results in a more natural-sounding track. Automation has also been used in place of compression in the second and last phrases, and the first word has a slight fade-in that reduces a troublesome "s" sound.

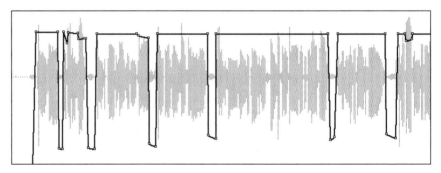

other tracks. If you have a vocal track with some background noise that's noticeable by its absence when it's automated out, then try reducing its volume in the dead spaces by 30–40dB rather than completely cutting it out.

The next step is to use volume automation to control dynamics. If you've comped tracks together, you may find that the volume of various phrases and words jumps up and down. You could try using a compressor to correct this problem, but I often get better results using automation. In many cases a little of both automation and compression is the best answer.

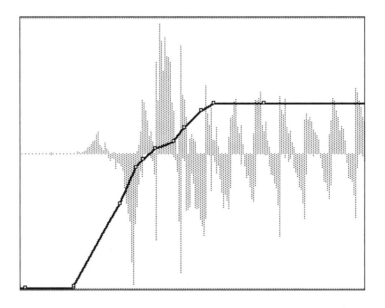

Figure 6-6

Using automation to reduce an overly strong "s" at the beginning of a word.

You can also use volume automation to reduce pops and other unwanted vocal noises. A common problem is sibilance (overly strong "s"-type sounds) at the beginning of a word. Sibilance is visible in a waveform display as transient spikes, and can be controlled by using volume automation to slightly fade into the word (see Figure 6-6).

A method for removing clicks and pops is to redraw waveforms. Some digital audio editors offer the ability to zoom down to the sample level and to redraw the waveform with a pencil tool. This can be an effective way of recovering what might be otherwise unusable tracks. When you look at audio while zoomed in down to the sample level, clicks and pops will stand out as abrupt spikes. Use the pencil tool to redraw the distorted portion of the waveform to look more like the sections immediately preceding and following it. Be careful when redrawing waveforms, as this is destructive editing, which means it's permanent. It's a good idea to make a backup copy of the track as a safeguard before attempting to redraw a waveform.

One last tip on editing vocals: Most digital editors allow you to move an audio track, or pieces of an audio track, in relation to others. This can be useful with a vocalist who has a less-than-impeccable sense of time (trust me, they're out there). Try nudging a word or two forward or backward in its track to help correct a phrase that sounds rushed, or work with phrases to pull a lazy vocal track into time.

While it's always best if you can capture a great take from your vocalist or musician, many times it just doesn't happen. Next time you're in that situation, rather than slaving endlessly trying to get your performer to deliver perfection, put your audio editing tools to work and see if you can't comp, automate, crossfade, and redraw the track to clean up subtle problems and tighten up sections of a performance. A great performance may be just a few mouse clicks away!

Going through the raw vocals for a remix can often yield more surprises than a box of chocolates. You honestly never know what a label is going to send you. Doug Beck has been there, and this piece should help give you the technical coping skills to deal with some worst-case scenarios.

August 2001
Vocal Tricks
What to do with over- or underproduced source material

One of the best things about producing dance music is the freedom to approach vocals in interesting and creative ways. Unrestrained from many conventions of pop production and traditional song structures, a dance music producer can routinely push beyond the usual vocal boundaries. In dance music production, for example, it's common to treat a vocal line like a synth part, even processing it beyond recognition. It's this interplay between the voice as an organic and as a synthetic instrument that makes vocal production one of the most satisfying aspects of producing dance music.

For all the creative latitude, however, your dealings with vocals in the studio can be fraught with landmines. Here are some of the pitfalls I've encountered, and some solutions that may help you.

OVERPRODUCED SOURCE MATERIAL
One difficulty I least expected when I started remixing was the "problematic *a cappella*." These basically fall into two categories: overproduced and underproduced. By overpro-

duced, I mean the *a cappella* is the stereo vocal track from the single, complete with sparkling, cavernous reverb, plus background vocal parts blended in, overlapping vocal phrases that would be much more workable if they were isolated. And no, you can't complain to the A&R person at the record company that you need the master reels and a budget for studio time so you can get the tracks you really want in a format that will make your job a lot easier. (Nor can you ask Shania or Mya to come over to sing the tracks you need.) You're stuck with this stereo vocal track. Here's what to try.

Before addressing any time-compression/expansion issues, I process the stereo vocal track through a stereo compressor and gate. Though there are no hard-and-fast rules to follow, the idea is to set the compressor and the gate to a point where the dynamics of the reverb effect are minimized. The amount of compression and the gate timing will of course vary, based on the amount and type of reverb used and the natural dynamics of the vocal part. You may find you need to adjust the settings for different parts of the song. In this case I usually make several passes as I record the vocal with different compression and gate settings, and then cut and paste the best-sounding sections of each pass into one stereo track.

Now that the vocals are "drier," I decide which sections, if any, can be put into mono. I strongly recommend this for parts where the lead vocal is mostly soloed, without excessive or prominent background harmony vocal parts (doubled melody is usually okay). For sections with prominent background vocals, try putting each section into mono, and listen carefully for phasing or other audio anomalies. Also, take the time to focus on whether the lead vocal melody seems more "up front" in the mix when the part is in mono. When you eventually mix the record, you can decide whether or not the lead vocal needs to stand out a bit more, or a bit less, relative to the background parts. I've also tried — albeit with varying degrees of success — layering the now mono track with the stereo track. This generally has the effect of thickening the vocals, which can be useful to contrast with an otherwise minimal track with a lot of available space in the midrange.

After time-compressing and locking up the various parts of the vocal to your track, you are free to experiment with all the wild effects you want. If there is still some residual reverb from the original vocal and you want to decrease it more, consider that a slight amount of distortion and over-compression tend to make the vocals seem more dry.

UNDERPRODUCED SOURCE MATERIAL

The "underproduced" *a cappella*, on the other hand, is essentially a single pass for every vocal track on the master reel, with no effects and tons of dead space. Aside from the painstaking process of locking up so many individual tracks to reconstruct the vocal arrangement, pitch problems that were corrected with Antares Auto-Tune during the mixing of the original single can suddenly appear. While I refuse to name names, let me just say that Auto-Tune has been a godsend for many a big-name vocalist, and for this producer as well. Before it was available, I would put the problem vocal parts in my audio editor, cut a phrase into small pieces, pitch-shift each piece to whatever degree was necessary, and splice words and phrases back together. (This is essentially what Auto-Tune accomplishes, but it does so instantly, thus saving me hours of very tedious editing.) I recommend obtaining a copy of the original single and learning the structure of the song, which will makes reconstructing the vocal arrangement much easier.

So what would the perfect *a cappella* contain? Ideally, I'd like a single mono pass of the lead vocal, in tune and in time, dry except for compression and perhaps minimal EQ. Any overlapping lead vocal tracks would be separate passes. If the background vocals were meant to be stacked in stereo and possibly doubled, I'd want a stereo pass of those tracks, but with no effects and no lead vocal in the mix. I'd especially like to have any interesting out-takes that never made it on the single, such as spoken words or sounds captured during the recording, and alternate takes that are more vampy or experimental. I'd also like to have "signature" musical parts isolated, such as a keyboard hook, a cool bass lick, or a prominent guitar line.

There are many factors unique to working with vocals in the dance music arena. The tools and technology available to us present opportunities for unprecedented creativity, as well as new difficulties and challenges to overcome. I would urge aspiring remixers and producers to explore working with *a cappella* vocals as much as possible, so you're ready when opportunities present themselves. I'm often asked about how to obtain an *a cappella* vocal. One easy place to find them is on vinyl or CD dance singles, which sometimes contain a partial or complete *a cappella* vocal track.

The marriage of a great vocal and a slamming track can be a powerful, magical thing. The more proficient you become at dealing with the dilemmas inherent in vocal production, the more your ideas will shine.

April 2004
CRYSTAL METHOD

Though their gear list includes some venerable vintage synths, the Crystal Method has managed to incorporate some recent innovations into their live and studio rigs, too. "With the Roland V-Synth," says Jordan, "we use the VariPhrase technology and the new filters. We took vocal samples that we already had in tracks and dropped them on the V-Synth, where we'd twist them up in very musical ways."

Good time-stretching and compression skills are the key to getting a vocal to work at your chosen tempo, but it's not just a matter of speeding or slowing the tempo in your DAW.

Regardless of whether you appreciate her contributions to modern pop music, it's hard to deny the phenomenal success of Britney Spears' seemingly endless stream of Top 10 *Billboard* Dance hits, so what better way to learn the essentials of adjusting a complex vocal than to find out how Doug Beck handled his Britney remix?

August 2002
Remixing Britney Spears
The impossible tempo and the temperamental a cappella

One of the most exciting moments for a producer/ remixer is when you're offered a remix project for a major artist — the kind of celebrity that everyone from your two-year-old niece to your grandmother recognizes. A celebrity so big that they even have a computer virus named after them. On the other hand, one of the worst moments you can experience is when you receive the *a cappella* (solo vocal) from such an artist, and you realize it may not work as a remix. It's either too slow to speed up or too fast to slow down: the tempo falls into that impossible range of 85 to 100 bpm. It's enough to make any seasoned remixer wince with pain, and a novice may just give up altogether.

Don't be too quick to give up. I find myself in these situations from time to time, but through countless hours of audio editing, I've found some ways to make even the most problematic *a cappellas* work. (That's not to suggest I'm successful 100% of the time, but I've sometimes succeeded when others have thrown in the towel.)

One recent challenge came courtesy of Britney Spears, when we were called upon by her label to remix her hit ballad "Not a Girl, Not Yet a Woman." Why, one might ask, would a perfectly respectable major-label record company even want to turn a sappy teen ballad into an uptempo dance record? It's important to remember that a dance remix can spread the appeal of a single, extend the life of the record on the charts, and hopefully cross it over to dance-format radio stations where such a song would not ordinarily get any spins. The record label, most of the time, doesn't even consider the tempo; they're just counting on you to help them achieve their marketing goals. If you can make this happen, you've got the edge. And all you need is an audio editing program that you're comfortable with, and plenty — and I mean plenty — of patience.

Any time you time-stretch/compress a vocal, especially when you have a considerable distance to go in tempo, your success depends on the tone and other unique qualities of a singer's voice. A vocalist who uses a lot of vibrato is going to give you more problems than one who doesn't. The tone of a singer's voice is a little trickier: You never really know how a particular vocal track is going to handle the time compression or expansion without actually trying it. It's also better to ask if the *a cappella* is available dry (no effects). Many times, when a studio is preparing an *a cappella* for remixing, you can request that they print it dry. The vocals will be easier to work with if you also request that the lead vocal be provided separately from any background vocal tracks. If there are many background parts, it's nice to get them comped (mixed down to a stereo track). Otherwise, it may be a real pain for you to match up, line up, then mix down six or eight different harmony parts from the individual vocal tracks. The comped backgrounds can save you an enormous amount of programming time, and there is really no downside to asking if it's available to you.

In the case of Britney's ballad, the original track was at 90 bpm. We wanted to get the vocal up to at least 125 bpm. Unfortunately, at 125 bpm the vocal sounded way too wobbly and effected. At 120 bpm, however, I found that the vocal sounded much better, with the exception of the longer, held-out notes and the ends of phrases that contained a lot of vibrato. I knew I could get away with a little weirdness in the vocal here and there (the track would mask some of it). But at the ends of phrases, a quirky vibrato would be way too noticeable and artificial-sounding. I knew I had some surgery to perform to get an acceptable vocal track.

Short of getting Britney in to re-sing the parts, here's what I decided to try. I took the 120 bpm vocal, chopped the audio file up into small words and phrases, and shifted the individual pieces around in a 125 bpm Cubase audio/MIDI session. After a couple of hours of painstakingly cutting and nudging the tiny pieces of audio, I finally had the vocal locked up nicely to a kick and hat pattern at 125 bpm. Everything sounded pretty good, except for the longer held-out notes and those ending phrases with vibrato. To remedy this, I experimented with the original 90 bpm *a cappella*, time-compressing it to several different tempos to see exactly how far I could speed it up without noticing any problem with longer notes and end phrases. After a few tries, I found that 100 bpm was as close as I was going to get, and it was still 25 bpm away from where it needed to be. Ouch!

Next, I took the new 100 bpm file and imported it into my session onto a track right below the vocal track I'd previously locked to 125 bpm. In the audio editor section of Cubase, I opened both of the tracks and sized the windows so I could work with the files simultaneously. I listened to the 125 bpm track from the top, and when I got to a long note or phrase that sounded bad, I chopped it out. Then I found the same part on the 100 bpm vocal. Because I had placed both tracks on top of one another in the audio editor, it was never too hard to find the part I was looking for. Once I located it, I cut and pasted it into the 125 bpm vocal track. Because of its much slower tempo, the substituted part now needed some serious editing. The notes were too long, sometimes running into the next line.

October 1999

THUNDERPUSS

Top remixers from pole to pole agree that vocals are paramount when it comes to crafting a righteous radio mix. Thunderpuss is no exception. Their remixes are chock-full of creative and catchy vocal effects. But before any cutting, pasting, or processing is performed, Barry Harris and Chris Cox spend hours massaging the *a cappella*. Chris explains: "Whenever possible, we use the dry version of the vocal and the separate background [harmony] tracks, because we often change the structure and the chord progression. We might darken things from major to minor, and if you're married to chords because of background vocals, you're stuck. Also, if you use a vocal that's wet, it doesn't time-compress as well. Dry, mono files compress a lot nicer."

Chris and Barry have discovered a clever solution for getting smooth time-compressed tracks. "The biggest problem with time compression is sustained notes," says Chris. "Take the Whitney Houston remix we just did, 'My Love Is Your Love.' It's at 82 bpm, a reggae record, and we had to turn it into a 128 bpm dance record. So if you were to time-compress that file and just throw it on as is, you're gonna hear — no disrespect — Stevie Nicks–meets–Belinda Carlisle 'billy goat' vibrato on the sustained notes. So Barry came up with an ingenious idea of comping [cross-cutting] the original and compressed tracks." "What I do," explains Barry, "is I put both the original 88 bpm track and the time-compressed track in [Mark of the Unicorn] Digital Performer. Then, listening to the 128 bpm track, I start replacing the sustained notes [in the time-compressed track] with the original ones. Whenever she sounds like a billy goat, that's when I comp." They also perform three-stage comps when necessary. Using the Whitney track as an example, they'd create a 108 and 128 bpm compressed version of the original, and then choose replacement notes from either the 88 or 108 bpm version — whichever sounded best. At times they've gone so far as to replace single syllables from words. Tedious, but it paid off.

This is where things got a bit tricky. I needed the end of the phrase to sound natural and end on the right beat. The only way to do this was to chop out a section from the middle of the substituted note, then shift the end section of the note back together with the beginning of the note. In other words, I had shortened the length of the note by slicing a chunk out of the middle to make it fit. I went through the entire lead vocal, line by line, and performed this same surgery every time I didn't like a long note.

After I finished with the lead vocal, I used the same process with the background vocal tracks. It took the better part of ten hours to cut, paste, nudge, and crossfade, but in the end it worked. I now had a usable, natural-sounding *a cappella* vocal at the target tempo of 125 bpm.

Obviously, this was one of our more extreme cases, and fortunately it doesn't happen all that often. It's reassuring to know there are so many incredible software and hardware tools available that can make almost anything possible in the world of audio editing, if you're willing to take the time and apply the technology to whatever audio problem you're facing. Still, every time a new project comes in, the first words out of my mouth are, "What's the original tempo?"

Used properly, pitch quantization and time-stretching can make a vocal fit your remix. Used *improperly*, they're fantastic ways to really mangle a voice and trip out your dancefloor. Here's my take on some of the more popular ways to process the human voice.

April 2002
Vocal Processing, Part I
Three techniques worth singing about

From a whisper to a scream — and everything in between — the human voice can convey more emotion in a single measure than even the most carefully crafted arpeggio or bass riff. Best of all, that emotion can often be harnessed and shaped via modern processing tools.

The trick is finding the right processor for the vocalist. Some voices benefit from effects that subtly support and reinforce the performance, whereas others shine when morphed beyond recognition. In this article we'll be looking at several approaches to creatively integrating the human voice into today's dance tracks.

PITCH QUANTIZATION
Few vocal effects have taken the music world by storm as effectively as pitch quantization. One of the most popular examples of this technology is Antares' award-winning Auto-Tune. Available as both a plug-in and a rackmount hardware unit, Auto-Tune can pitch-correct a questionable vocal performance, with minimal artifacts.

The way pitch quantization works is fairly straightforward. The user selects the song's key and mode, giving the processor a reference for applying the effect. Then, a vocal or instrument performance is scanned and the pitches are detected in real time. The pitch quantizer remaps the original pitches to the selected key, adjusting any offending notes while maintaining the formant characteristics of the original. Generally, the sensitivity and reaction time can be independently adjusted, so results can range from subtle and realistic to completely electronic. In some configurations, the effect is nearly transparent, giving the impression of flawless intonation.

While pitch quantization is handy for polishing lackluster vocals, the dance community has gone hog wild over Auto-Tune's ability to radically transform voices, giving sung — or even spoken — performances an otherworldly and decidedly cybernetic sheen. Arguably, the first mainstream dance track to popularize pitch quantization was Cher's "Believe." (Interestingly, some reports attribute the "Believe" effect to DigiTech's Talker pedal, but the end result is nearly indistinguishable from Auto-Tune.) More recent examples of this effect include Eiffel 65's "Blue" and Daft Punk's "One More Time" and "Digital Love."

More outrageous effects can be achieved by quantizing the vocal pitches to musically unrelated scales or by limiting the number of mapped pitches to three or four notes in the song's key. To emphasize the effect, some artists intentionally sing out-of-tune and include wild vibrato or sweeps in pitch, as these flourishes generate pitch-perfect glissandos and trills.

The latest round of computer processing tools has taken pitch quantization even further. Celemony Melodyne offers a revolutionary sequencer-like interface for arranging, re-pitching, and rephrasing multiple monophonic audio passages simultaneously. Tools like this allow producers to play new melodies or even chords with the recorded audio. Hardware fanatics can find similar functionality in Roland's VP-9000 and the latest versions of DigiTech's venerable Vocalist.

THE VOCODER

The vocoder has become a staple for processing vocals and thickening harmonies. The effect is immediately recognizable, with results ranging from hard robot voices (Afrika Bambaataa's "Planet Rock" is a good example) to shimmery synthetic choirs (the Cars, ELO, and the Buggles have all used vocoders to support and emphasize their background vocals).

Despite the ongoing popularity of the vocoder in modern dance music, Bell Labs originally created the vocoding effect in the 1940s as a possible means of compressing spoken material for transmission over phone lines!

While countless records have explored the more obvious uses of vocoding, I still routinely apply the effect to support lead vocals by doubling the vocal melody on a bright, sawtooth synth patch and using the lead vocal to modulate the vocoder's filter array. Subtly blending the vocoded result with the original performance adds a richness and depth to the vocals that's hard to duplicate by other means.

TIME COMPRESSION/EXPANSION

Time-stretching, as it's commonly referred to, allows you to modify the duration and timing of a recording without adjusting the pitch. Often, changing the tempo of a song for a remix is crucial to making it work on a dancefloor, as modern trance and house tempos start at 128 bpm.

Savvy users may have already discovered that expanding a track too greatly can add flanger-esque artifacts to the processed signal. If the objective is to retain the original performance's sound and character, these artifacts are often unacceptable. But if you're looking for a funkalicious effect to mangle and shape your vocals, time-stretching selected passages can add spice to an otherwise straightforward vocal.

Generally, expanding the length of a vocal to extreme ranges will yield the most interesting effects. The trick is making sure the results can be used in a musically relevant manner by experimenting on various sections of your track. I've found that legato passages and flowing rhythms work better than staccato, *sprechstimme* parts, as vocals with a lot of plosive consonants don't often survive the stretching process.

As you experiment, pay close attention to how the new phrasing relates to the rhythm and tempo of your track. Quite often, you can change the note durations of a phrase in a manner that makes sense in context of the song, without necessarily matching the rhythm of the original performance. Once you have a few vocal segments that work with your mix, sprinkle them throughout the track as transitions or breakdowns. Alternately, loop the stretched vocal, muffle it with a lowpass filter, and use it as a nested element that can be brought in and out of the mix by adjusting the cutoff frequency, panning, and/or volume.

So next time you're working with a vocal performance that needs a little "something extra," don't just slather on the reverb and delay. Grab that voice and make it yours.

Once your main vocals are in tune, in time and in place, it's time to start having real fun with the incidental parts. Here's one of my time-tested ways to trick out your extra vocal bits.

June 2002
Vocal Processing
What is digital glossolalia?

In the words of Dr. William T. Samarin, professor of anthropology and linguistics at the University of Toronto, "Glossolalia consists of strings of meaningless syllables made up of sounds taken from those familiar to the speaker and put together more or less haphazardly. . . . Glossolalia is language-like because the speaker unconsciously wants it to be language-like. Yet in spite of superficial similarities, glossolalia fundamentally is not language."

Glossolalia is often used to describe the vocalizations of the "speaking in tongues" trance state experienced by charismatic evangelists. It is also used to refer to the sacred utterances of various Native American shaman/priests.

What the heck does this have to do with remixing, you ask? Well, for one thing, most divas sound amazing when singing in glossolalia! One of my favorite vocal tricks involves taking a straightforward vocal and mutating it into a scat-like performance by intelligently slicing and dicing the syllables, then rearranging the components into an entirely new melody that can be used as a breakdown or transition, or even form the basis for a dub version of the remix. The best part of this technique is that it can be accomplished with hardware or software, using a sampler, digital recorder (with cut-and-paste functions), or full-blown audio sequencer.

WITH A SAMPLER

Begin by recording your vocal passage into the sampler. There's no need to capture the entire song. A single verse, chorus, or even a couple of lines will suffice. Once you have the vocals sampled, copy the entire vocal sample — as separate data — to several adjacent keys in your keymap. Don't simply assign the same sample to different keys. I like to use at least six to eight keys so there are more elements to play with.

Once the sample is copied and each instance assigned to a key, open your sample editor and adjust the start points so each sample begins at a different point in the vocal performance. In order to get the best results, try to avoid starting the sample at the beginning of a word. Instead, look for interesting syllables in the middle of words. Better yet, add a few ad-libbed bits like "uh" or "woo" if they're available. If you're running out of sample memory, set end-points for each of the segments (make sure you have enough material), then delete the unused parts of the sample using the truncate function.

When you're done with this process, you should have a series of pitched non-words loosely resembling your original vocal. Here's where the fun begins.

Create a new sequencer track for your sampler and start overdubbing your sequence — minus the original vocals. While entering your most Zen-like musical state, bang away at the keys. Play riffs, trills, whatever. Throw away your preconceptions and just flow. If you've set everything up correctly, you'll come across a pattern that makes sense both musically and rhythmically. Ideally, this pattern should be no longer than two measures. One-bar riffs work best for my personal style, but anything goes with modern electronica. Save this track, then cut and paste it wherever you want extra vocal spice.

WITH AN AUDIO SEQUENCER

This approach is considerably easier than working with a sampler, while also offering the ability to experiment visually with your vocal riff.

■ Create a new audio track in your sequence and import a copy of the lead vocal to this track. The copy should be aligned so it remains in time with the arrangement.

■ Now set your arrangement editor to snap parts to eighth- or sixteenth-note values. Using the scissors tool (Cubase, Logic, Sonar, and Pro Tools all include this feature), cut the vocal part into snippets of varying sizes, making sure to avoid complete words or phrases. The snipped bits should be long enough to capture the pitches, but short enough to be unidentifiable.

The resulting snips might look like Figure 6-7:

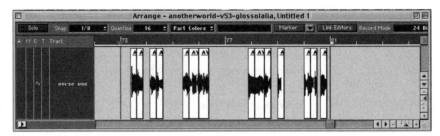

Figure 6-7

- Audition each snippet and delete the ones that sound rough. This should leave at least five or six samples to play with. More is better.
- Now put on your well-worn Zen baseball cap, set your loop points to a two-bar loop, and start the sequence. While the sequence plays, rearrange your vocal bits, listening to how they interact with each other. Eventually, you'll hear a tasty riff and shriek, "Eureka!"

The resulting rearranged snippets might look like Figure 6-8:

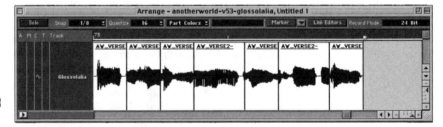

Figure 6-8

BUT WAIT, THERE'S MORE!

If all went well, you should have your vocalist "singing in tongues" and sounding like a digitally mutated Ella Fitzgerald. But don't stop there. Echo and reverb often sound good on parts like this, but you can get even more outlandish results by inserting a swept resonant filter, phaser, or flanger plug-in on the "glossolized" vocal. I just used this trick on my remix

August 2000
CHICANE

Great vocal processing on "Don't Give Up." You used Prosoniq's Orange Vocoder plug-in for that, right?
Yeah, but it's a fucking madman of a plug-in [*laughs*]. It has a complete mind of its own. Maybe it was because I was running everything VST off the processor, I'm not sure, but every once in a while it would go completely haywire. It would do all sorts of weird things. You'd have it playing right, and then it would go ballistic. It might decide to hold on a chord or go absolutely mad with distortion flying out of it. Or I might save it, and it wouldn't come back right. But eventually, when I got it to work, it was pretty cool.

What gave you the idea to vocode Bryan's vocals?
I'd discussed with him that it was always going to be a Chicane record. With Bryan's vocals being so distinctive, we didn't want it to come across sounding like a Bryan Adams record. We didn't want something where as soon as you heard the voice it was like, "Oh, that's Bryan Adams." So there's an element of disguise in there. I played around with it in different ways. The sound in the choruses is different than the sound in the verses, but, truth be told, the number-one reason for that is because the vocoder fucked up. Not any real deep meaningful artis-

of Beborn Beton's "Another World," applying a phaser to the result. The effect sounded wonderful. Spaced out, yet catchy. Yeehaw!

From electro to trance to hip-hop, vocoders are great way to freak a vocal track. That said, getting the most from a vocoder requires a bit of research and experimentation. In this piece, Jim Aikin rips away the curtain and shows you exactly how to implement this effect in your mixes.

August 2000
How Does a Vocoder Work?
Speak slowly and clearly into the device

A vocoder is not a very complicated device. You'll run into an assortment of bells and whistles on some models, but at its core the concept is simple. A vocoder splits a signal up into a number of narrow frequency bands, processes the bands separately, and then mixes them again into a single composite signal at the output.

THE FREQUENCY SPECTRUM

Before we get into the details, let's do a quick review on the nature of sound. Any sound can be analyzed as consisting of a number of sine waves at various frequencies and amplitudes. A sine wave is a tone that has no overtones: it's very pure, and has a colorless sound.

The frequency of an audio sine wave is measured in cycles per second — a quantity referred to as Hertz (abbreviated Hz). Higher frequencies are measured in kiloHertz (kHz), a term that means "thousands of Hertz." The lowest frequencies we can hear are in the 20Hz range, and the highest are somewhere between 15kHz and 20kHz.

Most sounds contain a number of sine wave overtones (also called partials) at various frequencies and various amplitudes. ("Amplitude" is a fancy word for loudness.) In the case

---

tic reason, it's just that I couldn't get the Orange to behave the same way twice. Rather irritating.

Do you recall what vocoder settings you were using?
I generally just pissed about with it. I'm very messy with the way I use my instruments and effects, really. If you asked me what I did a day after I did it, I probably couldn't tell you. I'm terrible with trying to remember my settings; I'm quite organic in the studio. What I can tell you is that on the vocoder plug-in itself is a little keyboard, and I input chords in reference to the key changes on the track.

Given the complications you described, did you have to capture the vocoder output to another source, for example, and then re-record the best bits?
Yeah, I had to do that in the end, because it was driving me completely skippy, so I put it on DAT and ended up winging it back into the computer. And also, it's mixed again with the normal [unprocessed] vocal. That worked out, because you get the best of both worlds. I mean, you get a bit of the disguised sound, but also you need to understand what's being said, so mixing the two together accomplished that.

March 1998
THE ANGEL

Angel developed several patches for the Alesis Quadraverb 2: "Some of them are vocal enhancer-type things, but there are a couple that are pretty tripped out, the kind of things you couldn't use on a regular basis." One of her programming tricks is to use plain old '60s guitar stompboxes in addition to her newer Symetrix 606 F/x Delay. "I have a whole bunch of guitar effects, cheap little pedals," she says. "But they all do something really special to a sound. I will literally use any effect on anything that I'm inspired to. People will be like, 'Oh my God, you can't put a vocal through that thing!' And I'll be like, 'Really?'"

of a pitched sound such as a piano, trumpet, violin, or square wave oscillator, the frequencies of the overtones tend to be whole-number multiples of the lowest frequency in the sound, which is called the fundamental. For example, a pitched sound with a fundamental of 200Hz would most likely have overtones at 400Hz, 600Hz, 800Hz, 1,000Hz, and so on.

We perceive pitched sounds as having the pitch of the fundamental. The higher overtones are not usually perceived separately. Instead, our ear blends them into a composite tone. The tone color, which is what allows us to figure out whether we're hearing a violin, oboe, trumpet, or human voice, is caused largely by the particular combination of overtones in the sound, and the changes in amplitude of the various overtones over time. For instance, when a guitar is picked, there's a burst of very high-frequency overtones (the sound of the pick) that dies out very quickly. The lower overtones, which are generated by the ringing string, die out more slowly. We can describe this phenomenon by saying that each overtone has its own amplitude envelope.

THE COMPONENTS

A vocoder uses three essential components — bandpass filters, envelope followers, and amplifiers. Let's look at each of these in turn.

When a signal is sent to a bandpass filter, the filter allows only the frequencies within a selected band to pass through. All other frequencies are blocked. For example, a bandpass

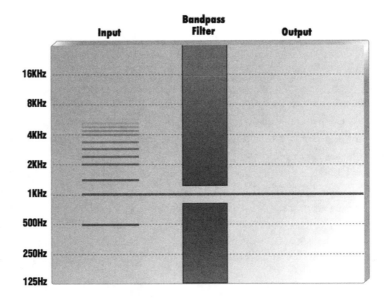

Figure 6-9
A bandpass filter allows sound energy to pass only if it is within a given frequency band. Here, the input of the bandpass filter consists of a tone whose fundamental is at 500Hz. The overtones are at 1kHz, 1.5kHz, 2kHz, and so on. But only the 1kHz overtone passes through the bandpass filter.

filter might be set to allow frequencies between 800 and 1,200Hz to pass through. Lower frequencies (such as 500Hz), and higher ones (such as 2,000Hz) will be blocked by this particular filter.

This example is slightly artificial. It's not practical to build a real filter in such a way that the sound energy at 799Hz is blocked while the energy at 801Hz is allowed to pass through the filter. A real filter will have a rolloff slope, which means that frequencies outside of the band will be attenuated (reduced in loudness) by an amount that depends on how far outside the band they are. If the rolloff slope is 24dB per octave and the bandpass filter's passband is between 800 and 1,200Hz, then the sound energy at 400Hz (one octave below 800Hz) will be reduced in level by 24dB. The steepness of the rolloff slope is one of the factors that affects how a vocoder sounds.

To continue our example, let's see what happens when we send a musical tone with a fundamental of 500Hz and a number of overtones through this bandpass filter. As shown in Figure 6-9, the fundamental (500Hz) will be mostly filtered out, because the lower cutoff frequency of the bandpass filter is 800Hz. The first overtone, however, is at 1,000Hz, so it will pass through the filter unaltered. The second overtone, which is at 1,500Hz, will also be filtered, because the upper cutoff frequency is 1,200Hz. The next overtone, at 2,000Hz, will be almost completely filtered out.

Figure 6-10

An envelope follower tracks the amount of sound energy in an input signal and outputs an envelope (a control signal) whose contour matches the shape of the input.

Input

Output

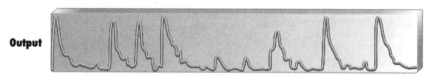

An envelope follower doesn't have any effect on an audio signal. All it does is sense how loud the signal is. It then sends out a control signal (see Figure 6-10) that corresponds to the loudness of the input. As the loudness of the input changes, the control signal changes in a matching way. The control signal has the same shape (contour) as the amplitude envelope of the incoming audio signal. An envelope follower may give the user control over its attack and decay characteristics. These two parameters determine how tightly the envelope tracks the changes in loudness of the input signal.

An amplifier is a circuit — or the equivalent in software — that controls the amount of gain of a signal passing through it. (You probably knew that already.) The simplest way to control the gain is to attach a knob to the amplifier, but many amplifiers in music devices are set up so that a control signal of some sort can change the gain automatically, in a hands-free manner. Old-style analog vocoders used voltage-controlled amplifiers (VCAs), and their envelope generators created analog control voltages (CVs). These days, most vocoders are digital-based, but you may see the term "VCAs" used once in a while to refer to the vocoder's amplifier stages.

THE VOCODER CONCEPT

A vocoder requires two input signals. One is called the speech signal and the other is called the carrier. Most synthesizer-based vocoders will let you use the internal synth sound as the carrier, with the speech signal being patched into an external audio input, but some hardware-based vocoders and all software-based ones also give you the option of using external signals for both the speech and the carrier. In either case, the operation of the vocoder is identical.

A vocoder operates as shown in the block diagram in Figure 6-11. The incoming speech signal passes through a bank of bandpass filters. These split the speech signal into a number of parallel bands, each band being limited to a narrow range of frequencies. Each band is then sent to its own envelope follower.

The envelope follower for each band measures how much sound energy there is in that band at a given moment. If the speech signal has one or more prominent overtones in a

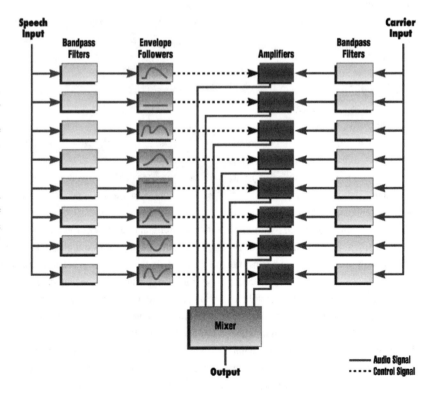

Figure 6-11
This block diagram shows how a vocoder works. The speech signal is sent through a parallel set of bandpass filters and then to a set of envelope followers. The carrier is sent through a similar set of bandpass filters, which are followed by amplifiers. The gain of each amplifier is controlled by one of the envelope followers.

given band, the control signal being sent out by the envelope follower will be high. If there are few or no overtones in that band that have a significant amplitude, the output of that particular envelope follower will be low.

At this point, we're finished with the speech signal. Essentially, it has been used as a multiband modulation source. It has been analyzed by the bandpass filters and envelope followers, and we're not planning to listen to it, so it can be discarded.

While the speech signal is being analyzed, the carrier signal is passing through its own bank of bandpass filters. These are set up so that their center frequencies are identical to those of the bank through which the speech signal passes. (Or at least, that's how they're usually set up; in some vocoders you can offset the carrier bands from the speech bands in one way or another to get special effects.) The carrier signal, like the speech signal, is split into a number of parallel signals, each containing a narrow band of frequencies.

The signals from the carrier's bands are then sent through a bank of amplifiers, and the output of each envelope follower is used to control the gain of one of the amplifiers. As Figure 6-11 shows, this causes the carrier's bands to be imprinted with the envelope shapes of the speech bands. The outputs of the amplifiers are then mixed back together so that we can listen to the carrier at the output.

The vocoding effect is the result of how the bandpass filters, envelope followers, and amplifiers interact. If the speech signal had a lot of overtones in a given band, the corresponding overtones in the carrier signal will pass through their amplifier, because the amplifier will be wide open. But if the speech signal had less sound energy in a given band, the envelope follower for that band will have a lower-level output, thus reducing the gain of the amplifier for that band. The overtones in the carrier signal that fall within that band will be given less gain. If the speech signal had no sound energy at all within a given band, the output of the envelope follower for that band will be at zero, and the amplifier will shut down, cutting off any overtones in the carrier that happen to fall within that band.

TECHNICAL CONSIDERATIONS

If you think about this description for a minute, you'll discover something essential about how a vocoder works: It can only subtract overtones from the carrier; it can never add new overtones. That's why Tip #1 advises you to use a carrier that has plenty of overtones. If you try to use something like a sine wave as the carrier — a flute line, for example — you won't hear any vocoding effect at all.

Early vocoders tended to have no more than eight or ten bands, because they were made with discrete hardware, and each band added expensive components. With a vocoder that's implemented in software, it's practical to have 16 bands or even more.

Vocoding works because the human vocal tract produces strong resonant overtones called formants. The overtones in the vowel "ee" are very different, for example, than those in the vowel "oo." This is what allows a vocoder to create the illusion of speech.

Human speech has important information in the extreme high register — consonants called sibilants (such as "s") and fricatives (such as "f"). Even a wide-open sawtooth-wave synth patch being used as a carrier is not likely to have enough energy in the extreme highs to model these consonants well. As a result, some vocoders have a switchable bypass for the extreme highs. This mixes the sibilants and fricatives from the speech signal directly into the carrier, increasing the intelligibility.

A few vocoders allow you to "crosslink" the envelope followers so that they'll open up the amplifiers corresponding to different bands. When you do this, you won't be able to understand the speech, but the carrier will still have a contoured, expressive shape. Crosslinking is especially effective when a drum loop is used as the speech signal. You can choose a band (such as the kick drum area) where there's a lot of energy and link it to a band in the carrier where there are some useful overtones. This band in the carrier will then acquire the same rhythm as the kick. When you do this, you're using the vocoder as a multi-band frequency-dependent gate with sidechain keying.

Other vocoders let you adjust the output levels of individual bands or the rolloff slope of the filters. Or you may be able to program a frequency offset between the carrier bands and the speech bands, sliding one set of bands up or down relative to the other in order to increase the intelligibility or create a gender-bending effect.

STEPS TO BETTER VOCODING

- Use a carrier that has plenty of overtones. A sawtooth-wave synth patch with the filter wide open is ideal. Wind sounds and white noise are also good. Anything that's bright and buzzy will work. Sounds that are muted or hollow generally won't work well.
- Set the level of the speech signal properly. If it's too low, you won't hear the effect. If it's too high, it may distort, and the distortion will throw audio energy into bands where it doesn't belong. This, in turn, will prevent the speech from being intelligible.
- If you can't understand the speech at the output, check whether your vocoder allows you to set the number of bands. Try using more or fewer bands.
- Try adding a bit of resonance, if this parameter is available, in order to narrow the bands slightly. Make sure the envelope followers are set to a fast attack and a medium-length decay.
- If your carrier is high-pitched, check whether the carrier bands can be offset in frequency from the speech bands. You may be able to get a more intelligible effect, at the expense of a little gender-bending or chipmunking.
- For added clarity, try blending a little of the speech input into the carrier. You may have to do this at your mixer rather than in the vocoder itself. If you're using a recorded speech track, you might want to clean up its pitches using a vocal pitch-correction effect so it will blend in better with the carrier. Better still, highpass-filter the part of the speech signal you're planning to mix with the vocoder's output (not the speech signal being sent to the vocoder's input), so that only the sibilants are heard.

Chapter 7
SOFTWARE-SPECIFIC TIPS

While the majority of the information in this book is platform-agnostic in the sense that it can be applied to almost any software or hardware tool, there are quite a few software tools available that are extremely well suited to dance music. Ableton Live and Sony Acid are the popular favorites for sample-based loop music (though Live's extraordinarily intuitive MIDI functions make it more of a true DAW). Because of its extremely comprehensive array of synthesis, sequencing, and mixing features, Propellerhead Reason has become a staple for electronica and hip-hop artists. The new kid on the block, Cakewalk's Project5, straddles the middle ground, incorporating a bit of everything in its rapidly evolving arsenal of groove-oriented functions. In this chapter, we'll dig a bit deeper into each of these programs with tips and tricks from industry experts with extremely deep knowledge of these products.

Kicking off the proceedings is a section on Acid written by the man who *invented* the product, Chris Moulios.

September 2000, revised April 2006
Sony Acid Hot Tips
Getting the most from Sony's ubiquitous prosumer platform

Anyone who has worked with sampled loops has surely experienced the pains of getting tempos and pitches locked down — especially in the old days before programs like Acid existed. Acid makes the once tedious tasks of tempo changing and pitch correcting a walk in the park.

Figure 7-I

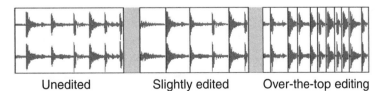

Unedited   Slightly edited   Over-the-top editing

SLICE & DICE

An inexperienced Acid user's project will almost always have all of the events starting and ending on loop boundaries, but you can slice, dice, and stutter your loops to achieve more creative results. The tools for effective slicing and dicing are the split and the event start offset.

To achieve the Ginsu knife effect, split a loop in strategic places and change the resulting split event's start offsets. The idea is to introduce variation so the loop doesn't just repeat *ad nauseam*. Do this every few bars and you'll get some much appreciated rhythmic variety. Take this technique to extremes: Up the tempo to 160, for example, and you get drum and bass. See Figure 7-1 for some examples of how this type of editing looks.

Acid has a few features that can make slicing and dicing easier. The "S" key is a useful keyboard shortcut for splitting events. Move the cursor to the place you want to split and hit "S". The Chopper tool, introduced in Acid 3.0, is a fun way to grab bits and pieces from a loop, and quickly splat them to the timeline.

There's also a quick way to change event start offsets, but it's a hidden feature. Hold down the Alt key, click on an event with the left mouse button, and then move the mouse left or right to change the event offset.

Figure 7-2

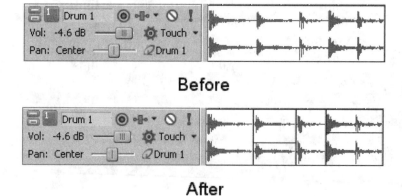

Before

After

ADDING DYNAMICS

Another trick to add spice to your loops is to split individual drum or instrument notes and add dynamics by using a volume envelope to change the event's gain. Think like a drummer and add accents to beats that happen before choruses or other important places. Figure 7-3 shows the before and after of this technique.

Figure 7-3.

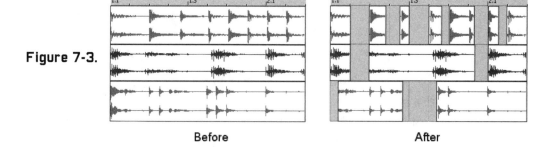

Before   After

SUBTRACTIVE ARRANGING

Acid makes it easy to keep layering loops until your mix gets way too busy. One way to "thin out" your mix is to use the erase tool to selectively remove portions of loop events (see Figure 7-3).

If you have multiple drum loops, try erasing the snares from one drum loop or the bass drums from another to get a tighter sound. Erase portions of instrument loops so they "take turns." This technique will not only make your arrangements more focused, but can make them more exciting as well.

Figure 7-4

Half or double this value.

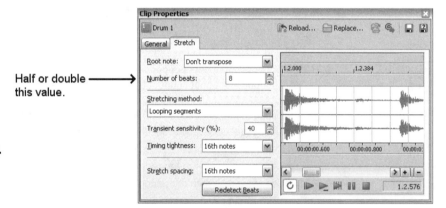

DOUBLE TIME/HALF TIME

By entering false information about the length of a loop, you can speed it up or slow it down relative to the project's tempo. In the Clip Properties, change the "Number of beats" parameter to half of its normal value for a loop that plays twice as fast. Double the "Number of beats" value for a loop that plays twice as slow (see Figure 7-4).

Figure 7-5

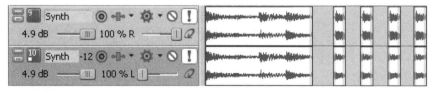

TRACK DETUNE

Here's an easy one: Duplicate a track and change the new track's pitch to make a thicker sound. Use octave intervals for pitched sounds (an octave lower often works well). For unpitched sounds, anything goes. Pan the tracks to opposite sides of the stereo field for a cool wide effect (see Figure 7-5).

TURN OFF ACID'S MAIN FEATURE?

Acid's time compression/expansion stretches loops without changing pitch. Sometimes, however, you want the "chipmunk" or "Darth Vader" effect that only slowing down or speed-

Figure 7-6

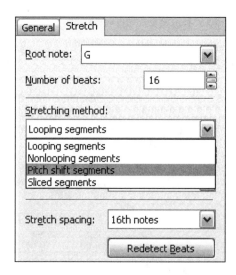

ing up loop playback will give you. In Acid Pro's Clip Properties page (Figure 7-6) you can change the stretch method to "Pitch shift segments" and then relive the days of sampler-based looping when pitch was king. When working with Beatmap files (typically song-length media, or audio which hasn't been trimmed to loop seamlessly), simply uncheck the "Preserve pitch when stretching" checkbox.

This effect can improve fidelity for drum loops that were recorded at a tempo close to the playback tempo. It's also a great effect when slowing down drum loops because it can help you achieve extra-low bass frequencies.

WORKING WITH OTHER PROGRAMS AND PLATFORMS

There are many ways to use Acid with other products, even products that run on different platforms.

The first way is to save a WAV or AIFF file of the entire mix and import that file into your multitrack recorder or sequencer. Just choose "Save As..." and pick the right format. Note that you can also mute or solo tracks before saving so you can separate parts for further mixing.

A second way, if you own Acid Pro, is to choose "Export Tracks..." from the File menu. This command was specifically designed for exporting files to other music workstations. It has two options. The first makes a long WAV or AIFF for every track that exists in your project. Each file contains the audio playback of the entire project as if the track were soloed. The second option makes a short WAV or AIFF file that is one iteration of each loop stretched to the project's tempo. This can be useful if you just want the stretching and wish to recreate the sequence of loop events in another program.

You can sync Acid to external hardware or computers. Generating MIDI clock is probably the best way to work with MIDI sequencers. Syncing to MIDI Time Code is probably the best way to link up with non-musical clocks such as SMPTE recorded onto analog tape. When attempting to link to external digital equipment (such as digital tape recorders or Digidesign Pro Tools), it's best to use a combination of MIDI Time Code and a hardware word clock.

Lastly, as of Acid version 5.0, you can use ReWire to connect Acid to other ReWire-capable programs. To use Acid as the ReWire Mixer (*i.e.*, the master), simply launch Acid, pull up the Insert menu, and select Soft Synth, then click the ReWire Devices tab and choose from your available ReWire client programs. You'll then need to launch the ReWire application (either via a button on Acid's Soft Synth Properties window, or by launching the application from your desktop shortcut). ReWire will synchronize the timelines of the two applications and feed the audio output of the ReWire device into Acid just like any other Softsynth. Acid has the added bonus of working just as well as a ReWire client, which is helpful if you want to connect to an application such as Cubase or Sonar, which operate only as ReWire masters.

> **Craig Anderton is another Acid guru, with hundreds of hours of editing and mixing experience under his belt. Here's his take on getting more out of your Acid mixes.**

February 2000, revised April 2006
Mixing with Acid
Some special tricks that will help your songs sound better

A lot of techno/dance/hip-hop/house musicians are using Sony Acid as their main multi-track machine. However, mixing those tracks down to a finished two-track master works a little differently in Acid compared to standard mixing processes; here are some tips on maximizing your Acid mixes.

FIX LOOP GLITCHES
Solo a repeating loop and listen carefully over headphones for any glitches or pops that occur at the loop point. If you hear something, zoom in until the loop shows the waveform. Usually the click results from a non-zero signal level at the splice point. (You generally want loops to repeat at a zero crossing; at the very least, the beginning and end of the loop must meet.) There are three ways to solve this:

■ Use the trimmer tool to trim the loop end into a silent region. However, because this shortens the loop, you can no longer extend the loop just by dragging the end with the pencil, as it will either push ahead or lag behind the beat. You'll have to copy the edited loop repeatedly by hand.
■ Use the volume envelope to add a very fast fadeout at the end. If that doesn't fix the click, add a short fade-in at the beginning instead. If that still doesn't work, add both. As with the above solution, you'll have to copy the loop repeatedly to extend it. Furthermore, lots of envelope action taxes the computer.

■ The best option is to open the loop in a digital audio editing program (Sony Sound Forge or Steinberg WaveLab, for instance). If you can't obtain a clickless loop by varying the loop points a bit, create a 5ms fade at the sample's beginning and/or end. This should eliminate loop-caused clicks without causing any audible discontinuity, but be sure to solo the loop after editing it and listen to the transition points to make sure you haven't introduced a perceptible volume dip.

Figure 7-7

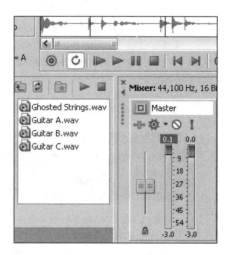

CHECK THE METERS

Before you start mixing, right-click on the meters for any outputs you're using, and select Hold Peaks. After you've finished mixing and are about to save your project as a mixed WAV or AIFF file (this is essentially your two-track master), play the entire tune, then check the meters (see Figure 7-7).

If the numbers are outlined in red, then the mixed signal has gone over 0, resulting in distortion. You therefore need to bring the master faders down by an equal amount (*e.g.*, if the meter reads +3.2, then you'd need to decrease the faders by 3.2 to compensate). If the meter numbers have a minus sign, then you're not taking full advantage of the available headroom. Bring up the faders until the meters register 0.0 for the highest peak attained during the piece (actually, I like to hit −0.1 to leave a little safety margin). Incidentally, you can adjust a master fader individually by shift-click/dragging it, or fine-tune the fader values with Ctrl-click/drag.

CONVERT RAM HOGS INTO HARD DISK TRACKS

If you need to free up more RAM (perhaps to run more plug-ins or just to make your computer happier), convert your longest loops into hard disk tracks. From the View menu, choose Clip Properties, then select the track or event whose clip you want to adjust. Change the Acid Type from Loop to One-Shot or Beatmapped. Although there's a limit to how many hard disk tracks you can run, the right balance of RAM-based (Loops) and disk-based (Beatmap and One-shot) clips gives the best overall computer performance.

AVOID IRRATIONAL PANNING & FX SETTINGS

With the focus on the track list, choose Select All from the Edit menu. Click on one track's pan control, and all tracks will show their pan controls. Review the settings, but don't adjust anything until you select only the track to be adjusted. Otherwise, you'll move all the pan faders simultaneously. Similarly, check the FX1 and FX2 settings.

ELIMINATE GLITCHES WHEN EXTENDING LOOP LENGTH

One cool Acid trick is to take a loop and double the number of beats (in the Clip Properties window). This extends everything out to twice its normal length, and interesting things happen when Acid tries to fill in the blanks. Sometimes it can't cope, though, resulting in a small spike that sounds like a tick.

Eliminating the tick requires some work, but it's worth it. Put loop markers around the loop, and solo it. Check the meters (as described earlier) to make sure you're using the maximum available headroom, then select Mix to New Track from the file menu. You now have a new loop that's double the length of the original, but still contains the glitch. Go into a digital audio editor, call up the new file, then draw out the click (it should be easy to find, as it doesn't look like the rest of the waveform). Drag the new file into the track list (or track view) and draw it in wherever the old file was, then delete the track with the old file. Done!

Kurt Kurasaki produces audio for Internet, multimedia, and game developers. But more than that, he's the author of Backbeat Books' highly acclaimed _Power Tools for Reason 3.0_. Here's a taste of Kurt's insights into the power lurking within Reason. If you're a Reason user and these tips get your juices flowing, you'd do well to check out his Power Tools book. It goes much deeper than space permits here.

February 2002
The Power of Reason
Try these signal routing and sequence editing tricks

When Reason first hit the streets, people who thought they knew what music software should look like were in for a jolt. It's been several years now, and Propellerhead Software's flagship program is being used by everyone from top film composers to teenagers with laptops and big dreams. If you're using Reason, the power user tips in this article should show you a few ways to squeeze more music out of it. If you're not — well, you're welcome to look over our shoulders while we get creative. You could even download the demo version (from www.propellerheads.se) and follow along.

If you haven't yet pressed the Tab key to take a detailed look at Reason's rear-panel connections, now is the time to do so. The control inputs and outputs on the various modules are a potent source of fresh musical effects.

The tips in this article will work with all versions of Reason, all the way back to version 1.0.

SUBTRACTOR UNISON MODE

If you've used a hardware-based analog-type synth, you know they can create a huge sound using unison mode. In this mode, several voices play the same notes. There's usually a unison detune parameter, which fattens up the sound by detuning each voice from those around it, Reason has an effect specifically designed to emulate this effect. While SubTractor doesn't have a unison mode switch, you can get the same results with a little extra effort. This trick is great for creating large stereo pads and sweeps and is a lot more customizable than the Unison effect alone.

Start with a riff in the sequencer playing a monophonic SubTractor lead or bass that you'd like to beef up. If the pattern is created using the Matrix, use the "Copy Pattern to Track" command in the Edit menu and move the MIDI sequence to the SubTractor sequencer track. Select the SubTractor track in the sequencer track list and select "Duplicate Track" in the Edit menu. Do this until you have at least four tracks.

Next, select the SubTractor in the rack and use the "Copy Device" and "Paste Device" commands in the Edit menu. This will give you several SubTractors, all playing the same patch. Go back to the sequencer and assign one of the new tracks to each of your SubTractors. Flip the rack over and connect each SubTractor to a mixer channel.

At this point you should be hearing the same riff as before, but louder, because it's being played by four or more SubTractors. To get the true unison mode sound, you need to detune the SubTractors from one another. Using the Cents parameter for each oscillator, tune the first synth up by 5 cents, the second one down by 5 cents, the third up by 10 or 15 cents, and the fourth down by 10 or 15 cents. You may also want to pan each SubTractor to a different spot in the stereo field. If the oscillators are phase-modulated by an LFO, you can further open up the sound by changing the rates and amounts slightly so each SubTractor has its own phase modulation.

Insert a few DDL-1 Delay Lines between some of the SubTractor modules and the mixer. Set the delay mode to "ms," the delay time to between 1ms and 10ms, and feedback to 0. Having the slight output delay on the modules will create a wider stereo image. It's not necessary to add a delay to each of the duplicate SubTractors, but each delay device should have a unique delay time within the 1–10ms range.

Several other effects can be achieved with this technique: octave doublings, unison chords, and so on. After tuning three SubTractors to different notes of a chord, try routing each of them through its own delay line, and give the delays different rhythmic time settings to create chord arpeggio patterns. (If you're using Reason 3.0, you can select all of your SubTractors and delay lines and use the Combine command to pack them all into a single Combinator module. After saving the Combinator preset, you'll be able to load your fat bank of SubTractors into other songs.)

A drawback of the multi-SubTractor technique is that any parameter changes you make must be duplicated for each of the SubTractor modules. If a filter change is desired, then the change has to be applied to each of the duplicate modules. This can be done with the "Copy Patch" and "Paste Patch" commands, but after using this you'll have to recreate the detunings. Another approach would be to route the SubTractor outputs through a submixer and send the submix outputs to an ECF-42 Envelope Controlled Filter, as shown in Figure 7-8. If you do this, open the SubTractor filters all the way, so the only filtering is coming from the ECF.

Figure 7-8
Here, several SubTractors are being routed through a submixer, and its output is being processed by an ECF-42 Envelope Controlled Filter.

This SubTractor configuration requires more CPU resources, but the dramatic change in the sound is worth the expense. What's more, the same technique works with the Malström synth.

REARRANGING REX LOOPS

Almost everyone finds the Dr:REX loop player an invaluable tool for adding realistic drum grooves to their Reason songs. But have you tried modifying the loops to create different rhythm patterns?

Load a loop, preferably one with several different drum sounds, into a Dr:REX player. Click on the "To Track" button to send the MIDI slice data to the sequencer. Select the Dr:REX track in the sequencer track list, and from the edit menu select "Duplicate Track." Repeat this until there are four copies of the track. The Transport Loop locators should be set to the length of one copy of the loop, unless you want to make a longer and more complex pattern.

Make sure the sequencer's arrow tool is selected. Set the resolution to 1/8 or 1/16 (eighth- or sixteenth-notes) and enable the Snap to Grid button. Drag the REX loop groups so the loops start on a different beat on each track. For example, try moving the groups to position offsets at 1.1.1, 1.2.3, 1.3.1, and 1.4.1.

Select the pencil tool and redraw the groups so each becomes a series of random-length short segments (between one and five eighth-notes in length). Draw similar (but not necessarily identical) group divisions for all four tracks of the REX data.

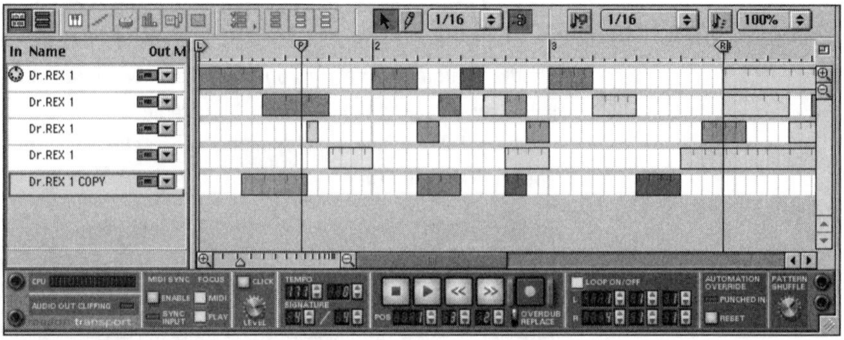

Figure 7-9
After duplicating a Dr:REX track and shifting the MIDI data by a few eighth-notes, chop the parts apart to produce something like this.

Click on the Play button to audition the current sequence of overlapping REX slices. A mess, right? But we're not finished. Enable the arrow tool again and start deleting sections from different tracks. You might end up with something like Figure 7-9.

When you have a beat you like, drag the segments all up to the original track. Once the rearranged loop data is on a single track, it can be accessed directly when you switch to sequencer edit mode. Double hits can be deleted and further timing changes can be made.

RANDOMIZING REX SLICES

The Alter Notes feature randomizes the timing of notes. It redistributes the note events within the area you've selected. Alter Notes can modify MIDI note events on any sequencer track, but this feature is well suited for randomizing the slice data of a REX loop.

Change the sequencer to edit mode so you can view the slice data of a Dr:REX track. Use the arrow tool to select a group of notes. From the Edit menu select "Change Events." Click on the Alter Notes "Apply" button. Depending on what group of notes you've selected, you may need to click the button a few times to hear noticeable or useful results.

Any number of note events can be selected for altering. With REX slice data, however, selecting from a limited range, perhaps half a measure, will yield the most effective results. Randomizing an entire measure of REX slice data may not be as useful as modifying part of the loop, because it may destroy your sense of where the downbeat is.

After randomizing the notes, try this: Lower the filter cutoff on the Dr:REX module, increase the filter resonance, and add some velocity modulation using the F.ENV knob. Now choose a few notes at random in the sequencer track and raise or lower their velocity values with the pencil tool.

SEQUENCED MODULATION

The control voltage (CV) and gate cabling feature in Reason works much like the CV and gate jacks found in modular synthesizer systems. As in modular synthesizers, Reason CV and gate signals can be interchanged with one another. In fact, the Matrix "gate" output also contains velocity data; it's not just an on/off gate, as it would be on a vintage synth.

One very practical CV technique uses the Matrix as a customizable LFO. The purpose of the Matrix Pattern Sequencer is to generate CV signals that can modulate parameters of other devices in the Reason rack. The Matrix is naturally synchronized with the tempo of the track. By creating a series of high-resolution patterns, you can generate a synchronized triangle wave (in effect, a slow LFO) as a modulation source.

Create a Matrix Pattern Sequencer and flip to the rear of the rack. Set the Bipolar/Unipolar switch to Bipolar mode, then flip back to the front of the rack and switch the Matrix to the curve display. Select pattern A1. Set the pattern steps to 32 and the resolution knob to 1/128. The higher resolution yields a smoother modulation curve, but the whole pattern will now be only one beat long. Before drawing the curve, copy pattern A1 and paste it to patterns A2, A3, and A4.

Select pattern A1 and enable the line tool by holding down the shift key. Start the curve at the zero crossing mark across the middle of the segment, and drag the cursor up to the maximum level at step 32. Switch to pattern A2 and draw the curve from the maximum level back to the zero crossing, again holding the shift key to get a straight line. Switch to pattern A3 and draw the curve from the zero crossing down to the minimum level. Switch to pattern A4 and draw the curve from the minimum level back to the zero crossing.

In the Sequencer, select the Matrix track and enter edit mode. Enable the pattern lane, select the pencil tool, and set the resolution to 1/4. In the pattern lane, select pattern A1 from the menu, and pencil in a pattern select event. Because this is the first event, the pencil will draw an event through the entire song. Select pattern A2 from the menu and at the second beat, pencil in a pattern A2 event for a quarter-note. Repeat this for patterns A3 and A4 at the subsequent quarter-note steps.

Switch to the arrow tool and select the measure with the A1-A2-A3-A4 pattern sequence. Copy and paste pattern select automation for the duration of the song, or for as long as you want the LFO sweep to continue.

As the song plays, the pattern select events will switch the matrix from one segment to another, and output curve will be a triangle wave LFO synchronized with the tempo of the track. The curve output signal can modulate any parameter that accepts a CV input. For example, it can modulate the panning on a mixer or delay module, or it can modulate the pitch or filter sweep of a SubTractor synthesizer. To get a longer sweep, reduce the resolution of the Matrix patterns from 1/128 to 1/64 or 1/32 and insert the pattern select events further apart.

LFO-TRIGGERED SAMPLER

This concept is more experimental. The LFO CV output signals can be used to modulate and trigger gate events — that is, notes. Using an LFO to trigger gate events in the NN19 can generate obscure, exotic textures.

Create an NN19 sampler and load a sample for playback. (Try using a sample like "CYM1 10HSH.aif" in the factory soundbank.) Cable the LFO modulation output of the NN19 to the NN19's own gate input. When you've made this connection, the LFO will trigger the sampler. Set the LFO type to square wave and adjust the rate to 42. Set the amp envelope release to 64 and the loop mode to "FW–BW."

Now add a SubTractor synthesizer to the rack. The SubTractor module will only be used

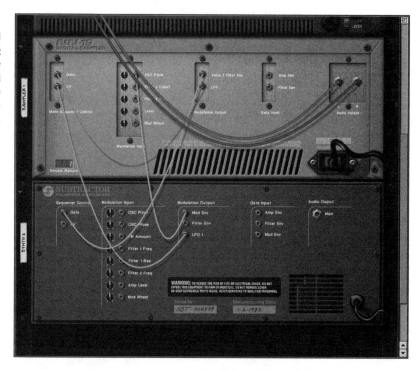

as a modulation control device, so its audio output should be disconnected. Cable the LFO 1 modulation output of the SubTractor to the mono sequencer control CV input of the NN19. Set the SubTractor's LFO 1 to the stepped random wave and adjust the LFO rate to 66. The LFO speed doubles every 12 steps, so 66 is twice the rate of 54 and four times the rate of the 42 you set on the NN19 trigger LFO.

The envelope modulation output can trigger gate signals on other modules. Set the NN19 filter envelope attack to 0, decay to 0, sustain to 127, and release to 0. Connect the NN19 Voice 1 Filter Env modulation output to the SubTractor's sequencer control gate input. Each time the NN19 is triggered by its own LFO pulse, the SubTractor will be triggered from the NN19 filter envelope.

Now connect the SubTractor Mod Env output to the NN19 OSC Pitch modulation input, as shown in Figure 7-10, and set the SubTractor's envelope rates to taste. The envelope from the SubTractor will modulate the pitch of the oscillator on the NN19. Many other routing configurations are possible — far too many to mention here.

COMPRESSOR WITH SIDECHAIN

The Comp-01 Compressor doesn't have a dedicated sidechain input, but with a bit of rewiring, you can perform side-chain ducking. The compressor is a stereo device, and the amount of dynamic change is dependent on the sum of the two input signals. This means we can use the left input for the side-chain signal and send the signal we want to compress through the right input and output.

Figure 7-11
This signal routing allows us
to create a de-esser for a
vocal sample. The EQ mod-
ule zooms in on the frequencies that need to be ducked.

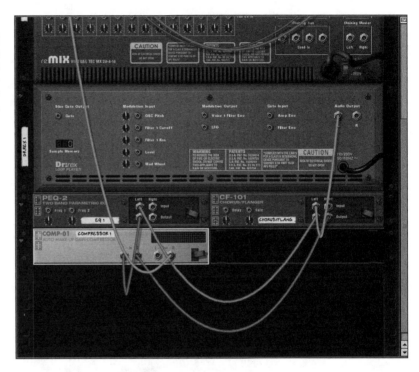

Figure 7-11
This signal routing allows us
to create a de-esser for a
vocal sample. The EQ mod-
ule zooms in on the frequencies that need to be ducked.

You can even create a frequency-dependent compressor effect using the side-chain concept. This configuration has useful applications, such as ducking snare hits from a sample loop or de-essing a vocal sample. To perform de-essing, create a Comp-01 Compressor, a CF-101 Chorus/Flanger (which we'll use as a Y-cable), and a PEQ-2 Parametric Equalizer. The patch is shown in Figure 7-11. [*Editor's note: In Reason 3.0, the MClass Compressor has stereo sidechain inputs, and the Spider Audio Merger & Splitter can be used in place of the CF-101. However, de-essing using the PEQ is set up as described here.*]

Connect the CF-101's left output to the PEQ-2's left input and the CF-101's right output to the Comp-01's right input. Set the CF-101 to bypass to split the input signal. Route the PEQ-2's right output to the Comp-01's left input.

The signal being processed should be connected to the CF-101's right input. The processed signal is at the Comp-01's right output. Set the Comp-01 ratio to 90, threshold to 72, attack to 0, and release to 19. The PEQ-2 should have both A and B enabled with both gains set to 127. Adjust the frequency and Q settings to the frequency range that empha-sizes the compression effect.

REVERSE REVERB
Try routing the output of a Redrum channel through a bypassed chorus/flanger [or Spider Audio] to split it. Send one output of the chorus/flanger to the input of a delay. The delay should be set to 100% wet with no feedback, so it will output the "dry" sound. Send the other side of the split to the reverb. Set the delay to some number of sixteenth-notes, and edit

the Redrum pattern so the notes are played the same number of sixteenths early. The dry sound will now be on the beat, as before, but the reverb return will be heard first.

MANAGING SONG PROJECTS

Reason Song Files can become very intricate, with dozens of audio files and loops involved in a production. Before starting a project, it's a good idea to build an organized directory structure for all the files that will be associated with the project.

Create a new folder with a name like "My Song." Within the project folder, create sub-directories for Reason song files, backup song files, Dr:REX loops, NN19 and SubTractor patches, samples, etc. Place copies of audio and loop files in the appropriate directories. Although the "Song Self-Contain Settings" option saves samples within a Reason song file, if the file becomes corrupt, everything including the samples may be unrecoverable. Saving each part of the song independently in a project folder could prevent a disaster.

Back up your project folder religiously. Backup song file and patch archives will establish a development history of the project, and provide a simple way to revert to previous settings.

> **Jesse Jost is a Project5 product specialist for Cakewalk, so it's safe to say that he knows Project5 inside and out. Here's his take on getting the most out of this powerful new entry into the sequencing world.**

August 2003, revised April 2006
Inside Cakewalk Project5
Getting more from Cakewalk's groove-oriented production suite

In this tutorial, we'll familiarize you with Project5's two most essential concepts, *signal flow* and *patterns*. Understanding these topics will help you wrap your head around the heart and soul of P5's workflow. Grasping P5's basics may require that you abandon some old notions about software sequencers.

SIGNAL FLOW

Signal flow ties together many important aspects of P5: MIDI filtering, audio mixing, effects, and the views. When you use P5 as an instrument host, the audio path originates with a DXi or VSTi, which is controlled by a rather sophisticated MIDI input filtering scheme. After that, the signal flows through a local effects chain and gain stage (mix level), possibly passing through an effects bus on the way, and terminates at the master gain stage, where the bits are conveyed to the computer's output and become analog audio.

Signal flow is managed in the Track Pane and Track Inspector. The Track Inspector provides an exploded view of the currently selected track, most importantly displaying the synth's arpeggiator, automatable widgets, and patch points for MIDI and audio effects.

Figure 7-12

Synths are initially patched into the Track Pane, which abuts the Track View. The Track Pane also serves as the mixing console and provides several features designed to accommodate an unfettered workflow.

BASIC CONCEPTS

One synth, one track. A one-to-one correspondence exists between softsynth and track; it's assumed that one track will be used for a single synth sound. Arranging, then, becomes a lighter task, since all of the patterns in a given track will go directly to that synth. Multitimbral instruments are readily accommodated by P5's *track layers* function. All tracks can spawn track layers, which can be assigned to different MIDI channels as well as store their own patterns for easy arrangement. In addition to this, individual patterns can themselves be assigned to any MIDI channel (more on this later).

MIDI input filtering. You can assign a specific MIDI port (which will be receiving a real-time performance from a MIDI controller) and MIDI channel for a track, facilitating the use of specific MIDI controllers for specific instruments.

Using the same port/channel for MIDI input for all of your instruments means that a single controller can be used to operate all of the instruments simultaneously. This provides the most direct method of layering multiple synth voices, making P5 a powerful softsynth workstation.

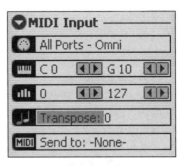

Figure 7-13

The Track Inspector provides other MIDI input filtering parameters, such as velocity, key range, and key transposition (see Figure 7-13).

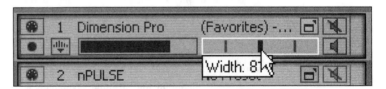

Figure 7-14

Mix controls. Each instrument output has its own gain stage, providing mute, solo, volume, pan, and width. Width (Figure 7-14), which describes the spatial image of a stereo sound, is not a parameter that's typically found in audio applications. With this parameter you're given the ability to create lush pads and sophisticated soundscapes. The Width control itself is nested within the Pan control. Holding down the Ctrl key while clicking and dragging invokes the Width control.

Figure 7-15

Audio output selector. The output selector (see Figure 7-15) appears on the Track Strip when you insert an instrument that has more than one audio output. As you scroll to select an output, the mix controls update to show the settings for the currently selected output. In order to keep a clean workspace, only one Track Strip is used for all the instrument's possible outputs. You can also select the output directly from the bottom of the synth widget in the Track Inspector.

Figure 7-16

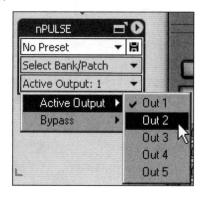

PATTERN BASICS

In contrast to most DAWs, P5's Track View contains patterns, not clips. It's fair to think of patterns as the atoms of your song arrangement. In P5, MIDI data lives inside a pattern, as does most audio. All patterns roll out and repeat at their specified loop points (like Groove Clips in Sonar). This makes song development easy.

Inside Track View, patterns appear as three different types (see Figure 7-16):

MIDI. MIDI events are lightly drawn on the pattern.

Groove audio. Audio groove clips are notched and roll out just like MIDI patterns.

Normal audio. Non-looping audio clips, such as imported or recorded audio, are not notched and do not roll out. A simple command (Ctrl+L) can change the selected clip into an audio groove clip.

Patterns are edited in the Pattern Editor, and consist of MIDI events and automation for your synths and effects. Sometimes you may want to have a pattern that's nothing but filter sweep automation, and strategically employ it throughout your arrangement.

When you make changes to a specific pattern, other instances of that pattern are also affected — this can be a terrific time saver. To dissociate a pattern from its siblings, simply select your pattern(s) and press U ("Unlink Selected Clips" from the context menu).

Figure 7-17

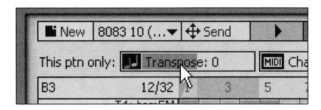

There are, however, a couple of attributes that do not affect linked patterns. These are called *instance attributes* and include MIDI channel and Pitch Transpose (see Figure 7-17). Transpose works on both audio and MIDI clips, by the way.

Figure 7-18

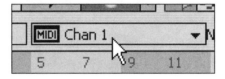

The MIDI channel of a pattern (see Figure 7-18) tells a multitimbral synth which voice to play (you can overlay patterns in tracks). Therefore, even patterns play a role in the MIDI filtering aspect of P5's signal flow.

With these concepts in mind, we'll get deeper into P5's synthesis and arranging features.

LOOPS/PATTERN BROWSER

The Pattern Browser is used for browsing and auditioning MIDI and audio. You can drag these assets directly from the browser and into your arrangement.

Out of the box, P5 provides you with hundreds of audio and MIDI patterns to get you started. Some of the drum patterns are designed to work with P5-specific synths, so let's hear how they come together by using the Pattern Preview function. Let's set up our workspace:

1. In the Track View, insert the synths Dimension (subtractive synth) and nPULSE (synth drum module).

2. Open the Pattern Browser.

3. Click on "Loops & Patterns."

Your screen might look something like Figure 7-19, with the Pattern Bin at the bottom right. Now let's audition some drum patterns:

4. Click on the nPULSE track so it becomes highlighted (current track = pattern preview track).

5. In the Pattern Browser, navigate to Drums > All; in the last column, click the preview control next to pattern "8083 10."

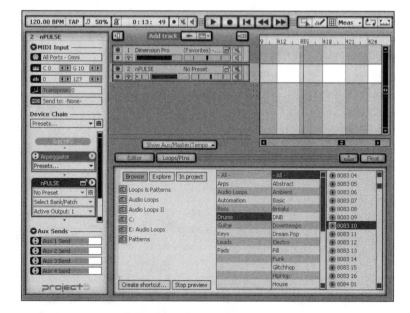

Figure 7-19

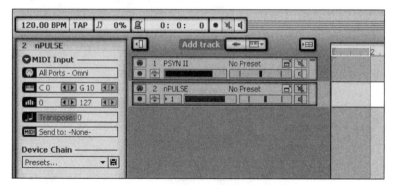

Figure 7-20

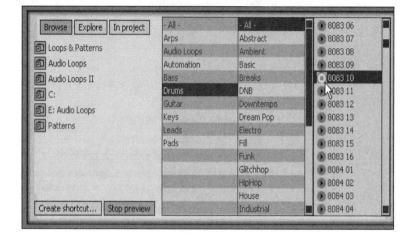

Figure 7-21

Feel free to preview other drum patterns, moving up or down the list. When you find a pattern you like, just drag it into the Track View, or better yet the Groove Matrix (see Figure 7-21). The Groove Matrix provides a useful way to preview multiple patterns simultaneously across tracks. Let's do this by dragging "8083 10" into the first cell on the nPULSE track and triggering that groove.

Figure 7-22

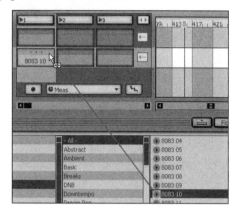

Let's add a melody to the Dimension track:

1. Click on the Dimension track so it becomes the new preview track.
2. On the Track Strip, select the Dimension preset "(Favorites) – Alien Piano 2."

Figure 7-23

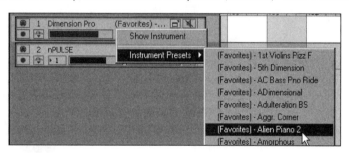

3. In the Pattern Browser, navigate to Keys > Keyboard Riffs > Key.Riff.Chord Progression.(1-14).
4. Click the pattern's preview control.

If you like the pattern, drag it into track 1's first Groove Matrix cell.

Preview tip: You can preview more than one pattern at a time in the Pattern Browser by holding down the Ctrl key while clicking on other patterns' preview controls.

DS864 PATCHES

The DS864 sampler supports Akai S1000/S3000, SF2, Kurzweil K2000, WAV, and AIFF formats. Each DS864 patch provides eight independent voices and eight assignable stereo outputs, which makes for some serious mixing and layering potential. It's all managed by the control cluster in the sampler's top left area.

Each of the eight patch layers contains a unique voice, but you can get up and running with just one layer. Multiple layers are useful for complex multitimbral patches — when the situation calls for a super-patch, you'll want to know how to create a multi-layer patch:

Figure 7-24

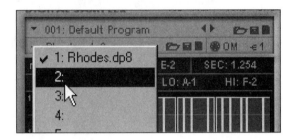

First, click on the layer menu and select one of the available eight channels (see Figure 7-24). Then load a new layer (*.dp8) from the layer browse dialog, opened by the adjacent Open control, to the right of the menu.

You should now have a 2-voice patch. You can specify unique MIDI channels and audio outputs for each layer. Note that all of the sampler's parameter settings (filters, envelopes, LFOs, etc.) are unique to each layer. When you have the program dialed in to your taste, save it using the Save control above in the topmost Program Control section.

Here's a quick-and-easy recipe for a killer piano sound that's light on resources:

1. Insert the DS864 and open the patch "Piano, Gold.ds8" (this is just a one-layer patch, so it's not too RAM-intensive).

2. In the Add FX section of the Track Inspector, click on the effects menu and select Effects > Project5 > Studioverb2.

3. In the plug-in's preset menu, select "Piano Room, Med."

Figure 7-25

Make no mistake, I'm an Ableton Live fanatic and have used it to create my original downtempo tracks under the name of Pizmo, as well as completed remixes for D:Fuse ("Living the Dream," if you're keeping track) and several others. Full disclosure: I also designed a huge portion of the sounds and MIDI clips that ship with the most current versions of Live and its hybrid FM soft-synth, Operator. The following two pieces apply to all versions of Live, but the first is specific to Live 3.

May 2004
Inside Ableton Live 3
Audio and arrangement gems from the vault of Preve

With its simple yet elegant interface, automatic time-stretching, and smooth pitch-shifting, Ableton Live radically transformed the way musicians create sample-based music. Artists such as BT and Josh Gabriel have embraced Live for its ability to create seamless dance sets as well as for its loop composition functions and plug-in architecture. Live's one-two punch of realtime sample mixing and full-on arrangement tools has made it the application to have if you work with lots of sampled material.

With version 3, Ableton took the possibilities even further. This update included features such as clip envelopes and real-time transposition of samples via MIDI, which give Live a degree of power that seasoned pros find indispensable. Yet even for the most experienced, this new flexibility can be daunting.

To help you explore Live's plentiful sonic options, here are some of my favorite production tricks and techniques for getting the most out of this revolutionary music tool.

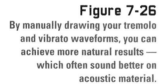

Figure 7-26
By manually drawing your tremolo and vibrato waveforms, you can achieve more natural results — which often sound better on acoustic material.

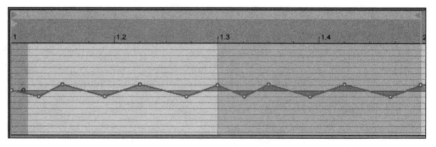

VIBRATO AND TREMOLO
Live's manual mentions the fact that the clip envelopes can also be used for LFO effects, but it doesn't delve deeply enough into the details, presumably since the clip envelopes always behave more or less like LFOs. Regardless, there are some classic LFO tricks that aren't immediately obvious when working with clip envelopes. For one thing, you can add vibrato to a vocal or instrumental part by selecting a pitch-transposition envelope and drawing a rapid triangle wave at various points in a loop to give the longer notes a sense of motion. Here's how:

1. Click on the audio clip.

2. Click the Transpose button in the Envelope pane of the lower window.

3. Select the Pencil tool in the transport bar.

4. Click on the envelope to set pitch or double-click on the envelope with the cursor to create handles, then drag the handles to the pitch you want.

If you want more synthetic vibrato effects, create a single-cycle triangle wave that lines up with the quantization markers and copy it throughout the entire sample or a section thereof. If you want to add a trill instead, switch to a square shape — the pencil tool is perfect for this — and stay within a few semitones of the original pitch.

If you prefer natural-sounding vibrato, skip the cut-and-paste approach and manually draw each point in the wave cycle. Don't try to finesse the timing or depth. Human vibrato doesn't sound mechanical, so it's important not to be too precise or you'll end up with artificial-sounding results. Try different speeds and amounts within each section, bearing in mind that real vibrato functions over a very limited pitch range. Keeping your modulation under a semitone in either direction is the secret.

Tremolo is similar to vibrato, but the envelope is applied to the volume of a sample instead of its pitch. The above rules also apply to tremolo, so try a few variations as you work. You may find that a track that appeared to need vibrato needed tremolo instead.

(MORE) REALISTIC PITCH-SHIFTING

While Live 3's clip envelopes enable you to re-pitch your samples to create new melodies, if you use the pencil tool exclusively for this, the pitch transitions will be quantized. This is fine for synths, but not vocals or real instruments, since they transition between pitches more smoothly. To get a more realistic effect, first add your transpositions using the pencil tool, then switch to "rubberband" mode (the "classic" automation mode, with breakpoints, etc.).

Using the rubberband editor, adjust the attacks and transitions so that some notes bend into others. Try different ramp angles, and leave some note events untouched; if you bend into every note, it will sound just as artificial as if you quantized everything, so take some time to see what works best with your samples.

PITCH-SHIFT XTREME

Alternately, Live 3's new extended transposition range allows for some truly extreme and unusual effects that are hard to duplicate otherwise, since they also remain locked in sync.

Try taking a standard drum loop and — using the transpose knob — raise the pitch by around 36 semitones. You should hear a bleepy, synthetic riff. Tinker with the pitch until it's close to the key of your track, then switch over to the transposition clip envelope. Using the envelope, use the pencil tool to tweak the pitches until you have a complementary melody.

You can also get interesting effects by transposing melodic instrument loops far outside their original ranges. Melodies in upper note ranges get a crunchy, bit-crushed sound when transposed downward by a large amount, whereas bass riffs turn into tweezed-out blips when transposed upward two or more octaves.

CLASSIC WAH

So you have a rhythm guitar sample that has a terrific groove, but what you really want is a wah-wah part. Not to worry, you can get darn good wah effects out of Live, but you need to know where to look.

Essentially, a wah pedal is just a foot-controlled bandpass filter. With that in mind, you can insert Live's AutoFilter plug-in, switch it to bandpass mode, then control the frequency with a clip envelope. The secret to nailing the classic sound is emphasizing specific beats, rather than simply slapping on an eighth-note pattern and letting it run. Examine the waveform as you listen to the guitar loop and note where the accents fall, then sharply increase the cutoff frequency at those points.

On the other hand, if you're working with strummed chords, you can apply an eighth- or sixteenth-note LFO-style triangle wave envelope to get that pimped-out sustained effect that sounds so sexy on downtempo love jams. For added realism, slow down the rate of undulation — just a tiny change works best — toward the end of the chord.

BEAT SPLICING

Live 3's clip envelopes make it easy to grab specific elements from a beat and merge them with elements from another loop, while keeping everything tightly locked. Here's how you do it:

1. Choose a loop that has a solid beat and clearly defined warp markers.

2. Switch the clip envelope to clip volume mode and — using the pencil tool — cut out sections of the beat, noting which sections were cut.

3. Find another beat that complements the original, and again make sure the warp markers are aligned to each beat.

4. Copy the envelope from the first beat to the second clip for use as a template.

5. Once the second envelope is in place, invert the envelope amounts for each section of the beat. This way, when one loop plays, the other will be silent and vice versa.

If you're not sure whether you like the results on a given pair of loops, try swapping in a different drum loop for one of the clips. Alternately, try adding a music loop for even more exotic effects.

Figure 7-27
By punching out holes every other 32nd-note, you can achieve that classic pulsed effect that sounds so darn good on power chords and background vocal pads.

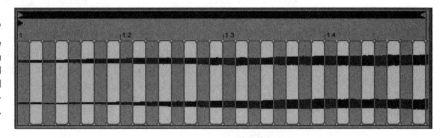

RHYTHMIC GATING

Similar to beat splicing, rhythmic gating is a classic DJ and remixing effect (sometimes referred to as "transforming") that sounds great on vocals and sustained passages. Live's clip envelopes — combined with the cut/copy/paste functions — make this technique ridiculously easy to implement. Next time you want to spice up a legato sample, try this:

1. Using the pencil tool, draw a quarter-note-length clip envelope at 32nd-note resolution. Alternate the volume for each segment from full volume to no signal. When the clip plays you should hear a quick sixteenth-note pattern, followed by the rest of the measure (either full on or silent).

2. Switch to the rubberband editor, then highlight that quarter-note segment and copy it throughout the entire one- or two-bar length of the sample. At this point, the entire clip should pulse at sixteenth-note intervals. This sounds especially dramatic on horns, vocals, and guitar power chords, as you see here.

3. Now switch back to the pencil tool and start experimenting with extending certain notes and/or silences (see Figure 7-28). While you can get great results with different note values, a good rule of thumb is to keep a few accents on either the downbeat or the two and four of your pattern. From there, you can start adding syncopation tricks like 32nd-note fills at the end of the pattern and so forth.

Figure 7-28
Tinkering with the rhythm of
your gating effect is a great
way to add syncopation
to a track.

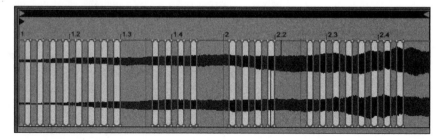

ACROSS THE GRAIN

While Live's warp markers are a terrific way to synchronize loops and tighten grooves, they're also a great way to mangle samples and beats. The trick is in using them the "wrong" way to achieve exotic granular synthesis effects.

Begin by switching the warp mode to Tones or Texture. Tones mode gives a smoother, more classic granular synthesis sound, whereas Texture adds a Flux parameter, which gives the overall sound a slightly chorused feel.

If you move the warp markers closer together, Live will expand the material between the markers, imparting a metallic flanger-ish tone to the sound. If you move them further apart, the results will be compressed, allowing you to rephrase musical loops in bizarre electronic ways that can be useful for glitch-hop effects.

Combining these two approaches and applying them to traditional drum loops allows you to create rhythmic effects that would be difficult or even impossible to achieve in any other software environment.

SEQUENCING

One of the coolest new features in Live 3 is the ability to map clips to MIDI note ranges, thus allowing you to play riffs and melodies with your sampled material. The upshot of this is that Live can now be used much like a traditional keyboard sampler and sequencer combo. Best of all, the process is relatively straightforward.

Figure 7-29
When a clip is configured in this manner, it's ready to go as a MIDI-playable tuned instrument. Power-users take note: If you set the quantization to anything other than "none," you can achieve real-time quantization of live playing — though you'll need to play a little ahead of the beat for best results.

1. Select a one-shot sample, like a chord hit or single instrument note. Assign the clip to a track and configure its MIDI key assignment so it covers a range of notes. (This is covered in the manual.)

2. In the Clip View section, set Launch Mode to "gate" and Quantization to "none." Leave Legato mode off. If needed, tune and transpose the clip so it tracks the keyboard correctly. With these settings, you should be able to play your clip like a "classic" sampler, with each note event triggering and transposing the sample accordingly, as in Figure 7-29.

3. Enter record mode, turn on a few drum loops, and start playing riffs with your new clip. When you exit record mode, switch to arrange mode. In the clip's track you should now see a series of clip events, each one transposed according to the notes you played.

4. If you want to quantize your performance, you can move the clip events to the appropriate locations. If the part has a good groove but just needs a few tweaks, hold off on this until step six.

5. Once you've got a part that fits your track, highlight all of the event segments and then consolidate the part by clicking on the Edit menu and selecting Consolidate. This will convert your clip sequence to a new audio file that can then be assigned to a new slot in your session view.

6. If your loop is fairly tight but needs a bit of adjusting, you can now use Live's warp markers to modify the timing of your loop to get a better feel.

While this technique isn't necessarily a replacement for traditional sequencing, it's really useful for the one-shot samples that are often found on soundware CDs. As with the other tips in this article, a little experimentation goes a long way.

ON-THE-FLY RATE & RESOLUTION CONVERSION

Unlike many sequencing environments, Live 3 is terrific at matching samples despite drastically different bit-depths and sample rates. Need to mix a 44.1/16 drum loop with a vocal at 48/16 and layer some crunchy 8-bit samples? No sweat.

Better still, if you're working on a track in another environment and need to add a few samples that don't fit the rate/resolution, Live has you covered. Just ReWire Live into your session as a client, then add your loops or audio tracks as needed. It's a quick and easy way to integrate samples that wouldn't otherwise fit without extensive conversion tinkering — and it's a huge time-saver when a project presents you with a bunch of 48kHz audio from a video soundtrack and you need to compose new material over it.

IMPORTING REASON LOOPS

If you use Reason in conjunction with Live, you've probably noticed that there's a ton of terrific loops in the Dr.REX factory library. While Dr.REX has some wonderful sound design features, Live's resources are useful for different types of effects, and its time-stretching algorithms generally sound a bit tighter than ReCycling your beats, especially when slowing material down.

The solution? Bring your favorite loops directly into Live.

1. In Live, select an unused track and switch the inputs to Reason (ReWire).

2. In Reason/Dr.REX, select the desired loop to import. Set Reason's tempo to the original tempo of the loop. This is usually indicated in the loop's name. Following this step ensures that the loop imports accurately.

3. Set Live's track to record and grab the loop. Once the loop is captured, be sure to save your set as self-contained in order to keep the audio file in an easy-to-find location.

You can do this with synth loops and other types of audio material as well, which is useful if you use Live as your primary tool for performing gigs. This way, you only have to run a single application for your performances, thus making the most of your CPU and RAM utilization.

KEEPING IT ALL TOGETHER

This tip is fairly basic, but I'm always amazed at how many users don't know it. If you work with a lot of soundware libraries or do a lot of recording, you should make sure that you always save your sets as self-contained. This puts all of your audio files in the same folder and makes backing up and/or transporting your sessions a breeze.

When doing this, the original filenames are preserved, which is generally a good thing unless you've got a ton of libraries that use filenames like "guitar1" and "bass-Cm" or whatever. If you're stuck with generic filenames, it's often helpful to include a plain text file in your set folder that contains a list of the libraries used in your project.

Finally, if you've used Reason or other audio apps in the creation of your Live set, be sure to include the associated song files in your project folder. This way, if you decide to go back and tweak something, the original source material will be available.

PRE-MASTERING

While it's fairly easy to get a slammin' groove out of Live, sometimes the final mixes don't pack the same punch as commercial releases.

Why? Well, for one thing, most commercial recordings are mastered. While the mastering process is complicated, and an in-depth discussion is beyond the scope of this feature, there are still some things you can do in Live to give your mixes a bit more polish.

To begin, try adding an instance of EQ Four to your master outputs. If your mix is too boomy, roll off the bass a bit. If it's too dull, use a high shelving EQ set at 12kHz with 2–3dB boost to add some shimmer. If the mids sound muddy, consider reducing the 500–700Hz range by 2–3dB. The key lies in not applying too much EQ at this point. Just a little nip and tuck will usually do the trick.

Once you've got your mix equalized and sounding smoother, add an instance of Live 3's Compressor II after the EQ. Compression will go a long way to giving you the loudness that makes mixes sound professional. Frankly, Compressor II is quite good at this and I use it frequently, despite the fact that I have other compressors at my disposal. Again, the secret lies in moderation. Too much compression can really kill a mix.

A good starting point for this compressor is the factory preset called "LongRelease." Be sure to adjust the threshold to best suit your material, as the preset is a bit too strong. Adjusting the release is helpful too, but if it's too short, you'll get nasty pumping artifacts. Use your ears. The end result should be a smooth-sounding mix that's a touch louder than the original signal and a lot punchier.

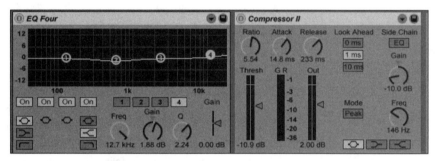

Figure 7-30
A time-tested signal processing path like the one above is a great starting point for getting a more polished sound from your mixes.

RAM VERSUS STREAMING

Generally speaking, Live is extraordinarily efficient at streaming long loops from a hard drive. But if you're working on a laptop, chances are that your drive is 5400 RPM or slower. This can sometimes pose problems when you're using Live as a portable recording studio.

While I've never had any problems on my PowerBook's 4200 RPM drive, I rarely run more than 13 or so tracks at the same time. I recently worked with a larger (21 tracks, to be exact) session that a friend had created in Live on his desktop system. Playing this many unlooped tracks simultaneously really pushed my laptop's hard drive, forcing me to turn off certain tracks periodically to keep everything flowing.

Fortunately, Live 3 addresses the shortcomings of slower hard drives with its ability to load entire samples directly into RAM. In order to do this, you simply toggle on the "RAM" button in the sample attributes window. Of course, you'll need a fair amount of RAM on your system, too.

The secret lies in not assigning all of your tracks to one mode or another. Instead, make the shortest samples in your arrangement RAM tracks and stream the longest audio files from your hard drive. If this isn't enough — and if your system has enough RAM headroom — experiment with RAM-enabling a few of your longer tracks. You may need to try several different combinations of RAM vs. HD-based tracks in order to get everything running smoothly, but it is possible, even on an older laptop — as long as you have enough RAM available.

Figure 7-31
Here's a screenshot of
one of my Live sets. Each
song is organized horizontally as a "scene." Clips with
the same color can be freely
mixed and matched, allow-
ing me to create complex
transitions between songs.
The filenames are intentionally blurred.

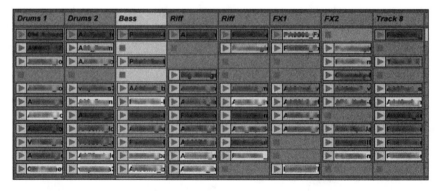

COLOR CODING

Many laptop artists structure their Live performances so that each scene (horizontal row) is its own track. They move downward vertically as they advance through their set. While this is a great approach, there's another trick that seasoned performers use to add even more variety and spice to their sets: color coding.

After you've created your set in the manner outlined above, spend a few hours determining which clips from different scenes work well together. Then assign each of these secondary groups of samples a specific color. Start by using colors that are easily differentiated at a glance, like red, green, yellow, and white. Some of Live's pastel color options are too muted to quickly spot in the heat of a performance.

By color-coding complementary clips, you can create a much more fluid-sounding set, integrating each scene into a more cohesive whole and increasing the overall sophistication of your performance.

Winter 2005
Power Tools for Live 5
Taking Live 5's synths and effects to the next level in your productions

Since 2004's addition of MIDI sequencing, Ableton's groundbreaking (some may say *paradigm-shifting*) software performance workstation, Live, has become one of the hottest DAWs for music production, real-time improvisational recording, and laptop-based performances. Live is no longer just for dance music and hip-hop, it's a true workhorse for creating tracks from start to finish.

Full disclosure: Over the past few months, I've worked with the Ableton crew on sound design and product development. As such, this has afforded me a deeper understanding of how to make the most out of this flexible environment. So without further ado, here's a slew of tips and tricks to help *you* get more out of your Live productions.

TIGHTEN UP

Ask any programmer how to lock down a really tight electronic groove and you'll almost invariably be directed to quantization. On most sequencers, the quantize function moves note-on events to the nearest sixteenth-note (or whatever resolution you've selected). This is all well and good, but the real secret lies in also quantizing the note-*offs*. That's where the precision lies.

I'm always amazed at how difficult most DAW manufacturers make adjusting this seemingly simple function, burying it under so many layers of menus that players give up in frustration. Not so with Live 5. Calling up the quantization feature includes a specific option for note-off quantization (see Figure 7-32). Huzzah! Next time you're working on a mix and the groove isn't quite snappy enough, select this feature when quantizing your track. You may be surprised at how much it cleans up the rhythms.

Figure 7-32
Live 5's new quantization features include amount, as well as quantizing note-off, which allows for really precise groove articulation.

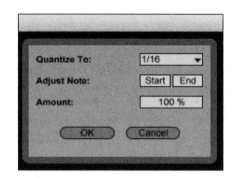

MAKING THE MOST OF CLIP ENVELOPES

Live's clip envelope feature enables the creation of complex rhythmic effects. Considering that every possible destination — volume, transposition, effect parameters, even synth parameters — is available, sometimes it's hard to know where to begin.

Here's a quick and easy experiment to help you familiarize yourself with the process. Start with Simpler's Monobass patch. Play a whole-note drone for one measure (Figure 7-33). Now switch to the clip envelope editor and select Simpler > Filter Freq (Figure 7-34). Start clip playback and draw a complex envelope shape. A quick shortcut to drawing interesting shapes is to start with the draw tool and draw a few large steps (Figure 7-35), then switch back to rubberband mode and add sweeps, aligning the break points to the quantization grid (Figure 7-36).

Figure 7-33
Using a sustaining whole-note allows you to better examine the rhythmic aspects of clip envelopes.

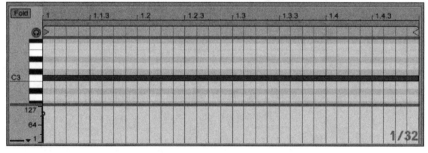

Figure 7-34
Select the Simpler device's Filter Freq envelope from the pulldown menu in the clip envelope section.

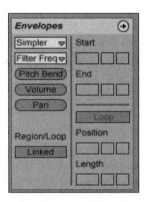

Figure 7-35
Using the draw tool is a great way to get a rough envelope shape with a minimum of fuss.

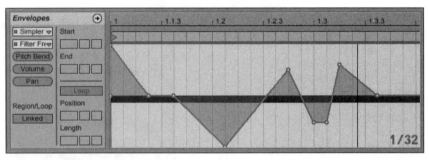

Figure 7-36
After you've got your basic envelope shape, switch to rubberband editing, then add or subtract breakpoints, making sure to align them with the quantization grid.

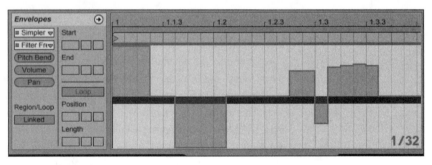

If all has gone according to plan, you should have a nifty rhythmic filter sweep happening. From there, highlight the entire envelope and copy it. Now switch to a different parameter, like resonance. Paste the envelope into the grid and move some of the envelope segments around, keeping them aligned with the grid. More complexity.

Now consider the possibilities of adding a few effects and automating some of those parameters.

Filters are obvious, so here are a few more exotic parameters to automate:

- Impulse transposition.
- Bit crusher: Downsample (soft mode).
- Erosion frequency and/or amount.
- Phaser frequency (LFO and envelope set to off) for custom phase sweeps.

- EQ midrange frequency for highly controllable bandpass sweeps and wah effects.
- Saturator base and/or drive.
- Ping Pong delay EQ frequency, especially on very wet signals with high feedback.

LIVE CLIPS AS PRESETS & ARCHIVES

One of Live 5's hottest new features is the ability to open up any Live set in the browser and import a clip. Warp markers, MIDI, instruments, effects, *everything* is preserved. Best of all, it's totally backwards-compatible, so if you've got an old bit you did in Live 3, no problemo.

While it's obvious that this feature allows for easy import of the collection of loops and sequences that Live 5 ships with, it's also good for a number of other things. Here's a sampling:

1. If you're like me, you probably have a bunch of half-finished song doodles lying about. Chances are, some of these experiments contain a few tracks that could serve as the basis for an entirely new song. The Live Clip feature makes importing these snippets a simple drag-and-drop affair with real-time preview, allowing you to focus on finding the best ideas by treating your back catalog like a customized loop library.

2. DJ-style performers can now stick all of their favorite tracks into a collection of Live sets, all organized by style, vibe, remixer, tempo, whatever. This allows them to bring only the sets they need to a gig, leaving their catalog hard drive safely at home.

3. Here's a related DJ trick: You can even drag an entire set's worth of clips and tracks into *another* set, creating a composite set that's limited only by your system's CPU, RAM, and hard drive. This also means that you can take an existing song or backing track, copy multiple clips that reference the same audio file, then set different loop markers for each clip, allowing you to switch between them — rearranging and remixing on the fly.

4. If you use clip envelopes often, you can now create a collection of presets that you can drag to a new track, then cut and paste the desired envelope pattern to an existing sequence or loop. To make previewing easier, apply the clip envelope patterns to sustaining drones, like those described elsewhere in this feature. This will allow you to hear the entire envelope without gaps, as well as separate the envelope's groove content from a pattern that may not jibe with the track you're working on, potentially causing you to overlook the perfect envelope.

MAXIMIZING CPU

Eventually, everyone hits their head on the ceiling of their CPU, which leads to frustration at inopportune moments. This happens even on the fastest systems. Here's a list of things to consider next time your CPU meter goes into the red.

First off, like many other DAWs, Live now includes a freeze function that renders a track or sequence — effects and all — allowing you to temporarily or permanently bounce a track to audio and free up most of the resources that track was using. If freezing isn't an option, here are some more CPU-saving maneuvers:

If you're using Simpler or Operator, check the voice assignment mode. Begin by selecting only the number of voices your sequence requires to play back without sounding

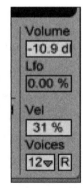

Figure 7-37
Both Simpler and Operator now include voice reassignment modes, allowing for more efficient polyphony allocation.

choppy. If you're using four-note chords, try setting it to eight or six voices. If that doesn't work, restrict the track to four notes and listen to the results. Be sure to set the voice mode to "R" (see Figure 7-37) too, as this will further optimize Live's voice reallocation algorithm.

While you're optimizing your synth tracks, check to see if the patch uses Simpler or Operator's "Spread" function. This sounds awesome and adds spaciousness to the track, but it also uses twice as many voices. If the Spread control is set to anything other than zero, turn it fully off and try a chorus effect instead.

If you have a few tracks that rely on Live's gorgeous new "complex" time-stretching algorithm, keep in mind that this mode uses considerably more CPU than the others. Use complex mode on only the tracks that truly need it.

If you're using EQ Four, turn off unused bands. Each active band uses a small bit of CPU, so turning off as many bands as possible will yield better overall performance.

On a similar note, if you have several heavily effected tracks, try using the device on/off automation function to turn on effects *only* when the track is playing. Shut them off between passages. This may require some experimentation, but it will often work if the arrangement isn't too complex.

If you're applying compression to a synth or drum part, try switching off the compressor and use the MIDI Velocity effect's compression tool to constrain the velocities to a limited range. This plug-in uses less CPU than Live's compressors, but can be used only on MIDI sequences.

CAPTURING THE MAGIC

I know several laptoppers who use Live's session view almost exclusively in their sets, manipulating effects and clips in real time, often while playing Simpler or Operator in accompaniment, to create a unique performance every evening. I also know a few DJs who have switched to Live for their mixes. Some performances are magical, others are so-so, but you never know until the end of the show if you captured that elusive energy. A great set could go by one night with no way to replay those moments. Right? Wrong!

I'm always amazed by the fact that many Live users don't think to turn on recording when they begin their set. When you do this, every gesture and nuance will be captured into an arrangement for later editing (if needed). If you're a purist, you can keep the flubs, or at least learn from them. If you're a perfectionist, you can go back and revise any awkward moments. Either way, a captured set can be tweaked, mastered, and then rendered as audio. This rendered set can then be burned to CD and archived or, better yet, sold at the next performance or even streamed online from your website. Either way, it's a potential revenue stream for industrious performers, and all it takes is an extra mouse click before you begin playing. So do it.

SIMPLER TRICK #1

Some users may find Simpler's single-oscillator design a bit limiting, but there are two easy ways around this:

If you just want to combine the sound with another layer an interval or octave apart, use the MIDI Chord effect. This effect is awesome for more than just Detroit techno chord stabs. If you just want to use two square waves an octave apart, this is the way to go.

If you need more flexibility, you can always copy your clip sequence to an adjacent MIDI track, create another instance of Simpler, and treat that as your second synthesis path. If you want to add the same effects to both synths without creating two instances of each, route the audio from both Simpler tracks to a separate audio track and process that track.

SIMPLER TRICK #2

While Simpler comes with a fairly wide range of presets, additional material awaits if you're not afraid to do a bit of programming yourself. Make sure you've installed Live's additional Impulse Live Pack, either as a download or from the included library CD. Then, in the browser, go to Live's Library > Waveforms > Drum folder. This is the Impulse drum sample library. There are tons of pitched samples in here waiting to be dragged into Simpler. With a bit of filtering and tuning, a tom or conga can become a bass patch. Or use one of the A-Triangles as a bell sound. E-Perc Sonar Triangle is great for atmospheric pads if you lengthen the attack and release and add some lowpass filtering to smooth it out and/or add character. And that's just scratching the surface of the Percussion folder.

SIMPLER TRICK #3

Many vintage hardware samplers allowed for real-time control over a sample's start point and loop parameters. On longer sampled passages, modifying the loop points can be used to create insane stuttered effects that can be manipulated as a performance or recorded and perfected. On shorter samples with only a few consecutive cycles, the results can range from bizarre hard-sync-type sounds to exotic pitchbends when the loop duration slips in and out of tune. Try assigning the mod wheel to one of Simpler's loop parameters and have at it.

Alternately, assigning the mod wheel to sample start allows you to skip over the attack portion of the wave data (if present), thus softening the sound for mellower passages.

IMPULSE TRICK #1

Here's an old-school MIDI trick from the days of really expensive hardware delays. You can create very precise echo effects on specific drums within the piano roll editor. Begin with an Impulse kit with a fair amount of velocity sensitivity on the desired drums. Then create a simple drum pattern or select one from the included Impulse clips.

Now select a drum hit and option-drag (or control-drag if you're on a PC) it over to the next eighth-note segment. While the new snare event is highlighted, grab its velocity slider and drag it down slightly. Repeat this process a few more times (see Figure 7-38). Now play the sequence. You should hear an echo on the drum, without the need to route it to a separate channel and apply a delay effect. For more examples of this effect, check out the Impulse clip library, specifically El Bee Jay and Free Electro.

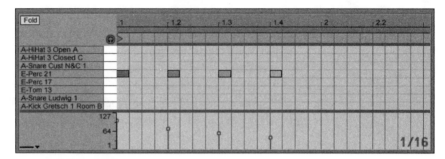

IMPULSE TRICK #2

While Impulse doesn't support velocity-switching or cross-fading between different samples, it's still capable of delivering realistic and organic drum grooves, once you understand how to tweak each drum's performance parameters.

For starters, transposition, stretch, filter cutoff, pan, and volume can all be modulated via velocity individually for each drum. What's more, you can apply randomization to transposition, cutoff, and panning. Adding a tiny bit of randomization — less than 5% — to transposition will work wonders at giving snares and hi-hats a, dare I say, "livelier" feel.

Applying velocity sensitivity to lowpass filter cutoff, volume, and transposition is another way to make your percussion more dynamic and responsive. The secret is to start with small amounts and increase the value as you develop your parts. Too much velocity sensitivity, especially on transposition or stretch, is terrific for exotic effects but not really suited to realistic drum grooves.

IMPULSE TRICK #3

Once you've got your kit tailored to your playing style, the next step lies in humanizing your sequences. Live 5's new quantization *amount* feature is the ticket here. By backing off from 100% to, say, 80–90%, you can impart a more nuanced feel, only correcting notes that are wildly off the mark while keeping the events that are closer to the pocket. As always, the secret lies in subtlety. If you lower the percentage too much, you may introduce unwanted slop. If it's set at 100% the timing will be perfect. While perfect timing is great for dance and hip-hop genres, it's often too robotic for rock or jazz.

IMPULSE TRICK #4

Here's a secret that every house and techno producer should know. That fat, crunchy kick that dominates hard dance tracks is basically distortion on a 909 kick. One of the coolest things about Impulse is that it has independent drive controls for every drum. Distortion being what it is, you can get similar kick sounds with the E-Kick 3 wave. Quite a few toms, like E-Tom 5, tuned lower, are useful for this too.

Another use for the drive control is to simulate old vinyl recordings. Start with a dry kit like All Purpose. Add a tiny bit of drive to every drum, enough to add some dirt without becoming true distortion. Now adjust the pitch of the kit slightly high or low to simulate turntable pitch-shifting. Follow Impulse with the Vinyl Distortion Dubplate preset and you're off to a good start at emulating the sound of greasy loops. If you've got CPU headroom, try sticking a Saturator before the Vinyl Distortion and try modifying a few presets.

EFFECTS TRICKS

Follow the Bouncing Envelope. Live 5's new Flanger and Phaser effects both have envelope-following algorithms that respond dynamically to changes in signal volume. These envelopes are awesome at creating exotic flange and comb filter effects on dynamic material. Drum loops are prime candidates, but the phaser's envelope is cool on leads and vocals too. Drop the flanger's "Wiggle" or "Metallic" presets on a busy drum loop and you'll get the picture. The phaser's "Enphasor" and "Zappified" patches are equally exotic-sounding effects that make use of this programming technique.

    Guided by Voices. Speaking of Zappified, this preset is an excellent example of the phaser's "space" mode. While many phasers provide control over the number of poles, which governs the slope or intensity of the effect, Live's new phaser delivers an Earth/Space option for the overall behavior of the phaser. Earth gives more of a classic phased sound, while Space is capable of more extreme effects like vocal formants and even bell-like textures. In the case of Zappified, the vocal formants are further enhanced by envelope control: Louder and quieter sounds impart a different vowel sound to the patch. This is especially pronounced when applied to bright sawtooth-based patches or distorted guitar leads. Check out the Tuvan Throat Simpler preset using a velocity-sensitive keyboard, or apply the Talkbox Solo audio group to a wailing guitar solo to hear this effect in action. As for the bellish textures that Space mode is capable of, slap the Great Buddha preset on a drum loop and dig the chimes.

    Digital Glitter. Another über-cool feature of the flanger and phaser is the inclusion of tempo-synced LFOs with multiple waveforms. Sure, we're all familiar with the traditional sine or triangle LFO sound on these effects, but things get really interesting when you venture into the uncharted territory of alternate waveforms. For example, old-timey sci-fi effects can be created by using a high-feedback flanger or phaser with a Sample & Hold LFO. The flanger's "Subotnics" preset is a great example of this sound, as is the "Twinkly Bitz" combo patch.

    Saturator. Another new effect, Saturator, delivers impressive distortion effects that previous versions of Live were sorely lacking, but that's just a small slice of the real action. Saturator also excels at warm-sounding analog effects too. Try using the clip or sine shapes and adding just a touch of drive to add punch and presence without mangling your signal. "Hot Tubes" and "A Bit Warmer" deliver the goods in this area. It's worth noting that this type of saturation delivers a form of dynamic compression as well, due to the way that the algorithm reshapes the original wave. Sound too good to be true? Try increasing the drive to its maximum while watching your meters. You may be surprised. It may not be an LA-22, but it's no slouch at adding warmth to classic compression/limiting applications.

    Beat Repeat. There's a lot of buzz surrounding the exotic Beat Repeat effect, and deservedly so. This effect blurs the line between a classic delay and more exotic plug-ins like Smart Electronix's cult hit, SupaTrigger, resulting in on-the-fly stutter edits that used to take hours, even days, to program effectively into a track. One of the coolest uses for Beat Repeat is applying it to a vocal track and letting it insert micro edits as the vocals play. The "Vocal Fun" preset was designed specifically for this application. However, since the effect is inserted randomly into a track, you may hear an awesome effect on a specific line once, then it's gone forever.

Not to worry, there's a way to let Beat Repeat do all the heavy lifting while you audition the results and sip tea. Here's how:

Select a vocal or lead track and apply the Vocal Fun patch. Then set the effected track's "Audio To" to another available audio track, set the destination channel's input to the effected track, and activate recording. Now play the vocal and record the results. Whenever you hear a cool vocal edit, jot down the time or bar number and continue. After a few passes, you should have a collection of ultra-exotic editing gestures that would have taken forever to develop and articulate. From there, isolate the sections you logged earlier and place them on their own track, removing Beat Repeat from the original vocal. Voilá! Several days-worth of work in a few minutes.

ARPEGGIATOR FUN

Live 5's arpeggiator is one of the slickest, useful implementations I've yet seen in a DAW. With tons of modes, various grooves, alternate retriggering, and gate options, as well as a few velocity options, it's capable of everything from emulated guitar strums to classic percolating effects.

One of the coolest, and least understood, features lurking within this beastie is the ability to use non-octave interval amounts so that your arpeggios cascade upward or downward in unusual ways. This is one of the secrets to understanding how Kraftwerk got some of their trademark sequenced effects way back in the '70s and early '80s. For example, check out the MIDI Effect Group called "TEE 4ths" and apply it to the "Warm Strings" Simpler preset. Then hit *any* note on your keyboard and hold it. If you're familiar with a little ditty called "Trans-Europe Express" — and if you're not, shame on you — you'll immediately be greeted by a sequence that's eerily reminiscent of the opening chord progression: a series of fourths that ascend upward by a fifth every half-note.

Which brings us to another useful trick: Try applying the Chord plug-in *after* the arpeggiator and tinker with the parameters as you hold one or two keys (more than that can lead to cacophonic results, so tread lightly here). Kraftwerk aside, this is also a quick shortcut to getting classic Detroit techno chordal effects, especially if you set up the chord plug-in so that it generates a minor seventh or ninth chord.

Chapter 8
MIXING

The previous chapters covered the essentials of developing grooves, adding loops, editing vocals, and designing or processing sounds. All that's left now is finishing the mix. Before we get into this process, there are a few things to consider.

First off, everyone has slightly different hearing (and slightly or radically different taste in mix styles). This is one of the reasons that there's so much variety throughout the range of genres that comprise "dance music."

Next, everyone has a different set of influences. Someone who's all about the gossamer pad clouds and hypnotic bass in trance is going to approach a mix very differently than someone who lives for the edgy crunch of retronica and electroclash. Ultimately, every genre has its own set of idioms and methods that define it.

Finally, everyone has a different rig, and the tools you have will define your capabilities. If you're exclusively using hardware (and some people still do — by choice), you're going to have a few more limitations in terms of processing capabilities, but that's cool, because some of the most important tracks ever released were done on decidedly unglamorous rigs. Limitations force you to be creative with what you have. On the other hand, someone who has an ultra-fast Mac or PC with loads of software runs the risk of tinkering with a mix until they've overproduced all of the energy out of it. Heaven knows, I've done that on more than one occasion.

With all of that in mind, there are still some tried-and-true techniques for getting a great mix no matter what your genre of choice is and no matter what gear you own. And that's what this chapter is all about.

So let's start with the basics. No matter how experienced you are, there's always something more to learn. If that weren't the case, why would you be reading this book?

In the first section, Craig Anderton outlines a simple set of processes that will take you step-by-step through refining and finishing your mixes.

March 1998
The Art of Mixing
Timeless techniques for constructing your mix

Mixing is not only an art, it's the crucial step that turns a collection of tracks into a finished piece of music. A good mix can bring out the best in your music — it spotlights a composition's most important elements, adds a few surprises to excite the listener, and sounds good on anything from a transistor radio to an audiophile's dream setup.

In theory, mixing should be easy: You just adjust the knobs until everything sounds great. But this doesn't happen by accident. Mixing is as difficult an art to master as playing a musical instrument. So let's take a closer look at what goes into the mixing process.

POINTS OF REFERENCE

Start by analyzing well-mixed recordings by top-notch mainstream engineers and producers such as Bruce Swedien, Roger Nichols, Shelly Yakus, Steve Albini, and Bob Clearmountain, as well as dancefloor-specific tracks by established producers like David Morales, Gabriel & Dresden, and BT. Don't focus on the music, just the mix. Notice how — even with a "wall of sound" — you can pick out every instrument because each element of the music has its own space. Also note that the frequency response balance will be uniform throughout the audio spectrum, with enough highs to sound sparkly but not screechy, sufficient bass to give a satisfying bottom end without turning the mix to mud, and a midrange that adds presence and definition.

One of the best mixing tools is a CD player and a really well-mixed reference CD. Patch the CD player into your mixer and A/B your mix against the reference CD periodically. If your mix sounds substantially duller, harsher, or less interesting, listen carefully and try to isolate the source of any differences. A reference CD also provides a guideline to good-sounding relative levels of drums, vocals, etc.

Match the CD's level to the overall level of your mix by matching the peak levels of the two signals. If your mix sounds a lot quieter even though its peaks match the reference CD's peak levels, that probably means the reference has been compressed or limited a fair amount to restrict its dynamic range. Compression is something that can always be done at the mastering stage — in fact, it probably should be, because a good mastering suite will have top-of-the-line compressors and someone who is an ace at applying them.

PROPER MONITORING LEVELS

Loud, extended mixing sessions are tough on the ears. Mixing at low levels keeps your ears "fresher" and minimizes ear fatigue. Loud mixes may get your juices flowing, but they make it more difficult to hear subtle level variations.

Many project studios have noise constraints, so mixing through headphones might seem like a good idea. Although headphones are excellent for catching details that you might not hear over speakers, they are not necessarily good for general mixing because they magnify some details out of proportion. It's better to use headphones solely for reality checks.

THE GEAR: KEEP IT CLEAN

Preparing for the mix begins the moment you start recording. One element in a great mix is recording the cleanest possible signal on each source track. If you're working with hardware, eliminate as many active stages as possible between source and recorder; many times, signal processors set to "bypass" may not be adding any effect, yet remain in the signal path. [*Editor's note: Modern software DAWs do not generally operate this way.*] If possible, send sounds directly into the recorder (for mics, use an ultra-high-quality outboard preamp) and bypass the mixer altogether.

Although you may not hear much of a difference when monitoring a single instrument, with multiple tracks the cumulative effect of stripping the signal path to its essentials can make a significant difference in the clarity of the overall sound.

THE ARRANGEMENT

Scrutinize the arrangement prior to mixing. Solo project studio arrangements are particularly prone to "clutter," because as you lay down the early tracks there's a tendency to overplay to fill up the empty space. As the arrangement progresses, there's not a lot of room for overdubs. Remember: *The fewer notes, the greater the impact of each note.* As Sun Ra once said, "Space is the place."

Here are some more tracking-related suggestions:

- Once the arrangement is fleshed out, sometimes it's good to go back and recut tracks recorded at the beginning of the project. Like many other people, I write in the studio, and often the song will have a slightly tentative feel because of that. Recutting some parts always seems to both simplify and improve the song, as I have a clearer idea of the song's direction than I did when I started.
- Try building a song around the vocalist or other lead instrument instead of completing the rhythm section and then laying down the vocals. Record simple "placemarkers" for the drums, bass, and piano (or rhythm guitar, or whatever), then immediately get to work cutting the best possible vocal. When you recut the rhythm section with the "real" parts, you'll be a lot more sensitive to the vocal nuances. It will be easier to feel where to add energy and where to leave a hole.
- Modern sequencers include digital audio capabilities that make it easy to lay down the vocal before you get too heavily into sequencing, so your sequenced parts can accommodate the vocals better.

MIXING: THE 12-STEP PROGRAM

Although there aren't any rules for recording or mixing, until you develop your own mixing "style" you may find it helpful to have a point of departure that's known to work. Here's what has worked for me.

You "build" a mix over time by making a variety of adjustments. There are (at least!) 12 major steps involved in creating a mix, but what makes mixing so difficult is that these steps interact. Change the equalization, and you also change the level because you're boosting or cutting some element of the sound. In fact, you can think of a mix as an "audio combination lock." When all the elements hit the right combination, you end up with a good mix.

Let's look at these 12 steps, but remember, this is just one person's way of mixing — you might discover a totally different approach that works better for you.

1. Mental Preparation

Mixing can be tedious, so set up an efficient workspace. If you don't have a really good office chair with lumbar support, it might be worth a trip to the local office supply store. Keep paper and a log book handy for taking notes, dim the lighting a little so your ears become more sensitive than your eyes, and in general psych yourself up for an interesting journey.

Take periodic breaks (every 45 to 60 minutes or so) to rest your ears and gain a fresher outlook on your return. This may seem like a luxury if you're paying for studio time, but even a couple of minutes of off time can restore your objectivity and, paradoxically, allow you to complete a mix much faster.

2. Review the Tracks

Listen at low volume to scope out what's on the multitrack. Write down track information. If you're mixing on a hardware console, use removable stick-on labels or erasable markers to indicate which sounds correspond to which mixer channels. Group sounds logically, such as having all the drum parts on consecutive channels.

3. Put On Headphones and Fix Glitches

Fixing glitches is a "left-brain" activity, as opposed to the "right-brain" creativity involved in doing a mix. Switching back and forth between these two modes can hamper creativity, so do as much cleaning up as possible — erase glitches, bad notes, and the like — before you get involved in the mix. Listen on headphones to catch details, and solo each track.

If you're sequencing virtual tracks, this is the time to thin out excessive controller information, check for duplicate notes, and trim overlapping notes on single-note lines (such as bass and horn parts).

To clean up tracks recorded on tape (digital or analog), consider bouncing them over to a hard disk recorder and doing some digital editing and noise reduction. Low-level artifacts may not seem audible, but multiply them by a couple of dozen tracks and they can definitely muddy things up.

4. Optimize Any Sequenced MIDI Sound Generators

With sequenced virtual tracks, optimize the various sound generators. For example, for more brightness, try increasing the lowpass filter cutoff instead of adding equalization at the console. One tip: With digital synths, keep the output volume control at maximum, as this usually allows for the maximum dynamic range. Reduce the level at the console if you need to. Occasional changes in a synth's level can be automated with controller 7 messages, but keep the loudest parts of the synth track at or close to 127, and adjust the synth's volume if necessary at the mixer. If you turn up the volume knob and then set a CC7 level of 32, you're compromising the instrument's dynamic range.

5. Set Up a Relative Level Balance Between the Tracks

Before you add processing, concentrate on the overall sound of the tracks — don't become distracted by left-brain-oriented detail work. With a good mix, the tracks sound good by themselves, but sound even better when interacting with the other tracks.

Try setting the levels in mono at first, because if the instruments sound distinct and separate in mono, they'll open up even more in stereo. Also, you may not notice parts that "fight" with others if you start off in stereo.

Figure 8-1
Different instruments take up different parts of the frequency spectrum.

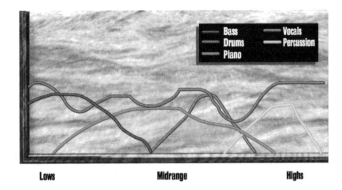

6. Adjust Equalization

Equalization (EQ) can help dramatize differences between instruments and create a more balanced overall sound. Work on the most important song elements first (vocals, drums, and bass). Once these all "lock" together, deal with the more supportive parts.

The audio spectrum has only so much space; ideally, each instrument will stake out its own "turf" in the audio spectrum, so that when the instruments are combined, they'll fill up the spectrum in a satisfying way. (Of course, this is primarily a function of the tune's arrangement, but you can think of EQ as being part of the arrangement.) One of the reasons for working on drums early in the mix is that a drum kit covers the audio spectrum pretty well all by itself, from the low thunk of the kick drum to the sizzle of the cymbals. Once the drums are set up, you'll have a better idea how to integrate the other instruments.

EQ added to one track may affect other tracks. For example, boosting a piano part's midrange may interfere with vocals, guitar, or other midrange instruments. Sometimes boosting a frequency for one instrument necessitates cutting the same region in another instrument. To have vocals stand out more, try notching out the vocal frequencies on other instruments instead of just boosting the EQ on the voice.

Think of the song as a spectrum, and decide where you want the various parts to sit (as well as their relative prominence; see Figure 8-1). I sometimes use a spectrum analyzer when mixing, not because ears don't work well enough for the task, but because the analyzer provides invaluable ear training and shows exactly which instruments take up which parts of the audio spectrum. An analyzer can alert you to an abnormal buildup of audio energy in a particular region.

If you really need a sound to "break through" a mix, try a slight boost in the 1 to 3kHz region. Don't do this with all the instruments, though; the idea is to use boosts (or cuts) to differentiate one instrument from another.

To place a sound further back in the mix, sometimes engaging the high cut filter will do the job — you may not even need to use the main EQ. Also, applying the low cut filter on instruments that veer toward the bass range, like guitar and piano, can help trim their low end to open up more space for the all-important bass and kick drum.

7. Add Any Essential Signal Processing

"Essential" doesn't mean "sweetening," but processing that is an integral part of the sound (such as an echo that falls on the beat and therefore changes the rhythmic characteristics of a part, distortion that alters the timbre in a radical way, vocoding, etc.).

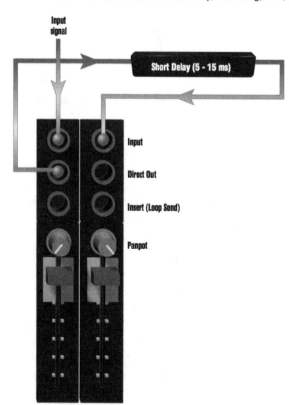

Figure 8-2
Creating an artificial stereo spread with delay. The delay input can come from the mixer channel's direct out or loop send (insert) jack, or you can use a Y cable to split the input signal into the mixer channel and the delay, and return the delay output to a second channel.

8. Create a Stereo Soundstage

Now place your instruments within the stereo field. Your approach might be traditional (*i.e.,* the goal may be to recreate the feel of a live performance) or something radical. Pan mono instruments to a particular location, but avoid panning signals to the *extreme* left or right.

For some reason they just don't sound quite as substantial as signals that are a little bit off from the extremes.

Bass frequencies are less directional than highs, so place the kick drum and bass toward the center. Consider balance: For example, if you've panned the hi-hat (which has a lot of high frequencies) to the right, pan a tambourine, shaker, or other high-frequency sound somewhat to the left. The same concept applies to midrange instruments as well.

Signal processing can create a stereo image from a mono signal. One method uses time delay processing, such as stereo chorusing or a short delay. For example, if a signal is panned to the left, feed some of this signal through a short (5–15ms) delay and send its output to another channel panned to the right (see Figure 8-2). When you do this, it's vital to check the mix in mono at some point, since mixing the delayed and straight signals may cause phase cancellations that aren't apparent when you're listening in stereo.

Another spreading technique involves EQ. Send a signal to two separate channels, but equalize them differently (for example, use a stereo graphic equalizer and cut the even-numbered bands with one channel and the odd-numbered bands with the other channel).

Stereo placement can significantly affect how we perceive a sound. Consider a doubled vocal line, where a singer sings a part and then doubles it as closely as possible. Try putting the two voices in opposite channels. After listening to the effect, change the panning to put both voices together in the center, and listen again. The center position gives a somewhat smoother sound, which is good for weaker vocalists. The opposite-channel vocals give a more defined, distinct sound that can really help spotlight a good singer.

9. Make Any Final Changes to the Arrangement
Minimize the number of competing parts to keep the listener focused on the tune and avoid clutter. You may be extremely proud of some clever effect you added, but if it doesn't serve the song, *get rid of it.* Conversely, if you find that a song needs some extra element, this is your final opportunity to add an overdub or two. Never fall in love with your work until it's done; maintain as much objectivity as you can.

You can also use mixing to modify an arrangement by selectively dropping out and adding specific tracks. This type of mixing is the foundation for a lot of dance music, where you have looped tracks that play continuously, and the mixer sculpts the arrangement by muting parts and doing major level changes.

10. Audio Architecture
Now that we have our tracks set up in stereo, let's put them in an acoustical space. Start by patching a good reverb to the aux send, and then add reverberation and/or delay to selected channels to give the normally flat soundstage some acoustic depth. By turning up the aux send for a particular channel and lowering the fader slightly, you can make a track recede to the rear of the soundstage.

Generally, you'll want an overall reverb to create a particular type of space (club, concert hall, auditorium, etc.), but you may also want to use a second reverb on single channels to add effects, such as a gated reverb on toms. But beware of situations where you have to drench a sound with reverb to have it sound good. If a part is questionable enough that it needs a lot of reverb, redo the part if possible.

11. Tweak, Tweak, and Re-Tweak

Now that the mix is on its way, it's time for fine tuning. If you use automated mixing, start programming your mixing moves. Remember that all of the above steps interact, so go back and forth between EQ, levels, stereo placement, and effects. Listen as critically as possible; if you don't fix something that bothers you, it will haunt you every time you hear the mix.

While it's important to mix until you're satisfied, it's equally important not to beat a mix to death. Once Quincy Jones offered the opinion that recording with synthesizers and sequencing was like "painting a 747 with Q-Tips." A mix is a performance, and if you overdo it, you'll lose the spontaneity that can add excitement. A mix that isn't perfect but that conveys passion will always be more fun to listen to than one that's perfect to the point of sterility. As insurance, don't throw out your previous mixes — when you listen back to them the next day, you might find that an earlier mix was the "keeper."

In fact, you may not even be able to tell much difference between your mixes. A veteran record producer once told me about mixing literally dozens of takes of the same song, because he kept hearing small changes that seemed really important at the time. A couple of weeks later he went over the mixes, and couldn't discern any difference between most of the versions. Be careful not to waste time making changes that no one, not even you, will care about a couple of days later.

One important tip is that once you've captured your ultimate mix, you should also run a couple of extra mixes, such as an instrumental-only mix or a mix without the solo instrument. These additional mixes can really come in handy later, if you have a chance to re-use your music for a film or video score, or need to extend certain sections long after you've archived the mix. Be prepared!

12. Check Your Mix over Different Systems

Before you sign off on a mix, check it over a variety of speakers and headphones, in stereo and mono, and at different levels. The frequency response of the human ear changes with level (we hear less of the highs and lows at lower levels), so if you listen only at lower levels, your mixes may sound bass-heavy or too bright at normal levels. Go for an average that sounds good on all systems. If you're mixing for a particular delivery system, you should consider mixing directly on that system — but if you aren't mix-

FADEOUTS

The secret of a good fadeout is to key it to the beat of the song. Let's suppose that you end a song with a long instrumental. One option would be to keep it at the existing volume for four measures, then fade out over eight measures. Also, a fadeout doesn't have to be continuous. You can turn a fader down a tiny notch, say, every two beats.

A linear fadeout is not necessarily the best option. A concave fadeout, especially on a somewhat long, instrumentally oriented piece, can leave listeners hanging on for more. The initial rapid decay tells them to listen closely; once they're hooked, you stretch out the ending. Convex fadeouts, on the other hand, usually don't sound very good, as the music feels like it's slipping away whether you want it to or not.

A return fadeout is when you fade something out, only to have it fade back in quickly before fading out again for good. This is the kind of trick you can use once every two CDs or so, and it does add variety. Probably the best implementation I've heard of this trick was when a song modulated up a whole-step during the brief time when the first fadeout had gone to zero volume. When the song came back, it had moved up a notch in terms of overall energy.

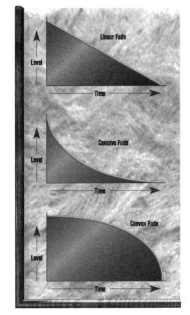

Figure 8-3
Linear, convex, and concave fadeout curves. The concave curve often sounds best.

ing there, be sure to test the mix on a representative target system.

With a home studio, you have the luxury of leaving a mix and coming back to it the next day when you're fresh, after you've had a chance to listen over several different systems to decide if any tweaks need to be made. One common trick is to run off some CDs and see what they sound like in your car. Road noise will mask any subtleties and give you a good idea of what elements "jump out" of the mix. I also recommend booking some time at a pro studio to hear your mixes. If the mix sounds good under all these situations, your mission is accomplished. Finally, if you're friends with a DJ at a well-equipped club, ask him or her to test out your mix early in their set before everyone arrives. This is really the best way to determine if your remix is ready for the world.

THE PERFORMER AS LISTENER

You may find that although you produced, played on, and engineered a piece, you never did really get to listen to it for pleasure. Well, now that the mix is over, give yourself a treat. Put on your final mix, and forget about analysis; just listen to the music. Pretend you walked in someplace and heard that music playing. What would you think of it?

Of course, maybe you'll decide you don't really like it after all. I've cut a couple of tunes where I listened back and wished I hadn't wasted my time, but that hasn't happened very often. Most likely, when you listen to your stuff you'll think it's pretty good, or you wouldn't have made it the way you did in the first place.

Don't be surprised if your feelings about a particular mix change over the months and years. Your tastes will change, and you'll learn more about mixing. But if you follow these steps, you should always be able to let yourself kick back and bask in the sound of your creation. You worked hard on it: You've earned the right to enjoy the fruits of your labor.

Since EQ is one of the fundamental tools in blending your tracks to create a good mix, let's take a look at what Mitch Gallagher has to say about the two most common types of EQ (graphic and parametric) and how each works.

April 2001
Graphic versus Parametric EQ
Understanding the differences

Whether you're working with live musicians, miked acoustic tracks, synthesized tones, or sampled instruments, equalization is probably an integral part of your sound-tweaking and mixing process. EQs are useful for shaping the overall tone of the sound, for correcting specific frequency-related problems, and for blending multiple sounds or instruments together. Several types of EQ are available; best known are the graphic and parametric types.

GRAPHIC EQUALIZERS

Any equalizer is a collection of filters that are used to boost and/or cut a range of audio frequencies. In a graphic equalizer, each filter is *hardwired* to a fixed specific center frequency. Multiple filters are arranged across the audio frequency range at regular intervals (1/3-octave, 2/3-octave, and 1-octave are the most common configurations), allowing you to adjust the entire spectrum by boosting or cutting the appropriate filter(s). A graphic EQ may have up to 30 or 31 bands available: The more bands, the finer the control you have. You're not given control over bandwidth, however.

The term *graphic EQ* comes from the way the EQ bands are arranged horizontally across the faceplate of the EQ. As you change the boost/cut level for each band, you're given a somewhat visual impression of what the equalizer is doing to the frequency spectrum — you can visually see the EQ curve you're creating by pushing the sliders up and down. But don't take the graphic representation created by the sliders as gospel. A variety of things may be going on behind the scenes, the main one being bands overlapping and interacting. Also, the slider positions don't reflect the frequency response of the incoming signal. If it's totally flat, then the sliders show the end result more accurately. If it's not flat (and what signal is?), then the slider positions are just a casual indication of the output signal's curve.

Graphic EQs tend to be easy to operate: You're really only given one parameter per band to fool with, and that's the amount of cut/boost per band. Graphics are useful for the overall sonic shaping of sounds, for correcting broad frequency-related prob-

FOR THOSE WHO DON'T LIKE AUTOMATION . . .

Automation offers many advantages for mixing. Yet despite these advantages, some engineers prefer not to use automation because they feel it destroys spontaneity and soul. And there's no law that says mixing should be hard-coded — some engineers consider it more of a performance process than anything else.

One engineer I worked with (and he had quite a few hits, too) used to work really hard getting his levels and EQ and reverb set just right. Then, when it came time for the final mix, he closed his eyes and rode the faders in time with the music. He was mixing from an 8-track master, and had each finger independently riding a fader to move it slightly in time with the beat. The difference was not obvious, but overall, it made songs come alive.

But you needn't restrict your playing to the level controls. Changing equalization during a piece can be great; try adding a little treble or midrange "bite" to an instrument during a solo. On fadeouts, sometimes you can make an instrument appear to fade out faster than other instruments by adding progressively more reverb to its channel via the reverb send.

Whatever you do, keep the mix lively and interesting, but keep it subtle, too. Even minute control changes can make a big change on playback. Don't just add gimmicks for the sake of effect; add them for the sake of making a more varied and musically interesting piece of music. Keep the levels dancing, and don't be afraid to experiment. — *Craig Anderton*

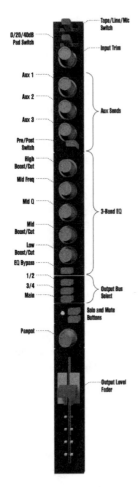

Tape/Line/Mic Switch

0/20/40dB Pad Switch

Input Trim

Aux 1

Aux 2

Aux 3

Aux Sends

Pre/Post Switch

High Boost/Cut

Mid Freq

Mid Q

3-Band EQ

Mid Boost/Cut

Low Boost/Cut

EQ Bypass

1/2

3/4

Main

Output Bus Select

Solo and Mute Buttons

Panpot

Output Level Fader

Figure 8-4

A mixer can look more than a little intimidating, if you've never worked with one before. Here's a breakdown that should help get you oriented. In addition to the master section, a mixer has a number of channel strips (eight or 12 or 16 or 24 of them, if not more), which are all functionally identical. They look more or less like the generic diagram at right.

The input section is at the very top. Here you choose which input to use (the instrument or mic input, plus the tape return if the mixer has an in-line design) and set the proper input level for your source with the input trim and/or the switchable pad.

Each channel will have one or more aux (auxiliary) send pots, which can be used for sending the signal to a reverb or other effect device. The amount of signal that will reach a particular effect is governed, in many cases, both by a pot in this section and by the corresponding master aux send level pot. The pre/post switch allows you to send to the effect either before or after the channel fader. A pre-fader send is useful if you want to bring the dry signal down without altering the amount that's reaching the effect.

This mixer has a three-band EQ with a fully parametric mid band; the fully parametric mid is not common, but it's useful. More often you'll see mid frequency and boost/cut knobs but no mid Q (bandwidth) control. Some mixer EQ sections allow the cutoff frequency of the low and high shelving to be adjusted, as well as the amount of boost or cut (shown here). The EQ bypass switch is another desirable feature not found on all consoles: It lets you compare the original sound with the equalized version.

This is a four-bus mixer, so the output bus select switches can be used to send the channel signal to busses 1 and 2, 3 and 4, or the main stereo output in any combination. Busses 1 and 2 are usually configured as a stereo pair (3 and 4 ditto), so the panpot can be used to bus to a single output: To send only to bus 3, for instance, select the 3/4 bus and then pan the channel hard left.

The function of the solo and mute buttons should be obvious. The advantage of hitting the mute button as opposed to pulling down the channel fader is that you don't lose the fader's level setting. If the mixer is a good one, the solo button will allow you to solo "in place," which means that the pan position set by the panpot is still used when the channel is soloed. By soloing several channels in place, you can hear selected tracks without losing their stereo relationships to one another.

lems, and for compensating for the acoustics in a room. In an EQ that has a larger number of bands, such as a 2/3-octave (15-band) or 1/3-octave (30-band), the filters are fine enough to do some surgical EQing tasks, such as taming feedback in a P.A. system or pulling a troublesome resonance out of a signal.

PARAMETRIC EQUALIZERS

Unlike graphic EQs, parametric models tend to offer only a few filter bands. Rarely will you see a hardware parametric with more than four or five bands (some software plug-in parametrics offer more bands). But you're given significantly more control over the EQ parameters with a parametric (hence the name) than you are with a graphic. A fully parametric EQ gives you three controls per band: frequency, which tunes the filter to a specific frequency area; gain, which adjusts the amount of boost or cut for the active band; and bandwidth, which adjusts how wide or narrow the range of frequencies affected by that band will be.

Unless you're just going to twist the knobs until you get a sound that you like, a parametric EQ requires a bit more knowledge and experience than a graphic. You'll need to have

THE GOLDEN RULE OF EQ

Ask an experienced engineer what primary EQ rule of thumb they follow, and the response will probably be, "Cut rather than boost." In other words, you're better off to reduce the gain on certain frequencies and then turn up the overall signal level than you are to boost the gain on some frequencies and then have to turn the overall signal level down. Why? Two reasons: First, any time you use an EQ, you're messing with the phase coherence of a signal, and boosting does more damage than cutting. Second, by boosting only some frequencies, you may be reducing the overall headroom available to the signal, requiring that you lower the average signal level to prevent distortion.

a basic idea of what center frequency you want the EQ band to operate at, and you'll also need to determine how wide the bandwidth should be for the tonal effect you want. If you use two bands in close proximity to one another, both set to wide bandwidths, they may overlap and interact.

Here's one easy way to determine what the center frequency for a given parametric EQ band should be. Turn up the gain for the band by 6 or 9dB. (Be careful of your overall volume level when doing so!) Set the bandwidth fairly narrow. Next, sweep the frequency for the band until you hear the area you want to equalize *pop out*. This is roughly where your frequency should be set (you may need to fine-tune it a bit). Next, adjust the bandwidth so the filter covers the range you want to work on. As you gain experience, this will become easier. Next, adjust the band's gain to taste. Keep in mind that 6dB is a pretty significant amount of EQ boost or cut, and that cutting is better than boosting. (See "The Golden Rule of EQ" sidebar.)

Parametric EQs can be used for overall sound shaping, but they tend to be better as problem solvers, such as removing an annoying resonance or boosting and cutting two tracks in complementary fashion to make them blend better or sit better in a mix. Parametrics also excel at surgical EQ tasks, such as notching out hum, curing troublesome feedback peaks, and taming sibilance, guitar pick noise, and other acoustic problems.

TECH TERMS

Bandwidth: The range of frequencies that a given filter in an EQ affects. In parametric EQs, bandwidth is adjustable. In a graphic EQ, the bandwidth normally increases as you raise or lower the gain on a filter. With large amounts of boost/cut, adjacent EQ bands may overlap. Some graphic EQs offer *constant Q*, which maintains the same bandwidth regardless of the amount of boost/cut added. This prevents adjacent bands from overlapping.
Center frequency: The frequency where the filter's boost or cut is greatest.
Gain: The amount of boost or cut applied to the signal.
Q: The terms "Q" and "bandwidth" (see above) tend to be used interchangeably with EQs. Q is the parameter used to define the width of the range of frequencies that a given filter affects. A high value for Q corresponds to a narrow bandwidth.

FINAL THOUGHT

Equalization is your friend! Used carefully and correctly, it can greatly enhance the tone of any audio signal, be it from a microphone, synth, or sampler. It can also be used as a tonal problem solver, helping to correct for frequency anomalies, noise, resonances, and peaks. Whether you should use a graphic or parametric EQ depends on your application, although for live work, graphics tend to be more common, while studios tend to favor parametrics. But use the type you have; there are no rules preventing the studio use of graphics or the use of a parametric with a P.A.

If I can leave you with one final thought on EQ, it would be to use it conservatively. It's easy to get carried away with equalization; after a while, our ears start to get numb to it. Plus, use the EQ's bypass button regularly so you know exactly how much boost and cut you're adding to your signals.

May 1998
KMFDM

Your gear list is extensive. Are there any particular pieces that were essential to the sound of Symbols?

The MS-404 [Doepfer analog synth] is definitely one of my favorite boxes, 'cause it's just so handy. Send it any sort of MIDI triggers, and it just goes on and on. When I'm doing the initial programming for bass and so on, I'm finding myself more and more using the [Clavia] Nord Lead. It's so handy when it comes to syncing the arpeggiator and those kinds of things. I would say that a good part of it is vintage synths, like mainly the [Sequential] Pro-One and [Korg] Mono/Poly. Other than that, it's mostly studio hardware. Everything goes through Manley compressors and Neve 1081s [EQ/pre-amps], and that really defines most of the sound. I've got my favorite settings on the Manleys that I hardly ever change, and everything pumps right through it.

What settings are those?

With the compressors, I look for a fast release, fast attack, and medium threshold, so you don't really suck out too much of the low end, but it still gives punch. It really pulls the stuff together, especially when you work with strange loops, like the stuff Bill would come up with — stuff that was recorded with a [Shure] SM58, mono, on a portable DAT machine or something. I would, for example, take that, copy it, and then run the whole thing through an [Eventide] H3000, harmonize each side up eight or nine cents, and compress it. But they're just the tiniest bit off and stereoized. A lot of the stuff I've been shooting for is making three-dimensional or stereo-type images. Like, I'd always go for a stereo bass, even though it might not be totally obvious. But it comes from both sides and hits you right in the chest.

> **Now that you understand the basics of EQ, let's dig a little deeper into how to apply these tools to your mix. Michael Cooper gets into the nitty-gritty of each frequency range of your mix elements.**

April 2000
Mixing and Remastering with EQ
Indispensable tips for equalization

Perhaps the hardest aspect of mixing is getting the equalization of the individual tracks just right, especially when your mix uses tons of tracks. The wrong EQ settings on just one track can compromise the entire mix. Every choice you make has an influence on the level of clarity, warmth, punch, detail, and overall spectral balance (the balance of frequencies) of your master.

By learning what effect each band of frequencies has on the sound, you gain a blueprint for crafting the perfect mix. But it will only be perfect if you can hear what's needed. Unfortunately, everyone is subject to ear fatigue. That's why remastering — doing a fresh master based on a mix that was completed earlier — can be such a lifesaver.

Remastering gives you a second chance to get the EQ right, after a song has already been mixed. Although doing a new mix from scratch (or editing the original mix, if you're working with a recorder or console that facilitates automated mixing) is always the best solution, the multitrack master tapes are not always available, and time and budget considerations may demand a quick fix. In such situations, applying stereo EQ to an existing master — part of the process of remastering — can greatly improve a mix. Just remember that whatever you do to the mix at this stage, it affects all tracks. For example, boosting high frequencies will not only make the lead vocal brighter, it will also hype the cymbals and guitars. Only by doing a new mix can you tweak each track independently.

But whether you're mixing or remastering, tweaking a specific band of frequencies will always have the same general effect on the sound. In this article, we'll examine the characteristics of different frequency ranges and discuss some practical examples of how boosting or cutting in these bands can improve your mix. Let's start with the bass!

BOTTOM FISHING

- **20–50Hz:** This is the "rumble zone." The ear doesn't hear too well down here; the lower part of this range is more *felt* than heard. This is where distant semi trucks live. The rumble you hear — or that shakes your house — when your neighbor is using heavy equipment a block away to put in a swimming pool is also in this zone. If you're unlucky enough to have been recording at the time, rolling off these frequencies by using low shelving EQ or a highpass filter should eliminate the problem.

  When the bass in your mix uncontrollably rattles closed doors and cupboards, this is the band of frequencies to cut. Conversely, if you want the seat of your chair to vibrate when the bass heads for the basement, this is the zone to (cautiously) boost. Check out "Tiger" on Paula Cole's album *This Fire* and you'll know what I mean. But unless you've got a subwoofer or full-range monitors that can accurately reproduce this audio band, you're better off leaving these frequencies alone. Otherwise, you may be adding way more bottom end than is needed. Too much energy in this band will quickly eat up headroom and force you to mix at a lower, wimpier-sounding level.

- **63–80Hz:** "Punch" is the operative word here. This mid-bass band is where you should boost in order to give bass and kick drum more impact and "size." This is also a good band to boost when you want to warm up a mix and beef up the bottom end without clouding vocals, guitars, and sax solos. But too much energy in this band can also rob your mix of headroom and cause cheap speakers to clip.

- **100–160Hz:** When congas, dumbek, and other hand drums produce a resonant boominess that rattles your fillings, this is usually the zone to cut. Conversely, if your big monitors spew plenty of bottom end but the bass guitar mysteriously thins out when you switch to your Yamaha NS10Ms, boosting a little in this region can restore warmth and weight to your mix on the smaller speakers. Just be careful not to overdo it, because too much energy in this zone can really make a mix boomy.

- **200–250Hz:** These frequencies are usually the culprit when acoustic guitar sounds too boomy. A little boost in this region can add warmth and body to a thin mix, but be careful — it can also make bass guitar sound cloudy and indistinct. The next time you're having trouble telling what notes the bass is playing, try cutting in this band instead of boosting the mids and highs. You'll get the clarity you were searching for *and* have a warmer mix than if you had hyped the high end.

MIDDLE GROUND

- **315–400Hz:** When the overall mix has a gauzy or veiled quality, this is usually the band to cut. The same goes for individual tracks like vocals — try cutting here first, instead of boosting mids and highs, to improve intelligibility of lyrics while retaining warmth.
- **500–800Hz:** This band is a bit difficult to describe in words, but too much energy here can cause a mix to sound hard or stiff. When the beater on the kick drum sounds like it's whacking a thick sheet of reinforced cardboard, start dumping these frequencies. A lot of hit records are engineered with this band de-emphasized, to give a nice V-shaped EQ curve (relatively hyped bass and highs, with mids cut) to the mix. But don't overdo it or your mix will sound thin.
- **1–2kHz:** This is the zone to boost when you want to improve intelligibility without increasing sibilance. Boosting between 1kHz and 2kHz can restore clarity and fundamental pitch to overly distorted, buzzy guitars. Conversely, when the mix starts to take on the characteristic timbre of car horns blaring, cut here to remove the glare.

THE TOP END

- **2.5–4kHz:** This is the zone where the human ear is most sensitive. That means two things. First, any track that needs to cut through the mix more will benefit by boosting this band of frequencies. Second, too much energy in this zone will cause ear fatigue sooner than in other zones.

When a mix is sounding harsh to your ears, check to see if you've got this audio band boosted on multiple tracks. It's a mistake many beginning engineers make, progressively cranking the highs as a mix unfolds to compensate for worsening ear fatigue and "cotton head." The next day, after your hearing has had all night to recover, your mix sounds edgy and sharply cutting. In general, it's better to cut other fog-inducing frequencies than it is to boost in the ear-fatigue zone. A clear mix is little consolation if it makes your ears bleed.

- **5–10kHz:** Most vocal sibilance lives here, although female sibilance can range as high as 11 or 12kHz. But although cutting in this band will squelch sibilance, it will also rob a vocal of nuance, articulation, and breathiness. For this reason, de-essing is usually a better strategy.

Boost at the upper end of this zone to bring out the sizzle on snare drum hits, the head strike on toms, and the click of a kick drum's beater. A little boost here can also give a nice silvery "ping" to plucked acoustic guitar strings. But once

DE-ESS FOR SUCCESS

A de-esser is a device that selectively lowers the level of "s" sounds in a vocal without affecting the rest of the track. Hardware de-essing is performed by a *sidechain compressor*. This type of compressor has an extra input called the sidechain input. Instead of sensing the level of the main audio signal and reducing the output when the signal passes a threshold, like an ordinary compressor, a sidechain compressor lowers the level of the main audio signal when the signal at the sidechain input rises above the threshold. (After triggering the compression, the sidechain signal is discarded. It's not mixed with the main signal.)

To perform de-essing, you split the vocal signal, passing one part through an EQ or highpass filter to significantly boost the frequencies in the 8–15kHz range, which is where the vocal sibilance is found. The output of the EQ is patched to the sidechain input while the unEQ'd vocal signal passes through the main signal path of the compressor. Whenever an "s" sound causes the signal at the sidechain input to peak, the vocal is compressed.

again, be careful. Too much boost in this zone can make a mix sound overly sizzly and biting.

- **12.5–20kHz:** This is the band where analog tape hiss and preamp noise are the most objectionable. A lowpass filter can often be used to roll off such noise on individual tracks, provided they're not percussive and have few highs (*e.g.,* electric bass and six-string guitar).

  A little boost here can really make cymbals scintillate. A moderate lift in this region can also give a mix a wonderful sense of airiness and transparency. Unlike with the lower high-frequency bands, the upper octave is usually a little more forgiving of boost: You can probably get away with more before the mix begins to sound brittle or icy.

MIX MASTER

In most cases, it's better to cut rather than boost. The exceptions are below 250Hz and above 12.5kHz. At these extreme ends of the audio spectrum, feel free to boost or cut as needed. But between approximately 300Hz and 10kHz, proceed with caution. Too much boost anywhere within this broad range can cause an instrument or mix to sound harsh, hard, or peaky.

For example, if a track sounds too cloudy, try dumping muddy lower frequencies instead of cranking mids and highs that might increase harshness. On the other hand, if a track sounds too cutting or edgy, roll off in the neighborhood of 2.5kHz to 4kHz rather than boosting low mids and bass. In most cases, your mix will sound warmer and smoother.

Of course, describing sound with words is an inherently subjective process. What one person perceives as boomy may sound gloriously fat to someone else. The above pointers are simply starting points for your own creative experimentation and troubleshooting. The more you tweak and observe the results, the better you'll get at hearing exactly what's needed on the next track or mix.

> **The art of panning and instrument placement is a relatively easy skill to learn, but requires some experience to master. Craig Anderton gives some excellent pointers in this article.**

April 2001
The Wide World of Panning
Placement is everything

Part of listening in the real world involves locating sounds in space. Although 5.1 surround sound excels at providing spatial cues, most of the music world still runs on stereo, which has been with us for four decades. Stereo's spatial options are limited to left, right, or somewhere in between, so we need to make the most of them.

Consider what happens when you sit down and play the piano. There's a definite sense of lower notes emanating from the left, and higher notes coming from the right. Also, the undamped high strings, which are on the right, ring faintly even when you play a note on the extreme left. Try recording a piano in mono, then again in stereo. If properly miked, the stereo version will be far more realistic.

Stereo placement (panning) isn't just about realism, though. It's also used to keep instruments from interfering with one another, as well as to add special effects. So let's look at some tips designed to help further your skills in the art of stereo.

AUDIENCE PERSPECTIVE OR PERFORMER PERSPECTIVE?

As you set up stereo placement for instruments, think about your listener's position. For example, for a right-handed drummer the hi-hat is on the left and the toms on the right. For the audience, it's the reverse. When mixing for a live-sounding track, I generally go for the performer's perspective, unless the object is to emulate a concert experience.

FREQUENCY RESPONSE & PANNING

Low frequencies are fairly non-directional, whereas highs are very directional. As a result, low-frequency sounds (kick, bass) generally sound better in the center of a mix, whereas higher frequency instruments (shaker, tambourine) can go further out to the left and right.

January 2006
MIGUEL MIGS

Whenever I use a hardware unit I run it through my Millennia Media Origin STT-1 preamps. They can switch between solid state or tube. If anything, that's my secret weapon for getting really warm sounds. I don't use that much compression, but I generally add a touch of EQ on most tracks when needed.

With synthesizers that have stereo outputs, keyboard split functions can be very useful for spatial placement. One option (especially if you're handling the bass line with your left hand) is to send the lowest split to the center, a middle split to left of center, and the top split to right of center. This is not necessarily the most realistic option with respect to imitating the real world, but hey, it's a synth. If there's also a bass part to contend with, then move the bass to center, and spread the keyboard from left to right (or right to left), going from lower keys to higher keys. This keeps your low frequencies spatially separated from the bass player.

The easiest way to spread a keyboard is if you can modulate the pan position from the MIDI note number. This creates a spread when you feed the keyboard's stereo outs to two mixer channels. However, unless the keyboard is the major focus of the music, you may want to narrow the final range a bit. For example, if guitar is another major melodic instrument in the piece, try spreading the guitar from left of center to center, and the keyboard from center to right of center.

PANNING & DELAY

When a delayed sound is placed in the same spatial location as the main sound, the end result may become somewhat indistinct if the echoes are on the same note that's currently playing. There are two main options: If your dry track is panned to one side of the stereo spread, weight the delayed sound (set to delay only, no dry signal) to the other side of the spread. If you're using stereo delay on a lead instrument that's panned to center, you can get some lovely results by panning one channel of echo toward the left and one toward the right. If the echoes are polyrhythmic, this can also give some lively ping-pong-type effects. Of course, this may sound gimmicky (not always a bad thing, mind you!), but if the echoes are mixed relatively low and there's some stereo reverb going on, the sense of spaciousness can be huge.

PLAN AHEAD

One way to pan is just to arbitrarily move panpots around until things sound good. But I prefer to plan ahead by drawing a two-dimensional diagram of the intended "soundstage," much like the way theater people draw chalk marks where characters are supposed to stand. When it's time to mix, using this diagram as a "map" helps me stay on track.

The further back I want to position the sound, the lower in level and, sometimes, the more reverb. Reducing the highs just a bit with a sound that you want to be distant also gives the ears an important cue. Closer sounds are louder, drier, and slightly brighter. You can also experiment with adding predelay to the reverb for a sound that you want to seem close to the listener. This works best when each of the main sounds has its own reverb. Be careful with adding one reverb to the entire mix: When done carefully, this can give a sense of space, but it's easy to overdo it, drowning your mix in mush.

WHEN MONO MATTERS

There are three reasons to pay attention to mono. One is that the final product may play over a mono system (well, you do want to hear your music on TV, right?). Another is that some techniques that create stereo from mono signals, or ultra-wide signals from stereo, can create mono incompatibility problems.

But the main reason for using mono is when you begin a mix: I suggest starting with all instruments panned to center. Don't do any stereo panning until you've used basic EQ with all instruments to make sure that each part stakes out its own part of the frequency spectrum. For example, if two keyboard parts clash in mono, initially use EQ to differentiate them, not stereo placement. If you're able to differentiate parts with EQ first, then stereo becomes the element that brings true spaciousness, not just separation, to a mix.

CREATING WIDER-THAN-LIFE SOUNDS

Many signal sources are essentially mono (voice, vintage synths, electric guitar, etc.), but there are ways to "stereoize" sounds. With a hard disk recording system, the easiest is to copy a track and "slip" it ahead or behind the original track to create a slight delay between the two, then pan the two tracks to opposite sides. In some cases, it's most effective to slip the original track ahead of the beat a bit and the copy a little late, so the two end up "averaging out" and hit in the pocket. But you can also use slipping to alter the feel. To drag the part, keep the original on the beat and slip the copy a little later. For a more insistent, on-top-of-the-beat feel, slip the copy ahead.

How much slip to add depends on the instrument's frequency range. If the delay is too short, the two signals may start to cancel each other and create comb filtering effects. This results in a thin, peaky sound, much like a flanger stuck on a few milliseconds of delay. Lowering the copied signal's level can reduce these negative effects, but then the stereo image will be less dramatic.

If the delay is too long, you'll hear an echo effect. This can also be useful in creating a wider stereo image, but then you have to deal with the rhythmic implications — do you really want an audible delay? And if the delay is long enough, the sound will be more like two mono signals than a wide stereo signal.

Thankfully, hard disk recording makes it easy to experiment. Just be sure to check the final result in mono. If the sound ends up being thin or resonant, increase the delay time a tad.

Another way to create wider sounds involves EQ. Split your mono signal into two channels, pan one channel left and one channel right, then give each channel its own EQ settings to create more of a spread. For example, if you use a high-shelf filter to boost 4dB starting at 2kHz in the right channel, cut the left channel by 4dB at 2kHz, using the same type of filter. As mentioned earlier, highs are more directional, so this will definitely tilt the channel toward the right of the stereo image. For a more extreme image, cut the bass in the right channel and boost it by an equivalent amount in the left channel. This will push the image further into both the right and left channels.

Stereo graphic EQs can also create a wider image. As one example, set up one graphic for full cut on even-numbered channels, and pan that to the right. Set up the other graphic for full cut on odd-numbered channels, and pan it to the left. This won't work successfully on instruments with limited ranges, like voice or a lead synth part. But with drum tracks, this technique can give a very unusual type of stereo imaging.

Every available parameter is an important part of shaping your sound. Spatiality is crucial, so put as much thought into placement as you do into levels, EQ, and other elements of mixing.

If you're adding processing to a bunch of your tracks, there's a fair chance that you may be damaging your gain structure, especially if the tracks aren't properly balanced in the first place. Here, Michael Cooper spells out some methods for keeping tabs on the gain. It's also worth noting that many of these tips are equally applicable to working with samplers.

November 1999
Managing Digital Levels
When enough is too much

As digital gear replaces analog recording equipment, understanding how to manage audio levels becomes increasingly important. There's a prevailing myth that recording in the digital domain entails nothing more than getting input levels as close to 0dB as possible. End of story? Not quite.

WHY SHOULD YOU CARE?
If you've ever pegged digital meters, you know that surpassing 0dBFS (0dB "full scale," or the top of a digital meter's range) produces nasty distortion. The trick is to get your levels

as close to 0dBFS as possible without going over and "crashing and burning." The higher your levels are, the greater the resolution of your signal. This translates into tracks with more detail, clarity, and depth (a sense of three-dimensionality), as well as a smoother and sweeter high end. Generally speaking, for every 6dB your signal falls below 0dB, you lose one bit of resolution. For example, recording a track at −7dBFS (7dB below full scale) on a 16-bit digital track will result in a recording with only 15 bits of resolution. Theoretically, that one lost bit cost you around half of the detail in your recording! (In reality, you're probably not getting 16 bits no matter what you do, but this advice still applies to getting the most out of your gear.)

Record at too low a level, and your track sounds harsh, thin, and veiled. Record just a tad too hot, and your track sounds like a chainsaw. And once you've finished recording, you're still not out of the woods. If you want your tracks to sound like a million bucks, you'll need to keep managing your levels while editing in a DAW and while mixing with a digital console. Remember, your digital reverb has converters in it, too, so you'll want to optimize its I/O levels as well. At every step of the production process, there's the potential to turn nectar into sludge.

The good news is that it's easy to avoid the pitfalls once you know what they are. Here are some simple rules to follow to keep your digital levels at their optimal settings.

LEVEL MANAGEMENT CHECKLIST

■ If you know a track will need compression or limiting, apply this processing before you enter the digital domain. By compressing a track before the signal hits the A/D converter, you can reduce peaks that might otherwise exceed 0dBFS. This, in turn, allows you to raise the overall level of the track (by turning up the output gain of the compressor), getting more of the signal into the top range of the converter, where you have more bits working for you.

Of course, whether or not you compress a track should always be an artistic decision. A compressor changes the envelope of a sound much as the attack and release stages of an envelope generator do. Arbitrary compression just to manage levels is a recipe for weird-sounding tracks. But if you know you'll want to compress a track for musical reasons, do it in the analog domain — before the A/D converter — for a more detailed recording later on.

■ The analog circuitry associated with A/D and D/A converters (such as the mic preamps in your digital console) often has slightly lower headroom (*i.e.*, a lower clip point) than the digital devices it serves. You might get distortion at a reading below 0dBFS, so use your ears! Instruments such as flute and recorder, which have high average levels and relatively low peaks, may distort at −3dBFS or lower. Don't be addicted to a −1dBFS or 0dBFS reading; turn the level down if it makes the track sound cleaner.

■ If you have to reduce your signal level to, say, −3dBFS on your digital mixer's input to avoid distortion, boost the track up to −1dBFS with a fader before the signal gets printed to your digital multitrack. This can improve the sonic quality of your recording if your A/D converters offer higher resolution than the storage medium (for example, if you're recording to 16-bit ADATs via 20-bit converters).

■ Tube condenser microphones can be fairly noisy (although the newer designs are much quieter than vintage mics). If you're recording a very quiet instrument with a tube mic, you may need to compromise your levels somewhat. Boosting your mic preamp to its maximum level just to get that –1dBFS reading may result in audible RFI (radio frequency interference) getting printed to your multitrack. In its most benign state, RFI sounds like static. At its worst, you'll actually pick up a radio program in progress. It's far better to present your A/Ds with a –6dBFS signal, boosting the signal up to full scale with a fader once you're in the digital domain, than it is to have a Charmin bath tissue commercial superimposed over your new age meditation music.

■ All circuits in the digital and analog signal paths may have different clip points. And digital meter readings don't always show distortion. Monitor all levels that approach 0dBFS cautiously. Never assume that a hot level that's okay in one device will not clip a second device just because the signal was routed between them in the digital domain with no gain change.

■ When inputting a full-scale signal into your digital mixer or DAW, beware of any additional processing that might nudge the signal over 0dBFS. For instance, if you're going to apply EQ boost to an already hot track, use digital attenuation before the EQ to lower the level first. Then check the post-EQ level to make sure you're still below 0dBFS.

April 2004
MAC ATTACK

Mac Quayle has been the programming genius behind countless remixes by Hex Hector, Victor Calderone, and quite a few others. More recently, Mac has stepped more into the spotlight, having remixed Madonna, Sting, Annie Lennox, and Beyoncé last year alone. At last spring's Winter Music Conference, Mac clued me in to a little trick he's been using to get some analog spaciousness into his digital mixes.

"The convenience of digital recording has transformed the way I work for many years now," says Mac. "But I do miss a certain quality to the sound of my analog past; and in my search for ways to recapture it, I've come across a method that's starting to become popular.

"The basic concept is this: An analog mix bus can sound better than a digital mix bus. I've read about complicated math describing why this is true, as well as why it isn't true. But I decided to let my ears be the judge, and at least in my setup, analog is the winner.

"I'll do all my mixing within the digital environment; then instead of mixing down to two tracks, I'll bring multiple outputs into an analog mixer and mix everything together there. I run Logic Audio on a Power Mac G4 with Pro Tools Mix hardware. I have two Digidesign 888/24 interfaces, which allow me 16 analog outputs. When I'm mixing, I split my tracks into eight stereo output pairs, usually grouped by instrument type (drums, keys, vocals, etc.), and I run those outputs into a Dangerous 2-Bus, an analog summing mixer designed specifically for this purpose (www.dangerousmusic.com). No processing takes place in the mixer, it just adds the outputs together using a high-quality analog mix bus. Then I take the stereo signal coming out of the 2-Bus and go through an analog compressor and finally back into the digital world through the A-to-D converters in my TC Finalizer. This technique could also work any number of outputs and any decent analog mixer with the faders all set at the same level. I'm amazed at how much difference this makes to the sound of my mixes; they're bigger and warmer, with better stereo imaging. It doesn't quite take me back to a vintage 24-track 2" tape machine through a Neve console, but it definitely sounds better than doing it all in the computer."

- Whether you're using software or hardware, learn your digital mixer's signal path. Religiously study the block diagrams until you've got the signal flow down pat. For example, the Yamaha 02R console's digital signal flow is attenuator > EQ > dynamics > fader, in that order. There are meters for you to eyeball at virtually every point along the chain, and you should! Watching post-fader meter readings on a channel that has hefty compressor gain may not reveal clipping if the fader is set below unity gain. You must look at the pre-fader (post-dynamics) level to ensure that the signal is not clipping before it reaches the fader.
- Use peak-hold metering wherever available. After you've run through a mix, check the "frozen" displays on every meter to hunt down any clipping distortion that might have slipped past you.

While all of the above may seem like a lot to keep track of, it will become second nature after you've done it for a while. The rewards are well worth the extra effort. A world of sweet, silky-smooth, fat, and detailed recordings awaits the discerning engineer.

In the mixing tutorial that kicked off this chapter, Craig Anderton touched upon the unorthodox use of road noise in evaluating your mixes. Here he goes much deeper.

March 2000
Bring On the Noise!
An unusual way to "road-test" your mixes

Do you want better mixes? Of course you do — having a decent mix can make or break your music. Even the best tracks won't come across if they're not mixed well.

Different people approach mixing differently, but I don't think anyone has described something as whacked-out as what I'm going to cover here. Some people will read this and just shake their heads, but others will actually try the suggested technique, and find that they're crafting tighter, punchier mixes *without* any kind of compression or other processing.

THE MIXING PROBLEM
What makes mixing so difficult is, unfortunately, a limitation of the human ear/brain combination. Our hearing can discern very small changes in pitch, but not small changes in level. You'll easily hear a 3% pitch change as being distinctly out of tune, but a 3% level change is nowhere near as dramatic. Also, our ears have an incredibly wide dynamic range — greater than 200dB. This is more than twice the dynamic range of a CD, for example. So when we use only the top 20–40dB of the available dynamic range in a mix, even extreme musical dynamics don't represent that much of a change relative to the ear's total dynamic range.

Another problem with mixing is that the ear's frequency response changes at different levels. This is why small changes in volume are often perceived as tonal differences, and why it's so important to balance levels *exactly* when doing A/B comparisons. Because our ears hear low- and high-frequency signals better at higher levels, just a slight volume boost might produce a subjective feeling of greater "warmth" (from the additional perceived low end) and "sparkle" (from the increased perception of treble).

The reason why top mixing engineers are in such demand is because through years of practice, they've trained their ears to discriminate among minute level and frequency response differences (and hopefully, taken care of their ears so they don't suffer from their own frequency response problems). They are basically "juggling" the levels of multiple tracks, making sure that each one is at an appropriate level with respect to the other tracks. Remember, a mix does not compare levels to an absolute standard: All the tracks are interrelated.

As an obvious example, the lead instruments usually have higher levels than the rhythm instruments. But there are much smaller hierarchies. Suppose you have a string pad part, and the same part delayed a bit to produce chorusing. To avoid having excessive peaking when the signals reach maximum amplitude at the same time, as well as better preserving any rhythmic "groove," you'll probably mix the delayed track around 6dB behind the non-delayed track.

The more tracks, the more intricate this juggling act becomes. However, there are certain essential elements of any mix — some instruments that just have to be there, and that are mixed fairly closely in level to one another because of their importance. Ensuring that these elements are clearly audible and perfectly balanced is, I believe, one of the most important factors in creating a "transportable" mix (one that sounds good on a variety of systems). Perhaps the lovely high end of some bell sound won't translate on a $29.95 boombox, but for the average listener, if you can make out the vocals, the leads, the beat, and the bass, you'll have the high points covered.

Ironically, though, our ears are less sensitive to changes in relatively loud levels than to changes in relatively soft ones. This is why most veteran mixers initially work on a mix at low levels: It makes it easier to tell if the important instruments are out of balance with respect to one another. At higher levels, imbalances are harder to detect.

ANOTHER OF THOSE ACCIDENTS

The following mixing technique is a way to check whether a song's crucial elements are mixed with equal emphasis. Like many other techniques that ultimately turn out to be useful, this one was discovered by accident.

My studio doesn't have central air conditioning, and my in-wall air conditioner makes a fair amount of background noise. One day, I noticed that the mixes I did when the air conditioner was on often sounded better than the ones I did when it was off. This seemed odd at first, until I made the connection with how many musicians use the "play the music in the car" test as the final arbiter of whether a mix is going to work or not. In both cases the background noise masks low-level signals, making it easier to tell which signals make it above the noise.

Curious whether this phenomenon could be refined further, I started injecting pink noise into the console while mixing. This just about forces you to listen at relatively low levels, because the noise is really obnoxious! But more importantly, the noise adds a sort of "cloud cover" over the music. Just as mountain peaks poke out through a cloud cover when viewed from an airliner, so do sonic peaks poke up out of the noise floor.

APPLYING THE TECHNIQUE

You'll want to add in the pink noise very sporadically during the process of creating your mix, because the noise masks high-frequency sounds like hi-hat. You cannot get an accurate idea of the complete mix while you're mixing with noise injected into the bus. What you can do is make sure that all the important instruments are being heard properly. (Similarly, when listening in a car system, road noise will often mask lower frequencies.)

Typically, I'll take the mix to the point where I'm fairly satisfied with the sound. Then I'll add in lots of noise — no less than 10dB below 0 with dance mixes, for example, which typically have restricted dynamics anyway. Then I'll start analyzing what I'm hearing.

By the way, pink noise is preferable to white noise for this application. Pink noise is weighted so that there is equal energy in every octave, while white noise is weighted so there is equal energy at all frequencies. Pink noise has a lower perceived pitch, which makes it more suitable for masking the fundamental frequencies of ordinary instruments.

While listening through the song, I pay special attention to vocals, snare, kick, bass, and leads. It's very easy to adjust their relative levels, because there's a limited range between overload on the high end and dropping below the noise floor on the low end. If all the crucial sounds make it into that window and can be heard clearly above the noise without distorting, you have a head start toward an equal balance. If you can hear a hi-hat or other minor part fairly high above the noise, it's probably too loud.

I'll generally run through the song a few more times, carefully tweaking each track for the right relative balance. Then it's time to take out the noise. First, it's an incredible relief not to hear that annoying hiss! Second, you can now get to work balancing the supporting instruments so they work well with the lead sounds you've tweaked.

Although so far I've only mentioned instruments being above the noise floor, there are actually three distinct zones created by the noise: totally masked by the noise (inaudible), above the noise (clearly audible), and "melded," where an instrument isn't loud enough to stand out or soft enough to be masked, so it blends in with the noise. I find that mixing rhythm parts so they sound melded can work if the noise is adjusted to a suitable level.

FADING OUT

Overall, I estimate spending only about 3% of my mixing time using injected noise. But often, it's the factor responsible for making the mix sound good over multiple systems. Mixing with noise may sound crazy, but give it a try. With a little practice, there are ways to make noise work for you.

With your levels and EQ in place, it's time to finesse the effects. We've touched upon effects throughout this book, but if you're still scratching your head, check out this roundup of descriptions penned by none other than the ubiquitous and talented Craig Anderton.

March 1998
The FX Files
How to Use Effects in the Studio

Effects are to recording as spices are to cooking — they can really enhance whatever's already there, but you have to remember that a little goes a long way. Yet a lot of people aren't really that familiar with their effects; they just dial up a preset and hope for the best.

If you understand how these devices work, you can use them much more effectively. The following roundup of common effects should clue you in not only to what they are, but to their crucial parameters, annoying quirks, and some hot applications.

COMPRESSOR/LIMITER
Profile. A compressor/limiter (C/L for short) evens out dynamic range variations by amplifying soft signals to make them louder, and/or attenuating loud signals to make them softer. The result is less level difference between soft and loud signals. A compressor/limiter can be used, for instance, to tame the sharp percussive peaks on a snare drum track, allowing the drum sound as a whole to be boosted to a higher level in the mix without overloading the master tape. With a vocalist who tends not to keep an even distance from the mic, some gentle compression will give the vocal track a more uniform presence.

How it works. Once the input signal exceeds a user-settable threshold, compression starts to reduce the output level. As a result, increasing the input signal does not increase the output level by an equivalent amount. For example, with a *compression ratio* of 2:1, every additional 2dB of input level above the threshold results in only 1dB of additional output level.

Crucial parameters. *Threshold* sets the level above which signals will be compressed or limited. Signals that lie below the threshold are not processed.

Ratio selects how the output level changes in relation to the input once the input exceeds the threshold. The higher the ratio, the greater the amount of compression, and the more "squeezed" the sound. Extremely high ratios put an absolute "ceiling" on the signal. This is called *limiting.*

Output adds gain to offset the lower level caused by restricting the dynamic range.

Attack sets the reaction time to input level changes. A longer attack time "lets through" more of a signal's original dynamics before the compression kicks in. For example, increasing the attack time retains the initial "thwack" of a kick drum.

Release determines how long it takes for the C/L to return to its normal state after the input drops below the threshold. With short release times, the C/L tracks very slight level changes, which can produce a "choppy" sound.

Annoying habits. Over-compressing results in a thin, unnatural sound, and brings up the noise floor. Don't add any more compression than you need.

Hot tips. When it's used with other effects, place the compressor early in the chain if possible, so that it doesn't bring up the noise from previous stages.

■ If it seems like there's been a sudden increase in compression but you didn't increase the compression amount, then the input signal going to the compressor may have increased.

■ Some music from the '60s featured a drum sound that sounded like it was "sucking" and inhaling. To create this effect, apply lots of compression with an extremely short release time.

■ Compressing a mix that includes both drums and sustained bass tones can cause the bass to "pump," dropping audibly in level whenever a drum hit occurs.

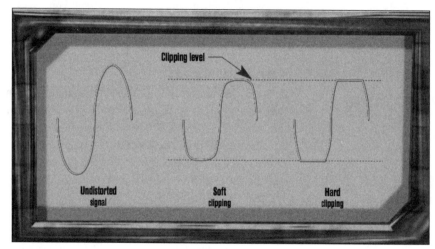

Figure 8-5
An undistorted signal compared to soft- and hard-clipped versions.

DISTORTION

Profile. Distortion mimics the way an amplifier behaves when overloaded, so it's a popular effect for guitar. However, distortion can also spice up drums, synthesizers, and even vocals.

How it works. Not all types of distortion (tube, transistor, digital, etc.) sound the same. Some devices include a tube stage or other analog distortion circuit that can be modified under computer control. Others use DSP to emulate particular types of distortion.

Most musicians prefer "soft" clipping, where the output signal becomes progressively more distorted as the input signal level increases. With hard clipping, the output signal remains undistorted up to a certain point, then becomes extremely distorted as the input increases past that point (see Figure 8-5). Hard clipping sounds harsher.

Crucial parameters. *Sensitivity, drive,* or *input* determines the amount of signal level needed for the onset of distortion. Maximum sensitivity gives the most distortion.

Output. Since distortion often adds a great deal of amplification, the output parameter trims the effect's output level back to something reasonable.

Tone controls. Some distortion effects include tone controls. Distortion adds harmonics to the signal, increasing the high-frequency content; pulling back on the highs reduces shrillness, while boosting the bass gives more depth. Some distortion effects let you EQ the signal before it hits the distortion stage, which can shape the distortion.

Annoying habits. Because of their high gain, distortion boxes can generate a lot of hiss. Noise-gating the output can be useful. Also, because most distortion devices are designed for guitar, it's hard to find stereo models for mixing applications.

Hot tips. Patch a distortion unit into a mixer's aux bus, and bring the returns back to the mixer. To add some "bite" to a channel, turn up its aux bus send to taste.

■ A little distortion can really increase the punch of drum sounds.
■ Distortion can make a synthesizer sound a lot more "rock and roll." Add some crunch to organ patches that use rotating speaker effects.

EQUALIZERS

Profile. An equalizer (EQ) emphasizes (boosts) and/or de-emphasizes (cuts) certain frequencies to change a signal's timbre. The amount of boost or cut is expressed in decibels (dB). Equalization is used to tame objectionable overtones in individual sounds, and also to avoid conflicts between sounds in a mix. Suppose you're playing a rhythmic piano part behind a vocalist, for instance, but since the piano and voice occupy a similar frequency range, they conflict. The solution: Pull back on the piano's midrange somewhat to make room for the vocal.

How it works. Equalizers use filter circuits that pass (ignore) certain parts of the frequency spectrum and boost or cut others. The four most common filter types are lowpass (passes all frequencies below a certain cutoff frequency while reducing those above), highpass (passes frequencies above the cutoff frequency while reducing those below), bandpass (boosts only the frequencies around its center frequency, while ignoring or reducing higher and lower frequencies), and notch (frequencies close to the notch frequen-

Figure 8-6
A graphic representation
of parametric equalizer
parameters.

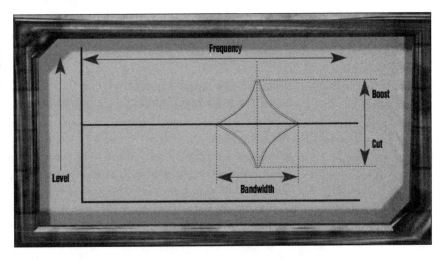

cy are reduced, while frequencies higher and lower than the notch frequency pass through to the filter output). The range of frequencies affected by the boost or notch is called the *bandwidth.*

There are several types of equalizers. *Shelving equalizers,* which are found on even a basic mixer, boost or cut all of the frequencies above (high shelving) or below (low shelving) their assigned cutoff frequency. The cutoff frequency may be adjustable, or it may be fixed. The *graphic equalizer* uses multiple bandpass filters to split the audio spectrum up into a number of bands, with an individual boost/cut control for each band.

A *parametric equalizer* is a highly sophisticated form of tone control. Unlike the graphic equalizer, which can boost or cut only at certain fixed frequencies, a parametric can boost or cut at any point over a continuously variable range of frequencies. In addition, the bandwidth is variable, from broad to sharp (see Figure 8-6). There are also *quasi-parametric* (also called *semi-parametric*) equalizers, which include frequency and boost/cut controls but no bandwidth control.

Crucial parameters. *Frequency* sets the specific part of the audio spectrum where the boosting or cutting will occur.

Boost/cut determines the amount of equalization effect at the selected frequency.

Bandwidth, resonance, or Q determines whether the boosting or cutting curve is sharp and narrow or gentle and broad. Narrow bandwidth settings (equivalent to high resonance or Q) affect a very small part of the audio spectrum, while broad settings process a wider range.

Annoying habits. Some equalizers do not include bypass switches, making it difficult to compare the equalized and unequalized ("flat") versions of a sound. Also, some equalizers have a fixed bandwidth, which always seems too narrow or too broad for the intended application.

Hot tips. Frequently compare the equalized and non-equalized sounds. You don't want to get into a situation where you boost the treble a lot, which makes the bass seem thin so you boost that, which then makes the midrange seem weak so you boost that, and so on.

Always use the minimum amount of equalization necessary. Just a few dB of change can make a big difference.

DELAY EFFECTS: FLANGING, CHORUS, ECHO

Profile. Time delays can produce various effects, including flanging, echo, chorusing, tapped delay, and stereo simulation. Some devices provide dedicated separate effect algorithms for each function. Others simply include a general-purpose time delay effect that is flexible enough to provide these different effects. Phasing, flanging, and chorusing are produced using extremely short delay times, so that you never hear anything that sounds like a delay. Nonetheless, a delay is the basis of the effect.

How it works. Time delay effects record the input signal into digital memory, then read it out a certain amount of time later. Feeding some of the output back to the input recirculates the delayed sound, thus creating a repeating echo effect. *Modulation,* which varies the delay time, produces an animated kind of sound by raising and lowering the pitch of the delayed sound as the delay time sweeps back and forth between a maximum and minimum value.

Crucial parameters. *Initial delay* sets the amount of delay time. With echo, this is the time interval between the straight sound and the first echo. With flanging and chorusing, modulation occurs around this initial time delay. Some devices let you synchronize the delay time to MIDI song tempo. Another option is a tap function, where hitting a switch or button sets the delay time interval.

Balance, mix, or *blend.* This parameter adjusts the balance between the straight and delayed signals. If you set a simple chorus algorithm to 100% wet, you may not hear any chorusing effect, because the chorusing is created by a slight pitch offset that occurs between the dry and delayed signal as the delay time is modulated. Richer-sounding chorus algorithms use multiple delays, so you'll still hear the effect when the balance is at 100%.

Feedback, recirculation, or *regeneration.* This parameter determines how much of the output feeds back into the input. With echo, minimum feedback gives a single echo; more feedback increases the number of echoes. With flanging, adding feedback increases the effect's sharpness, much like increasing a filter's resonance control.

Sweep range, modulation amount, or *depth* determines how much the modulation section (normally an LFO) varies the delay time. A wide sweep range is most important for dramatic flanging effects. Chorus and echo don't need much sweep range to be effective. With longer delays, adding a little bit of modulation provides chorusing, but too much modulation will cause detuning effects. Many of the echo (long delay) algorithms found in effects hardware have no modulation.

Modulation type. The modulation usually comes from periodic waveforms such as triangle or square waves, but some devices include randomized waveforms and/or envelope followers (where the modulation tracks the incoming signal's dynamics).

Modulation rate sets the speed of the modulation LFO. Typical rates range from 0.1Hz (one cycle every ten seconds) to 20Hz. For standard chorusing, a modulation rate of 2Hz or less would be standard; faster rates are used mostly for unusual effects. With flanging and chorusing, modulation causes the pitch of the modulated signal to go slightly flat, return to the original pitch, go slightly sharp, then return to the original pitch and start the cycle all over again.

Annoying habits. The delay time readouts on older models are not always 100% accurate. Also, changing delay times via MIDI while the device is processing a signal invariably results in burping and belching as the delay flushes its memory and refills.

Hot tips. To add vibrato, set a short initial delay (5ms or so), monitor the delayed sound *only,* and modulate the delay with a triangle or sine wave at a 5 to 14Hz rate.

- To create a comb filter, mix a straight signal with the same signal passing through a short, fixed (unmodulated) delay. Try an initial delay of 1 to 10ms, minimum feedback, no modulation, and an equal blend of processed and straight sound. Then turn up the feedback to increase the filtering.
- For mono to pseudo-stereo conversion, set a stereo chorus depth parameter to maximum and rate to minimum (or off). This creates a stereo spread without the motion that would result from having a higher modulation rate.

■ To calibrate the echo repeat time to a particular rhythmic value, such as an eighth- or quarter-note, the following formula translates beats per minute (tempo) into milliseconds per quarter-note (echo time):

60,000/(tempo in bpm) = delay time in ms

PITCH TRANSPOSER

Profile. The pitch transposer synthesizes one or more harmony lines from an input signal. Simple pitch transposers are limited to parallel harmonies, while more sophisticated models can produce "intelligent" harmonies if you specify a key and mode (major, minor, etc.).

How it works. A pitch transposer essentially cuts a signal into tiny pieces, then glues them all back together — in real time, except for a few milliseconds of processing time — so that they take up less time (the pitch is shifted up) or more time (the pitch is shifted down).

Crucial parameters. *Transposition* sets the harmony line's pitch interval, typically in semitones but with an additional fine-tuning control.

Blend or *mix* sets the balance of the original and transposed signals.

Feedback, regeneration, or *recirculation* feeds some of the output back to the input to create stepped harmonies and other special effects.

Intelligent harmony settings. These consist of key and scale data so the pitch transposer generates harmonies based on the rules of harmony for the specified scale.

Annoying habits. It takes a lot of processing power to do pitch transposition, and the sound often suffers from audible imperfections. For example, there might be a fluctuating tremolo effect, or occasional glitches. The greater the degree of transposition, the more objectionable the problems.

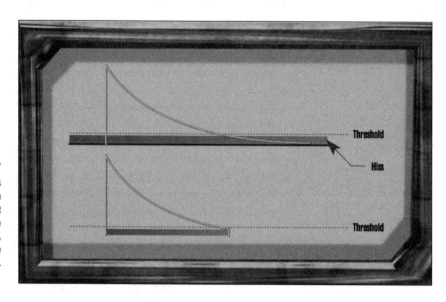

Figure 8-7
The upper diagram shows the signal before gating. In the lower diagram, note that although we've masked the noise while the gate is open, the decay cuts off more abruptly than normal.

Hot tips. Even if your transposer doesn't offer "intelligent" harmonization, you can often change the transposition amount via MIDI by using continuous controllers as you play.

■ For glissando effects, set the transposed pitch very slightly higher than normal (a few cents), then advance the regeneration control. This recirculates and pitch-shifts each note, thereby initiating a stepped upward glissando effect (the harmony pitch control controls the step interval).
■ Pitch transposers can produce good flanging/chorusing effects. Set the pitch control for a very slight amount of transposition (1 to 20 cents or so) and add regeneration to taste.

NOISE GATE

Profile. The noise gate helps remove noise and hiss by shutting off the audio whenever the input signal drops below a certain threshold. As a bonus, some noise gates can also do special effects.

How it works. The presence of a loud musical signal masks hiss, which becomes audible only during quiet parts — usually when the music is not playing. Setting the threshold just above the hiss level will allow the signal to pass whenever its level exceeds the threshold, but will block the output when the signal level drops below the threshold, which should happen mostly when the signal consists solely of hiss (see Figure 8-7).

Crucial parameters. *Threshold* or *sensitivity* determines the level above which the gate opens. High threshold levels are useful for special effects, such as removing substantial amounts of an instrument's decay to make a more percussive or gated sound.

Attenuation. Some noise gates feature adjustable attenuation for the gate-closed state. With less attenuation, the gate doesn't shut down all the way, so some of the low-level signal will still pass through.

Decay time sets a fadeout time for the audio when the signal drops below the threshold.

Attack time works in reverse: When the input signal exceeds the threshold, the noise gate opens up over a specified period of time, causing the signal to fade in. Generally, you want the attack time to be as fast as possible, so that the beginnings of percussive sounds aren't missed.

Key input. This allows a separate audio signal (not the signal being processed) to open and close the gate.

Annoying habits. Sometimes the gate drops out parts of a signal that you do want to hear. Also, noise gates work best on signals that don't need to be cleaned up too much. Eliminating noise that's too loud can also mean nuking substantial portions of the signal.

Hot tips. If possible, avoid using noise gates for noise reduction, since they tend to destroy low-level dynamics.

■ The key input is very cool for special effects. For example, gate a sustained chord with a kick drum beat to "chop" the chord into rhythmic slices.
■ For a huge drum sound, mic the drums so they include a lot of room sound, compress the hell out of the signal, then gate it with a high threshold. This lets bursts of room sound through, but eliminates the reverberant decay.

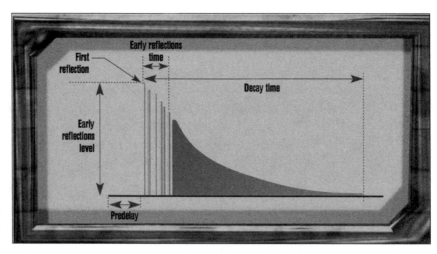

Figure 8-8
Common reverb parameters.

REVERBERATION

Profile. Reverb simulates the sound of audio reflections bouncing around inside an acoustic space (*e.g.*, large hall or auditorium). Digital reverb can also create spaces that don't exist in nature.

How it works. Digital reverb processes audio through an algorithm that creates a series of delays with filtering, similar to the reflections that occur when sound waves bounce off of the walls and ceiling of a room.

Crucial parameters. Figure 8-8 graphically illustrates the basic reverb parameters.

Type determines the kind of reverb to be emulated: room, hall, plate, spring (the classic "twangy" reverb sound used in guitar amps), and so on. Except in the case of convolution reverbs, the word used to describe the type is only a rough indication of the sound quality, and shouldn't be taken literally.

Room size determines the room's total volume. Changing this parameter often changes other parameters, such as low- or high-frequency decay.

Early reflections level. Early reflections are closely spaced discrete echoes, as opposed to the later "wash" of sound that constitutes the reverb's tail. This parameter determines the level of these initial echoes.

Predelay sets the amount of time before the first group of reflections or room reverb sound begins, and is usually set to 100ms or less. A longer predelay setting gives the feeling of a larger acoustical space.

Decay time adjusts how long it takes for the reverb tail to decay to the point of inaudibility. There may be separate decay times for different frequency bands, allowing you to more precisely tailor the room's characteristics.

Crossover frequency is a parameter found only on units with separate decay times for high and low frequencies. It determines the "dividing line" between the highs and lows. For example, with a crossover frequency of 1kHz, frequencies below 1kHz will be subject to the low-frequency decay time, while those above 1kHz will be subject to the high-frequency decay time.

High-frequency rolloff. In a natural reverberant space, high frequencies tend to dissipate more rapidly than lows. High-frequency rolloff helps simulate this effect.

Mix, balance, or *blend.* Sets the mix between the reverberated and dry signals.

Diffusion is a "smoothness/thickness" parameter. Increasing the diffusion packs the early reflections closer together, giving a thicker sound. Decreasing the diffusion spreads the early reflections further apart. Some reverb units call this *density,* and some diffusion controls affect all reflections, not just the early ones.

Annoying habits. Even the best digital reverbs don't really sound like clapping your hands in a cathedral. An acoustic space is still the best way to do reverb. A poorly designed reverb algorithm can have a too-regular pulsing quality, or add high-pitched ringing to certain notes.

Hot tips. Different instruments can sound better with different reverb settings. For example, low density settings can be problematic with percussive sounds, since the first reflection could sound more like a discrete echo than like part of the reverb. Increasing the density solves this. However, low density settings can work very well with voice by adding more fullness.

■ A track with no reverb will often sound dry and brittle, but it's easy to overdo the reverb. Sometimes the best reverb is just a taste of a very short room algorithm, mixed so low you can't consciously hear it.

■ To create a "bigger" sound, set the low-frequency decay longer than the high-frequency decay. For a more ethereal sound, do the reverse.

■ *Convolution* reverb plug-ins, which model actual acoustic spaces, are more DSP-intensive than traditional digital reverbs, but they can create a more vivid sense of space.

TREMOLO

Profile. A tremolo provides a periodic amplitude change, causing the sound to pulsate.

How it works. A modulation source, such as a triangle or sine wave, controls the output amplitude.

Crucial parameters. *Modulation amount* or *depth* determines how much the modulation section varies the amplitude.

Modulation type. Some tremolos include different modulation waveforms.

Modulation rate sets the modulation frequency.

Annoying habits. With plucked sounds, the tremolo will cause some note attacks to disappear, which may affect the rhythm.

Hot tips. Tremolo is the driving sound behind surf guitar, but it was also used on vocals back in the '60s, when people were so stoned they thought it actually sounded good.

■ Stereo tremolo units can be set up to do automated panning. To create panning, the modulation of the left and right channels is out of phase, so that the output signal shifts from left to right and back again in the stereo field.

EXCITER

Profile. An exciter increases brightness, but it's not the same as EQ. The result is a brighter, "airier" sound without the stridency that can sometimes occur when the treble is simply boosted.

How it works. Different processes vary, but one popular model adds subtle amounts of high-frequency distortion. Another boosts the highs whenever the midrange frequencies in the input are loud. Sometimes phase changes will also factor into the sound.

Crucial parameters. *Exciter frequency* sets the frequency at which the "excitation" kicks in.

Exciter mix varies how much "excited" sound gets added to the straight sound.

Annoying habits. People usually turn the exciter up too much, and ruin otherwise perfectly good-sounding songs.

Hot tips. Don't process an entire mix through an exciter; that's usually overkill.

■ For best results, drive the exciter with an aux bus and add subtle amounts for various channels, as needed.

VOCODER

Profile. A vocoder creates "talking instrument" effects.

How it works. A vocoder has two inputs, the *carrier* input for an instrument, and the *modulator* input for a microphone or other signal source. Talking into the microphone superimposes the frequency spectrum of the modulator input on whatever is plugged into the instrument input. It does this by opening and closing bandpass filters.

Crucial parameters. *Carrier input level* sets the level of the carrier signal (duh).

Modulator input level adjusts the modulator signal level.

Balance sets the blend of mic with vocoded sound.

Highpass filter adds directly into some high frequencies from the mic channel directly into the output. This increases intelligibility by mixing in the sibilants ("s" and "th" sounds, for instance) from the carrier, since these consist of very high frequencies that are not usually present at significant levels in the carrier signal being vocoded.

Annoying habits. The filters are so sharp, it's easy to overload them and get horrible distortion. And please don't call them vo*cord*ers.

Figure 8-9
Series, parallel,
and series/parallel
configurations.

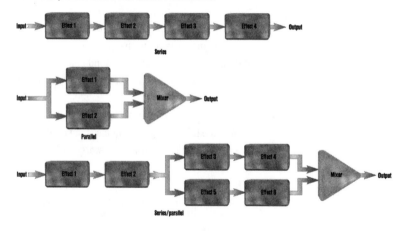

Hot tips. Vocoders are good for much more than talking-instrument effects. For example, play drums into the microphone input instead of voice, and use this to control a keyboard playing sustained chords.

■ For best results, the instrument being processed should have plenty of harmonics. Distorted guitar works well as a carrier for vocoding, as does a wide-open synthesizer sawtooth wave or even white noise.

SIGNING OFF

Signal processors are really cool, but when you add MIDI control or automation, they get even better. Few people have truly exploited the possibilities inherent in today's effects and multieffects, so get creative — you may discover an incredible signature sound that will be uniquely your own.

> **Make no mistake, when it comes to remixes, effects can often be as important as the musical parts and rhythmic grooves. Here, Greg Rule offers a few additional tips and tricks for applying your effects in unique and dramatic ways.**

May 2001
Fun with Effects
Don't serve your cake without the icing

A while back, I had the pleasure of remixing the song "Liberty" by the seminal industrial band Clan Of Xymox. I had loads of fun with the string and vocal effects processing on that one, so I thought I'd share a few of those techniques with you. To hear the complete remix, scan your favorite CD shop for Clan Of Xymox's *Liberty* CD-single on Metropolis Records.

MULTIPLE EFFECTS

Complex setups may require patching several different boxes together. Hardware devices can be connected in series or parallel; with software plug-ins, parallel effects are normally instantiated on aux send busses. Parallel setups always require a mixer (although some multi-effects include the mixer, either invisibly or as another effect), but allow more flexibility. For example, bass through wah-wah sounds thin because the wah blocks the bass frequencies. However, feeding the wah-wah into a mixer in parallel with an EQ set to boost the bass frequencies gives the best of both worlds.

With series effects, order does matter. Generally, dynamics processors (compressors and limiters) either go at the beginning to create a smooth, sustained signal for subsequent effects, or at the end to minimize level variations generated by the other effects.

LINE-SPECIFIC VOCAL PROCESSING

Some of us have fallen prey to the "set it and forget it" approach to vocal processing — yours truly included. Listening back to some of my first remixes, I'd sometimes find one good delay and/or reverb patch and let it coast from start to finish. Boooorring. I got wise to this, though, and started to focus more on effects. Instead of using one or two effects throughout, I started exploring ways of giving each section its own color: a lo-fi edge for the verse, for example, a swept filter and delay for

DELAY EFFECT GLOSSARY

Delay time: The time that elapses between the original sound and when the delayed sound is heard.

Doubling: A process of overdubbing two takes of the same part onto separate tracks and mixing them together. Since the performances aren't quite identical, they create a fuller and more interesting sound. With effects processors, short delay times (10–50ms) are used in an attempt to achieve similar results.

Echo: A signal delayed by a long enough time that it can be heard as a distinctly separate event is sometimes called echo. More often, however, it's simply called delay.

Haas effect: A psychoacoustic phenomenon in which delay creates an apparent change in left/right balance. When an identical signal is sent to the left and right channels at the same volume, but one side is delayed by a few milliseconds, our ears perceive the sound as coming from the side that arrives earliest. The strength of the effect depends on the amount of delay.

Multi-tap delay: A type of stereo delay with multiple delay occurrences at user-determined intervals. Each of the taps has its own delay time, output level, panning, and (sometimes) feedback amount.

Ping-pong delay: A type of echo effect in which a repeating delayed sound alternates between the left and right channels of a stereo image.

Regeneration: A setting on a delay unit that determines how many times a delayed sound repeats before it fades out. Also known as feedback.

Slapback: A type of delay where only a single delay repeat is heard, and the delayed sound is nearly the same volume as the original. Slapback delay times are generally short, around 80–150ms.

the chorus, some vocoding on the bridge harmonies, and so on.

For the "Liberty" remix, I decided to go one step further by applying a different effect to each line of the chorus. The catalyst for doing this was the song's chorus lyric: "The heart of gravity." When I heard those words, I immediately thought of a descending pitch-shift effect that implied heaviness or downward motion. I love using plug-ins, so to create this gravity effect I launched GRM Tools' Pitch Accum plug-in, put on my Mad Scientist At Work cap, and attacked those onscreen sliders. In no time I had the descending dive-bomb effect I was looking for. I was careful to retain a small amount of the original dry vocal, though, so the melodic reference wouldn't be obliterated.

Once I had the gravity effect sorted out, I started toying with the other vocal phrases in the chorus. A layer of sandpaper grit was applied to the line "I guess it's gonna be" with Bomb Factory's SansAmp plug-in. The wah-wah effect on the "question of my liberty" phrase was done with Bomb Factory's Moogerfooger Filter plug-in. A touch of reverb and a tempo-synced delay were also applied for subtle sweetening.

Not every remix will benefit from this type of line-specific processing, but the next time you're about to "set and forget," think twice. Are you doing it because it's what the song needs, or is it because you're running out of gas and just want the mix to be done? Don't let the latter be the reason your remix misses the mark.

SANDBOX STRINGS

The minor, descending string part you hear in the chorus of my "Liberty" remix was played on a Kurzweil K2500. The original sound was silky-smooth, but I later decided that a lo-fi, Victrola-like treatment would help give the strings a spookier, more sinister sound. Here again, I scanned my plug-in menu and found the perfect tool — Fusion:Vinyl from Opcode.

In addition to letting you apply scratches, pops, rumble, hiss, wear, and record warp, Fusion:Vinyl also provides bandwidth and compression controls. When I dialed in a couple of pops and clicks, cranked the compression, and decreased the bandwidth dramat-

June 1997
CHEMICAL BROTHERS

When using effects, do you try to perfectly match the delays with the bpm of the song, for example, or is it more a feel process?
It's just whatever feels right. I mean, I can never find my bpm tempo chart. It just doesn't matter, really. Sometimes I'll set the Roland [Space Echo] delays, and you get a loose kind of feel. The way we make drum loops move, the way we put movement into them, is to put a lot of little short delays on them, and then play around with the delay times. And then when you get everything grooving together, you record it. As long as it sounds good, that's all that matters.

ically (which downgraded the quality to AM-radio grade), the spook quotient went through the roof.

If you don't have Fusion:Vinyl, there are other ways to accomplish this evil effect. Use EQ or a highpass filter to zap the low end from the track. Peel a few layers off the top too. If you have a compressor, go ahead and squash the sound even further. Finally, layer a looped vinyl noise sample with the EQ/compressed track. I used an E-mu Planet Phatt module, for example, to produce a very convincing Victrola-like horn part for a Hypnotic Records compilation by doing exactly what I described above.

The moral of the story: Even though we have gorgeous, 24-bit tools at our disposal, there are times when taking a backward step is just what's needed to give a track an extra edge.

Gone too far with your mix? Did it sound better a few hours — or days — ago? This is a common pitfall, even for seasoned remixers with a boatload of credits. In this section, Doug Beck describes how he got out of a similar bind with one of his remixes.

May 2000
Subtractive Mixing
Tips for bailing out a troubled track

It happens to everyone eventually. You spend hours slaving over a track, meticulously poring over every detail. Yet after spending all of this time, you have a nagging feeling that something is not quite right. Is that kick flamming? Are the synths perfectly locked with the groove? Is the bass too loud? When I find myself in this situation, it's almost always the case that I've spent many, many hours over the course of several days working on one track, and I can't figure out what's wrong — if anything. I reach a point where I'm not sure if I've just created a masterpiece or a piece of something else. Most likely it's something in between, of course, but I'm just too close to it to get an objective handle on it.

This happened to me again recently. After six days of producing a new vocal dance track, something just didn't seem right. The worst moment was when the artist listened to the track and said, "Hmm . . . I can't put my finger on it, but it doesn't make me want to dance." Gulp. That's ugly. At this point I clearly needed a break from working on this record, so I decided to put it away for a day or two, then come back and approach it with fresh ears. Here's how I fixed it.

JUST FOR KICKS

The kick drum wasn't as tight as it could be. On my first listen, I discovered the kick drum was a little too boomy for the rest of the track. When I soloed the drum tracks it sounded fine, but as I brought the bass and synth tracks back in, it didn't feel tight. There was a sloppy-sounding, boomy decay to the tone of the kick drum, and it sounded progressively lazy with each beat of the four-bar loop. I tried to EQ some of the offending frequencies out of the kick, but after a few minutes it became clear that I was going to have to replace the kick drum. Ordinarily this wouldn't be a big deal — just bring up the sequence and replace the kick, right? Wrong! I had printed all of the tracks to audio files, and was mixing in another room. To further compound the problem, this particular kick loop had another percussive element in it, one with a feel we really liked. We had pretty much built the rest of the percussion around it.

I went back to my studio and called up the sequence in Cubase. Because the original kick was a loop, I had two choices: Find another kick loop with the same kind of feel or find a good kick sample and program a kick track that matched the feel of the original. I decided on the second approach, so my first step was to solo the loop and program my new kick with the same pattern and feel. This was fairly painless because of the groove quantize feature on my sequencer. Locking down the basic pattern of the groove was simple enough; the only tedious part was that all of the kick fills needed to be completely reprogrammed. Next, I printed my new kick track to audio, brought it into the mix room, and imported it into my original track. Everyone noticed the difference immediately. The whole track seemed to tighten up.

Note about audio files: When I print my sequencer tracks to audio files, I like to start every track at measure one, regardless of what measure that particular part actually begins in the arrangement. This makes importing your files into Pro Tools or Vegas or whatever you're using much faster. Let's face it: Hard disk space is really cheap these days, so you might as well keep it simple. I've also found that recalling a mix is much easier if everything has been printed to audio. There's always that one synth patch that doesn't seem to sound the same no matter how careful you were about archiving it, but if it's recalled from an audio file, it's exactly as you remember it.

SIMPLE SYNTHS

There were too many synth tracks. In the course of recalling the mix, I started muting different parts in different sections and liked what I heard. I ended up stripping down the arrangement considerably, and took some parts out completely. This opened up the track, and made a big difference in the overall sound of the record. The parts that remained had much more impact as well. For example, a stabbing synth hook sounded cleaner, brighter, and fatter than it had, because I pulled out a pad that had been fighting with it in the same frequency range. Now the synth hook really cuts through the mix, without being too loud.

There was definitely a lesson here, and though many of us took it to heart long ago, I think we could all benefit from a little reminder: Less can be more! This is particularly true in the world of dance and house music. In big dance clubs, where it really counts, the best-sounding records are almost always the most minimal.

With all of the great synths available (both hardware and software), it's easy to over-do it, and I overdid it on this one. There were simply too many synth parts stepping on each other. Just a few great parts can go a long way, and aural clutter only distracts from the groove (not to mention the vocal). On the happy occasion when I find myself with too many good ideas for one track, I need to remember that I don't have to use all of them. I can save some of them for the next record.

DRY IT OUT

There was too much FX processing. I generally like processing on my synth tracks, espe-cially for lead sounds. I find that effects can really enhance a sound and have a significant impact on the feel and the vibe of a track. However, the track I was working on benefited tremendously from backing way off on the delays and reverbs. As soon as I pulled back the heavy effects, the track tightened up. The timing felt better, and there was less mud-diness in the midrange. Every track is different, and some elements of a mix clearly ben-efit from delay, reverb, exciter, whatever. In this case, however, I was surprised at how much better my track sounded with the barest of effects. Just because you have all of the cool plug-ins and effects boxes, it doesn't mean you need to use them on every sound in your track.

In the end, I was surprised at how much better I felt about the record after making these few changes. Because I went back to it with fresh ears and a fresh perspective, the track was saved. It's very easy to get caught up in the spirit of creating, and of course it's a necessary part of making music. It's probably wise, though, to remember to take a step back, and take a deep breath or a day off — whatever gives you a little distance. Your work will probably be the better for it.

Sometimes it's best to limit your mix to its essentials from the get-go. Of course, there are innumerable ways to approach streamlining your sound. Here, Rob Hoffman adds his two cents on how to tighten and refine your mixes before they jump the tracks. Feng Shui indeed!

September 2001
Mixing Feng Shui
The art of creating space in your mix

Want to make your mixes sound larger than life? The key to big mixes is space and move-ment. I'm constantly striving to create more space within a mix, and I'm often asked by clients and mastering engineers how I achieve this. It can be a very difficult process, especial-ly in a remix with lots of tracks, but here are a few tips. Call it "Mixing Feng Shui."

One simple technique that I use begins during tracking. Listen to each sound and determine how much stereo information is present. If it's a stereo synth patch, for exam-ple, track it in stereo. I know this can eat up a lot of tracks on your recorder, but for now let's forget about such limitations. If the patch doesn't have much stereo information, now is the time to either remedy that or decide to track it in mono. I often make quick adjustments to my patches as I'm writing and then again during tracking. One trick is to turn on another tone, select a similar waveform, and let that one auto-pan or alternate pan. Turn the volume down on this new tone so as not to overtake your original sound, but simply add some movement to the patch. You can decide for yourself about filter and envelope settings, but I generally copy them from my main tone.

During the tracking process I examine all of my sounds for buzzing, hums, clicks, and pops. While it's rare for any one sound with a buzz to ruin your mix, they can all add up. Now is the time to correct any anomalies. Quite often these noises smear your stereo image. I once had to re-track a song for Bruce Swedien because the previous engineer on the session hadn't paid attention to such details. It was amazing how much clarity and detail became apparent after I got rid of ground hum and a few noisy synths.

I like to pan instruments that are tracked in stereo full left and right. I then let my kick, snare, bass, and vocals stay straight up the center. The holes in between get filled with mono percussion and mono synth sounds. This usually provides a well-balanced stereo sound field.

The next weapon in the battle against clutter is EQ. I generally apply EQ in the mix, but not during tracking. My favorite weapon is the highpass filter. One lesson I learned from my mentors Bruce Swedien and Chris Lord-Alge is to clear out the bottom end so the bass and kick have room to breathe. I usually start filtering all tracks individually (that's right, no one escapes) at around 100Hz. Let your ears be the judge. I engage the filter and begin sweeping the frequency up. For hi-hats and light percussion, I'll often filter up to 300Hz or even higher. By doing this I'm clearing out some extraneous buzz and hum, and cleaning up the muddy end of the audio spectrum. My mastering engineer has told me that not doing this is the most common mistake he hears today. He's often having to cut in the 200–500Hz range to clean up the low to low mids on his clients' mixes. Filtering the kick and bass is a case-by-case scenario, but I generally like to filter kicks up to 80Hz and give them a little boost at 120Hz — unless it's an 808-style kick, in which case I move my filter frequency lower. For bass EQ I like to filter up to 100Hz, boost at 120Hz, and then usually add a boost at 1–2kHz for definition. Generally this provides plenty of punch without a lot of muddiness.

Another space-creating technique I use is automated panning and panning delays. I like to take mono sounds and give them a bit of movement throughout the song. This works especially well with transition sounds such as snare rolls, reverse cymbals, and wind chimes. My favorite panning delay box is the Electrix Mo-FX. You can sync the delay to MIDI clock and have the delays pan back and forth across the stereo spectrum. Movement keeps the listener's ear busy searching for new sounds, making the aural experience more exciting.

So far we haven't mentioned reverb, the standard mix tool for creating space. In general I use two reverbs in my mix: a short plate-style program and a long hall. I use my reverbs to create realistic space. Usually strings and pads pass through longer halls to recreate the feeling of a live string section in a great recording space. I send vocals and solo instruments through the smaller plate or sometimes even just an early reflection program to give the illusion of a smaller space. I use stereo reverbs only — that is, reverbs that have discrete left and right inputs versus reverbs that sum their inputs or only look to the left side for input. This allows me to add reverb to a given track but not smear or lose the track's direction within the mix.

One problem I often encounter is solo or lead instruments that really don't have any stereo information, but need to occupy a large amount of space in the mix. Reverb and delay have been the traditional cures for such a dilemma. However, with the advent of plug-ins, we now have more elegant cures. My current favorite is Waves PS22 Stereo Maker. This plug-in can be used on any mono source to create a wonderfully wide sound spectrum.

January 2006
MIGUEL MIGS

Once I get a groove going the ideas just start flowing. With today's technology, I mix as I compose in order to keep the vibe flowing. Running everything though the Waves Ultramaximizer while you mix may be a bit unorthodox for traditional engineers, but it's how I get my sound.

Another trick I use during intros and breakdowns is to build the mix with mono instruments and suddenly explode to a full stereo mix. I'll keep my loops and percussion limited to a small space in the stereo spectrum, then, as the mix builds, I'll introduce elements panned a bit wider than center. As the final build and release comes around, I'll un-mute my stereo tracks. This technique is a great way to end a breakdown section. The contrast between the small mono breakdown mix and the full stereo mix makes tracks sound huge.

These techniques can truly help your mixes sound wider and bigger than the average engineer's.

After your track is arranged and the final mixdown completed, it is then mastered. Mastering is an arcane process that's equal parts art and science, with a dash of Zen for good measure. Not surprisingly, the more you understand how mastering works, the better your mixes will make the transition into the real world. Craig Anderton has a few choice words on how to make sure your mix is ready for that final polishing stage.

December 2000
Mixing for Better Mastering
Ingredients and special sauce

Judging by the email I get, mastering your own recording projects at home has become a hot topic. One question I received recently was particularly thought-provoking — whether doing a great mix would eliminate the need for mastering. Theoretically this is possible, but the analogy I'd use is putting dressing on a salad. You could put a certain amount of dressing on each piece of lettuce, tomato, etc. When they're combined, you should have the same results as putting dressing on the entire salad. This would be like optimizing every track and assuming that when they're put together, the mix will sound "mastered."

But in my experience, I've never heard a mix — no matter how good — that couldn't benefit in some way by a little judicious mastering.

Nonetheless, there are techniques you can use while mixing to make the mastering process go more smoothly, which is the subject we'll tackle in this month's column.

MATCHING TIMBRES

If you use loops in your music, be aware of loops whose characteristics are wildly different from those of other loops that you're also using. For example, let's suppose most of the loops were taken from a drum machine you use, but you also inserted a few commercially purchased drum loops. It's likely that the latter were already "pre-mastered," perhaps with some compression or treble-boosting. As a result, they may sound brighter than the loops you created.

If you decide to boost the track's overall brightness while mastering, the commercial loops will now seem "over the top" in terms of treble. I had this happen once when re-mastering a stereo track where everything needed a little extra brightness except for a hi-hat loop. It took forever to use notch filtering to find just the hi-hat frequencies and reduce those, while boosting everything else.

This kind of inconsistency can also happen if you use a lot of analog synths, which tend to have a darker sound, mixed with a few digital synths, which tend to be brighter. This will also cause problems when mastering, because if you bring down the highs to tame the digital synths, the analog synths will sound much duller; if you bring up the highs, the digital synths may screech.

The solution is simple: To ensure that changes made during mastering will affect all sounds pretty much equally, bring the "minority" tracks into timbral alignment with the majority of the track's timbres before mixing. However, don't go overboard with this. Some differences between tracks need to be respected. You might want a particular track to sound brighter or duller than others, regardless of any equalization done while mastering.

TAMING THE PEAKS

Another issue involves peak vs. average levels. A lot of engineers use compression to increase a tune's average level during the mastering phase, thereby making it seem louder. (Regrettably, some engineers and artists take this to an extreme, essentially wiping out all of a song's dynamics.) To understand the difference between peak and average levels, consider a drum hit. There's an initial huge burst of energy (the peak) followed by a quick decay in which the amplitude drops. You will need to set the recording level fairly low to make sure the peak doesn't cause an overload, and this will result in a relatively low average energy.

On the other hand, a sustained organ chord has a high average energy. There's not much of a peak, so you can set the record level such that the sustain uses up the maximum available headroom.

If you look at an entire tune, you'll likely find that it has areas with high peaks, and also areas where there is high average energy. Suppose you're using a hard disk recorder and playing back a bunch of tracks. Of course the stereo output meters will fluctuate, but you may notice that at some points the meters briefly register much higher than for the rest of the tune. This can happen if, for example, several instruments with loud peaks hit at the same time, or if you're using lots of filter resonance on a synth and a note falls on the resonant peak. If you set levels to accommodate these peaks, then the rest of the song may sound too soft.

You can compensate for this while mastering by using limiting or compression, which brings the peaks down and raises the softer parts. However, if you instead reduce these peaks during the mixing process, you'll end up with a more natural sound, because you won't need to use as much dynamics processing while mastering.

The easiest way to do this is to play through the song while mixing until you find a place where the meters peak at a significantly higher level than the rest of the tune. Loop the area around that peak, then, one by one, mute individual tracks until you find the one that contributes the hottest signal. For example, suppose a section peaks at 0dB. You mute one track, and the peak goes to –2. You mute another track, and the section peaks at –1. You mute a third track, and the peak hits –7. Aha! That's the track that's putting out the most energy.

If you have envelope-based mix automation, dive into waveform view for that track and insert a small dip to bring the peak down by a few dB. Now play that section again, make sure it still sounds okay, and check the meters. In our example above, that 0dB peak may now hit at, say, –3dB. Proceed with this technique through the rest of the tune to bring down the biggest peaks. If peaks that were previously pushing the tune to 0 are brought down to –3dB, you can now raise the tune's overall level by 3dB and still not go over 0. This creates a tune with an average level that's 3dB hotter, yet is not squashed by any kind of compression or limiting.

GETTING RID OF SUBSONICS

Unlike most analog recording, digital can — and sometimes does — produce energy well below 20Hz. This subsonic energy has two main sources: downward transposition/pitch-shifting, and DSP operations that allow control signals, such as fades, to superimpose their spectra onto the audio spectrum.

I ran into this problem recently when doing a remix of a soundtrack tune. I was adding some limiting to the finished mix, and in some sections the level went way down, as if some hugely powerful signal was overloading the limiter's control signal. Yet I couldn't hear anything out of the ordinary.

Looking at the two-track mix showed something interesting: a massive DC offset. After a bit of research, I noticed that these dips corresponded to places in the song where there was a long, rising tone. I had transposed the tone down by several octaves so it sounded like it was coming up from nowhere, but that transposition had moved it down so far into the subsonic region that it created a DC offset. That's the signal to which the limiter was responding.

So I used Sonic Foundry's graphic equalizer plug-in to insert a super-sharp highpass cutoff starting at 30Hz. When I redid the mix, the DC offset was gone.

Now that my curiosity was piqued, I called up a spectrum analyzer window and started looking at some of the files that had been subjected to multiple DSP operations. Sure enough, in a few cases there was significant energy below 20Hz. After a while this can add up, robbing available headroom and possibly causing intermodulation problems with audible frequencies. Since then, I've started using batch processing functions (available in Steinberg WaveLab, Sony Sound Forge, and other programs) to run all files used in a project through a steep low-cut filter. In some tunes this doesn't make too much difference, but in others I've noticed a definite, obvious improvement in headroom and overall clarity. You can use a sharp low-cut filter with already mastered material to cut out subsonic frequencies, but it's much better to do this type of processing before the files are mixed together, as this can lead to a cleaner mix.

Okay, now your tune is prepped for mastering. Hopefully, as a result of these techniques, any processing required for mastering can be more subtle, so you'll end up with a clearer, more natural sound — but one that still packs plenty of punch.

While we live in an increasingly digital world, any die hard DJ will quickly tell you that vinyl remains a huge part of the wonderful world of dance music. Here Joey Donatello breaks it all down in an insightful summary of why vinyl is still cool, how it's mastered, and the esoteric differences between US and European vinyl mastering techniques.

April 1997
Alive and Extremely Well
Believe it or not, vinyl still matters

It is my firm belief that even though technology is moving faster than ever, vinyl records will be around for a long, long time. Or at least until Elvis makes another record. Vinyl is a sound, a feeling, a science. I have been fortunate to visit many clubs around the world, and I'm happy to report that vinyl is still "King" in danceland. Sure, most commercial clubs are now CD-equipped, but a few holdout independent dance labels still don't manufacture CDs; it's vinyl only.

What is vinyl? Well, for starters, it's plastic — clear plastic, to be more precise. Vinyl for records starts out clear, and then other elements are added to change the color and composition. Vinyl records can be made up of many types of chemicals, some harmful. Around 1980, the Environmental Protection Agency cracked down on the way vinyl records were made, and so pressing plants had to follow strict EPA guidelines for the manufacturing of vinyl records in the United States. That was a good thing, not only for the environment, but because the vinyl got stronger and more durable.

Let's walk through the basic steps of pressing a record. First, your tape is sent to a mastering house for EQ, compression, and to cut a reference master (also called an acetate). This acetate allows you to listen to how your record will sound before it gets sent to the

June 1998
ARMAND VAN HELDEN

One of the remixes that defined Armand's early career was "Spin Spin Sugar" by the Sneaker Pimps. Here's what he had to say about its creation.

Tell us about your "Spin Spin Sugar" remix.

Well, it's funny about that one. When it came in, I didn't know who the Sneaker Pimps were. You know, this is the life I live in New York. I don't know much about alternative groups. I didn't know who Tori Amos was either. I didn't even know who the Spice Girls were until six months ago. So you understand, I live a very urban life. But my manager asked me about it, and I got a cassette. That's how it started.

And the Sneaker Pimps hadn't really broke–through in the States at that point.

No, they hadn't hit anywhere, so it wasn't a priority at all. But I finally sat down with the cassette and peeped it out. And I said, "Ya know what, this could probably work. This is half-speed of house. I could put a house beat right over this." Her vocal was 60, 62, or maybe 64 bpm. Real slow. But if you double it, it's 128.

So you didn't have to time-stretch?

I didn't have to do anything, which was good. So, as soon as I got the DAT from Virgin, I put the whole *a cappella* in [Opcode] Studio Vision, and when I put a beat over it I got chills. I'm like, "This is going to be nasty! This is going to be dope."

Describe how you built this remix.

The thing to remember, with me, everything you hear in that mix is a sample. I'm talking everything! There are no loops. Here's my process: When I do a mix, I'll put the *a cappella* in the computer, I'll set the bpm, and just put a simple beat in. I can take any kick and snare, lock it tight, and that's where I start. From there I go to my Roland 760 and I literally fill that thing up with samples in a matter of an hour and a half. I've got about a hundred seconds stereo in it, and I just fill it up with mad beats, bass, notes, stabs, whatever quirky little sounds. Everything that's in my mixes comes from someplace else. I love the art of sampling. You can listen to "Spin Spin Sugar" and never know where I got anything from. That's the art of it. Drum and bass is based on that. That's where that shit comes from. All the stuff that Roni Size does, which is musically now so respected, is a sample.

So even that big bass line in your "Spin Spin Sugar" remix was a sample?

Yeah. But actually that bass came from their DAT. And that's another thing, see, like with the Tori Amos [remix] too, that bass was from her bassist or whoever was in her band. So it all depends on what I get on DAT. In the Sneaker Pimps case, I had a five-minute track of bass, and I just grabbed that one little thing off it.

pressing plant. Second, after your approval, the mastering house cuts a master lacquer, which then goes to the plating house, where the "Mother" is created. To ensure the freshness of the lacquer, the Mother gets shipped next-day to the plating house. The plating house makes a stamper (or "Father") copy, which is used to stamp or press the vinyl into records. Many Fathers can be made from the Mother, but a Father has only so many stamps before it wears out.

And now a few facts about vinyl. Vinyl does not like extreme temperatures, nor does it like high frequencies and phase problems. A record has grooves, and that is where the sound comes from. The groove size is determined mainly by volume, EQ, and length of audio. If you look at grooves through a microscope, they vary in size due to the volume, EQ, and length of audio cut into the vinyl. A good guide to follow with a 12" 33-1/3 rpm record destined for the club is to cut 12-minute sides. The longer the side, the smaller the grooves, thus a lower overall volume level. On 45 rpm speed, seven to eight minutes is cool for a 12". If you think about it, this single groove has to carry a stereo signal up through a single needle. That is a lot to ask of a piece of metal, and that's why your stereo spread is reduced, as well. The stereo spread on a record is about 20 to 30% less than on a CD. The groove can't handle the separation.

Have you ever noticed that a vinyl record from Europe sounds much better than a record pressed domestically? Why is that? It's simple, really. In 1964, the RIAA [Recording Industry Association of America] and some electronic equipment manufacturers got together to discuss stereo signals. Up until then, records and equipment were mono. To press records and process a stereo signal, a new EQ curve had to be created for the United States. At the time, Europe had a curve that worked and sounded great, but the U.S. had to do it their way. So with the advice of the manufacturers, the encoding and decoding process of vinyl mastering and audio signal were compromised just to save a few dollars on parts. The American curve is shown at left and the European on the right.

 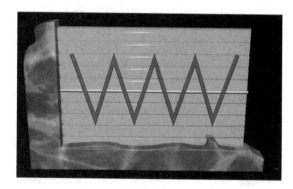

What does that mean? Knowing that vinyl does not like high frequencies, the U.S. curve boosts the high end during encoding; thus more high end is sent to the cutter head (bad), and then cut out on the decoding end. The European curve is much smoother-sounding all the way through, allowing you to cut a louder record (good).

Knowing all this, why would you even want to press a vinyl record? All I can say is drop the needle on a record, then compare it to a CD. It's a sound, a feeling. Nothing feels like vinyl. Vinyl is a hands-on medium that has a sound all its own.

I fear future generations of deejays and musicmakers might never know the enjoyment vinyl has to offer. But for now I feel good, because as fast as technology may move, it's still slow enough to assure that vinyl will be around for as long as I am. And that's all I can ask for.

Acknowledgements

I'd like to begin by thanking my partner, Seabrook Jones, for putting up with my increasingly hectic schedule, especially during the crazy final weeks of finishing this tome.

I'd also like to thank my entire family — Papa, Suzi, Som, Ami, Niki, Anjuli, Karen, Marion, and Elly — for encouraging me to pursue my dreams. Many musicians are surrounded by discouragement from family, friends and associates. I'm genuinely grateful that I don't have do deal with that.

Kudos to Josh Gabriel, who is always ready and willing to talk music, technology, and life at a moment's notice.

Of course, the Backbeat team — Richard Johnston, Jim Aikin, and Amy Miller (for sorting through a decade of archives) — all deserve a round of applause for giving me the opportunity to make this dream a reality.

This is beginning to sound like an acceptance speech, but I'd be remiss if I didn't give the nod to a few of the DJs who have helped to shape my career. Teaming with Roland Belmares resulted in several Top 10 Billboard Dance hits over the past couple of years, while working with Licious The Diva has brought me new insights into rocking a dance floor. Additional thanks to all the Austin-based DJs who pump my tracks at peak hours, notably Jason Jenkins, Filthy Rich, Scot Free, and Chris Allen.

Last but not least, I'd like to give a shout out to my peeps Jason, Travis, Andy, and the rest of the gang at Little City, the best little coffeehouse in Texas! These folks turn me on to the latest indie pop, as well as helping me maintain my caffeine buzz as I write. After three books and countless *Keyboard* articles, I just can't imagine writing anywhere else!

Index